BUDOFF

Microcomputers in special
education

MICROCOMPUTERS
IN
SPECIAL
EDUCATION

MILTON BUDOFF
JOAN THORMANN
ANN GRAS

**BROOKLINE
BOOKS**

Library of Congress Cataloging in Publication Data

Budoff, Milton, 1929-
  Microcomputers in special education.

   1. Computer-assisted instruction.   2. Exceptional
children — Education — Data processing.   3. Microcomputers.
I. Thormann, Joan, 1945-   .   II. Gras, Ann, 1926-
III. Title.
LB1028.5B79   1984   371.9'043   84-7596
ISBN 0-914797-07-7

Published by
Brookline Books, Inc.
29 Ware Street
Cambridge, MA 02138

Printed in the United States of America at Braun-Brumfield, Inc.

Table of Contents

1. Introduction and Overview   3

Section I. Microcomputers: An Introduction to the Technology

  2. Origins of the Species Computer   13
  3. The Computer at Work   27
  4. Languages and Packaged Software   51

Section II. Microcomputers: Applications to the Instructional Process

  5. Computer Assisted Instruction in Special Education   77
  6. Authoring Languages: Promises and Pitfalls   91
  7. Integrating Computer Assisted Instruction
     into Instructional Scenarios   99
  8. How Special Education Teachers Use Computers
     for Instruction   111
  9. Evaluating and Selecting Software   129
10. Tips for Introducing Teachers and Children
     to the Computer   141
11. The Computer as Helper:
     For Teachers and Administrators   165
12. Microcomputers: Making the Technology
     Work in Schools   185

References   199

Appendix 1. Hardware Features and Technical Considerations   203
Appendix 2. Software Evaluation Form   225
Appendix 3. Resources   229

1

Introduction and Overview

For the second time in two weeks, an excited school principal told me that a new Brand X microcomputer had been purchased. When I asked her how she planned to use it, she said she wasn't sure. The microcomputer would be stored until someone figured out what to do with it!

Are such stories commonplace? It appears that they are. Schools purchase and use microcomputers with few soundly developed purposes in mind. The proliferation of microcomputers creates the temptation of school personnel to leap on the microcomputer bandwagon. Horror stories can be told of microcomputers sitting idly in a storeroom gathering dust or becoming property of zealous "computer nuts" on the faculty (Beck, 1982).

The microcomputer revolution, the increased sales as the hardware costs drop sharply, and the dramatic publicity about the applications of microcomputer technology to business and technical areas are exerting tremendous pressure on schools to incorporate this technology into their curricula.

While the computer is very powerful for many applications, it is still limited for educational applications. Used thoughtfully with a sense of its strengths and its limitations, the computer can have substantial impact on instructional practices in the special needs classroom and can help many students, especially those who have considerable difficulty learning in school.

The dynamic and evolving nature of microcomputer technology leaves many questions unresolved. It allows schools to define their concerns as they become involved. It challenges administrators and teachers to make carefully thought through decisions about hardware and software, and instructional applications.

Microcomputers in Special Education allows you to accomplish these tasks. It provides background about the computer technology, the applications of computers to special education and specific instructional applications more particularly, and suggestions as to how schools might proceed in adopting the technology. Microcomputer technology can be viewed for special needs persons from two perspectives. Microcomputers can be used (1) for instructional purposes and (2) as a prosthetic device, that is, as a means to minimize or counteract the effects of a disabling condition. These two views require different books.

This book focuses on instructional applications for handicapped students. It provides a largely nontechnical presentation, so readers who choose to skip Section I, which presents background on the operation of computers, can do so without penalty. Section II discusses special education applications. Appendix 1 provides a brief discussion of technical terms.

The Developing Technology

Despite the current excitement about microcomputers in education, computers in the classroom have not brought about the revolutionary changes anticipated during the past two decades. Until recently, the cost of instructional computing was excessive because expensive telephone hookups and computer specialists were required to communicate with very large *mainframe* computers in remote places. The equipment tended to suffer repeated breakdowns. The systems held much promise but were of high cost and unreliable.

Microcomputer systems have solved many problems of the mainframe computers. Microcomputers are low in cost, easily transportable (many are portable), highly reliable, and usable by computer novices for specific applications requiring little or no programming knowledge. They have sound and graphics capabilities, as well as the ability to interface with audiovisual equipment, such as videodisk and videotape recorders, voice synthesizers, and character readers that read existing print. These options offer virtually unlimited possibilities for developing exciting and creative courseware for children — especially those with special educational needs and/or disabling conditions. Classroom teachers can become familiar with micrcocomputers easily, and use them to develop customized lessons to meet particular children's needs.

The large number of computers purchased means that many new companies, virtually new industries, have emerged to write and market software and hardware. This very competitive market results in frequent announcements of new software, devices, and even new generations of equipment. The incentives to develop and market software and hardware increase geometrically as the volume of purchasers mount.

The Power of the Computer

These developments increase the likelihood of the computer becoming a powerful instructional tool in the classroom. Schools have been forced to jump on this almost irresistible bandwagon and have responded by purchasing microcomputers at a rapid rate. This interest is also apparent in special education. Over 4000 people attended a 1983 Council of Exceptional Children conference on the applications of microcomputers in special education. The Office of Special Education Programs and the rehabilitation research programs of the United States Department of Education have recognized the potential of this technology by funding many projects intended to make the technology applicable to the needs of special education students and disabled persons.

The key to the power of the computer is the excitement it generates in special education children. Sections of this book report anecdotes from teachers. They indicate that special education students are really turned on by their interactions with a computer. Teachers testify that students produce substantially more work using a computer, in a more focused way and for longer periods, than when working with more traditional materials, e.g., workbooks. These are important insights into the power of the computer because special needs children frequently produce little or no work.

While most schools invest in computers for general education, they are likely to be more immediately beneficial for students with remedial and special educational needs since the limited software currently available is for drill and practice. Special education students will work on these exercises and find them interesting and exciting. The experience of success and mastery can be very exhilarating to students who feel they are poor learners. This excitement is a powerful motivator to work on the computer: To demonstrate their competence, to interact with it, to have it offer them praise or criticism, to create on it. This enthusiasm, harnessed, can help the student develop a sense of independence and competence, based on the knowledge that the student can learn by his own efforts.

By contrast, students who learn easily are bored by drill and practice exercises once they have solved them. The problem formats are often unchallenging and, as a result, alienate bright students. These students want courseware that involves them in tasks that are challenging; instructional software that is in very short supply.

Simply scheduling students for computer time, regardless of their intrinsic interest in the computer and without consideration for the instructional value of the time, risks alienating the child who was initially excited by this new tool. The computer can be discarded by children who are bored with uninteresting interactions. The current plight of the computer game market illustrates this dramatically. Children have turned away from computer games in droves, exhibiting ennui for these games in 1984 as dramatically as they exhibited excitement in 1982. This disillusionment inhibits and sabotages acceptance of the computer.

The Best Approach

Our concern is that teachers and administrators understand the nature of the technology, what can realistically be accomplished with the computer, and what cannot be done, at this point in time. While the power of the technology and the sophistication of teachers to use it are developing, we must be careful to structure the educator's and student's exposure to the computer and the expectations surrounding it. We are concerned that the computer be perceived positively. Computers can make a meaningful contribution to the learning process even now; more so, when more interesting and useful courseware and applications become available.

We plead for planned use of the microcomputer in instruction with students, especially those with special needs. Educators need to take care in introducing the student to the computer, actively manage the child's exposures to it, and, most important, think about maintaining the child's sense of meaning and excitement from the contact. For many children, especially those who have experienced learning problems for an extended period, the introduction can be very easy. But teachers need to formulate a plan, to provide a sense that the computer is part of a total instructional strategy or program. The child should not simply be placed at the computer for a number of periods a week, without regard to the instructional quality of the experience.

The proper approach to using the computer is to identify the distinctive roles it can play in instructing a child in a particular skill or content area. Its roles should be carefully thought through and should enhance the power of an instructional plan. It may be used to foster motivation for a student who works fitfully. It may, because of its "dumbness," force the student to learn by an interactive process of correction and teaching. An instructional plan or scenario should involve a teaching process with a series of steps in which the computer may be used for particular tasks on the road to mastery. The student may learn the basic format of a long division problem in class. He may then shift to a workbook to practice solving these and more complex long division problems because workbooks are economic and useful teaching devices. Completion of the workbook assignment may prepare him to match wits with the computer to continue practice of long division in a drill sequence or game format.

In sum, uses for the microcomputer in classrooms, and especially in special education classes, must be viewed critically. Since applications are still evolving, use must be considered within the scope of current thinking which is "state of the art," rather than firmly grounded. Schools should proceed slowly, thoughtfully, and be self-critical. They should approach the technology gradually, preparing teachers and administrators for selected applications. Special education administrators and teachers must view the technology realistically, and explore the broad range of possible uses while becoming comfortable with the technology. The commercial hype tends to undercut critical thinking; one comes to believe the uncritical claims.

Microcomputers in Special Education serves as a road map for the reader. In addition, it provides an understanding of the broad range of possible uses and the best approach to this new and rapidly-evolving technology.

Section I provides background information about computer technology. Chapter 2 discusses the origins of the computer and the logic by which it works. The third chapter discusses how computer hardware works: the central processor; input devices like the keyboard; and output devices like the disk drive, printer, and video monitor. The fourth chapter discusses the nature of computer languages, and how these become operations and applications software for the computer: How they make the dumb instrument into a functioning mechanism.

Section II, the bulk of the book, is concerned with the applications of microcomputers in special education. Chapter 5 defines and illustrates the various modes of computer assisted instruction (CAI). Such CAI modes are described as drill and practice, tutorial, educational games, simulations and demonstrations, software aimed at teaching problem-solving skills (e.g.,

LOGO), and the application of word processing (a powerful application that can stimulate writing and improve language arts for children who are seriously deficient). Chapter 6 discusses the nature, promise and pitfalls, of authoring languages which are intended to allow computer novices to write lessons for students.

Chapter 7 suggests scenarios for integrating the computer into classroom instructional practice. It discusses the logic of instructional scenarios and provides examples for the reader to consider and apply. Instructional scenarios are scripts constructed by teachers which incorporate the unique roles of various instructional modes, e.g., computers, in an instructional plan for a student with specific needs. By thinking of instructional scenarios we are arguing that computers, like workbooks, flashcards, tape recorders, classroom presentations, or just plain old books, have unique strengths that can be harnessed for teaching. The computer should not be the only mode for teaching the particular skill or for knowledge acquisition but should be integrated into an instructional plan. It is our belief that technological innovation has largely failed to be well integrated into instructional practices during the past decades because it is superimposed on the teaching-learning process without a sense of the distinctive roles it can play.

Chapter 8 presents a review of actual practices reported by special education teachers and administrators in a statewide survey in Oregon in 1981-82. It serves to highlight the actual experiences teachers cite about their work with microcomputers in special education settings. Their comments about how they introduce students to microcomputers, schedule them, use instructional materials, and the advantages and disadvantages they cite about software are instructive to the teacher, practitioner, and administrator.

Chapter 9 presents guidelines for evaluating and selecting software: First, the general characteristics relevant to the needs of special education students. It builds on the more general discussion of software languages and applications software in Chapter 4.

Chapter 10 provides tips on how to introduce the computer to educators and students. Teachers can deal with the technology at several levels, depending on their familiarity, comfort, or sophistication, as they design or construct these instructional scenarios. In their first contacts with the computer, teachers may use it for very limited ends, e.g., for drill and practice. As they become more familiar with its capabilities, they may come to think more complexly about the contribution of this technology to their instructional efforts.

We suggest there are three levels of competence one can reasonably expect of educators: those who gain a minimal familiarity that allows them to become comfortable with the computer; those willing to use applications software in their classrooms; and those who are really involved and work to master and apply the technology in school. These three levels of skill require different types of training, support, and encouragement, which are outlined in this chapter.

Introducing students to the use of the computer also requires different approaches based on ability and interest level. Chapter 10 also suggests approaches to introducing students and useful introductory software.

Chapter 11 reviews the helping roles a computer can play in storing and accessing data about students and educational programs, ensuring fair and nondiscriminatory assessment, generating individual educational plans, and in managing the instructional processes and the administrative paperwork. Suggestions are provided about how to implement a system for performing some or all of these functions within a school district.

The last chapter deals with the preeminent problem: how to make informed and intelligent decisions while the technology is still rapidly evolving. The hardware becomes more powerful each year as does the range of peripherals applicable to handicapped and disabled learners. The instructional software currently available admittedly has limitations but software developers are showing promise of greater innovation, especially as the capabilities of the mass-marketed machines increase.

In Chapter 12 we focus particularly on the importance of building a staff capability to use microcomputers with special needs students that a slow immersion into the technology offers the school district. The common practice is to purchase microcomputers and hope the staff will somehow learn on their own, sometimes with orienting in-service workshops. This unprepared introduction has frequently left the staff behind, raising anxieties and generating a sense of helplessness and vulnerability, especially since inevitably, there are students who understand the technology better than the teachers.

A suggested reading list is included at the close of each chapter. The references are gathered at the end of the text, preceding the appendices.

Appendix 1 briefly details hardware features and technical considerations. Appendix 2 presents a sample software evaluation form. Appendix 3 is a listing of resources.

We argue that while the technology is developing, school districts familiarize their staff with microcomputers and help them understand how to apply the technology with special education students, to explore its applications and uses. The teacher's familiarity will allow more intelligent decisions to be made since they will be based on experiences with students. When computers are to be introduced, staff will feel ready to implement the technology because they are knowledgable and interested in having them in their classrooms.

Microcomputers represent great promise for special education in instructional applications. In this book we provide direction for how this promise may be realistically harnessed at a time when the technology is rapidly evolving.

Suggested Reading

Bennett, R.E. Applications of microcomputer technology to special education. *Exceptional Children*, 1982, *49*, 106-113.

Browning, P., & Nave, G. Computer technology for the handicapped: A literature profile. *The Computing Teacher*, 1983, *10*(6), 56-59.

Cogen, V. The computer's role in education and use with the exceptional child. *Mental Retardation*, 1969, 7(4), 38-41.

Hannaford, A. Microcomputers in special education: Some new opportunities, some old problems. *The Computing Teacher*, 1983, *10*(6), 11-17.

Hofmeister, A.M. Microcomputers in perspective. *Exceptional Children*, 1982, *49*, 115-121.

Hope, M. How can microcomputers help? Special education: Forward trends. *British Journal of Special Education*, 1980, 7(4), 14-16.

Podemski, R., Hush, S., & Jones, A. Microcomputers and the disadvantaged: Why we're missing a great opportunity. *Electronic Learning*, 1983, 2(6), 20-22.

Taber, F.M. The microcomputer: Its applicability to special education. *Focus on Exceptional Children*, 1981, *14*(2), 1-16.

Section I
Microcomputers:
An Introduction
to the Technology

2

Origins of the
Species Computer

Overview

Computers are an exciting and inescapable feature of modern life, and they are becoming more exciting and more inescapable all the time. Computers today can respond to spoken instructions, "talk," make music, draw graphs, paint pictures, play chess. They manage our bank accounts, diagnose our illnesses, analyze international affairs. Enthusiasts look forward to the day when computers will "learn" and "think" just as humans do; others consider this a most frightening prospect. At present computers remain under human control, although we are becoming ever more dependent on these children of technology.

Forecasters predict that, before many years, computers will be as commonplace in American homes as television sets and as essential in American classrooms as blackboards. Computer literacy has already become a concern of many educational systems. Some high schools are making it a condition for graduation; some colleges require that every student own a personal computer. Yet as recently as 1975 most of us rarely heard the word "computer," and when we did we thought of math geniuses, giant organizations, and $100,000 price tags.

Where did this phenomenon come from, and where is it going? Can we predict its future by viewing its past? Both past and future are fascinating subjects. However, since the primary goal of this book is to look forward, we will look back just long enough to identify some of the people who made computers possible, and to consider the external influences that led inevitably to the computer revolution. You may agree in the end that computer technology and its role in our lives have become self-energizing — continually adding to the very forces that drive them onward.

To put some reasonable limits on our historical review, let's consider a small computer such as might be found in a classroom today, identify its important elements, and look briefly at their origins. In the next chapter we can look more closely at how these elements work together.

THE CPU: The computer's brain, where the real computing goes on

BINARY: The CPU's language, all 1s and 0s

LOGIC: The difference between a computer and a calculator

PROGRAMS: Sets of instructions that use logic to control the computer's operations

LANGUAGES: Make writing programs easier through the use of vocabulary and syntax that are more like human language than binary

MEMORY: Can be short-term, long-term, variable, or permanent

I/O: Input and output for two-way, people-computer communications

The CPU

The work center of every computer system is its Central Processing Unit (CPU). The computer revolution began when it became possible to put this processor on a chip less than a square inch in area and as thin as cardboard. This chip, which you can buy for as little as $4, can perform one million (1,000,000) calculations in one (1) second.

The chip is quite useless, of course, until one adds a good number of other things, just as the human brain is trapped and mute without voice, eye , ears, memory, or sense of touch. But even with the other hardware that makes the computer into a powerful *system*, the total price can be less than that of an imported ten-speed bicycle. The low cost of a "computer on a chip" can be traced to two factors: The main ingredient of a chip is silicon, which is more common than sand, and these chips are produced in enormous quantities.

There are a number of chip manufacturers in the field today, but the first was Intel, whose 8080 processor chip, introduced in 1973, ushered in the computer revolution. The 8080 was made possible through a totally new technology of semiconductors, transistors, crystal diodes, and integrated circuits. (Fortunately, one does not have to understand any of these terms to use a computer.)

But before a computer could be put on a chip, it was necessary to build a computer in the first place—a good many, in fact, with each design an improvement in some way over its predecessors. This is necessary because it is virtually impossible to tinker around and rebuild a computer on a tiny chip. So before Intel could tool up for 1974, their design engineers had to know exactly what should go into a computer, and how and why. Before the *revolution* could begin, there had to be an *evolution*.

Some trace the computer's beginnings to previous centuries, but the first true working computer was the Mark I, started in 1939 under the joint sponsorship of Harvard University and IBM and finished in 1944. You would not recognize its kinship with our classroom computer. It was a 55-foot-long electromechanical monster, and its thousands of relays made a noise variously compared with "a roomful of ladies knitting" or "an auditorium of tin crickets." Mark I took all of one third of a second for an addition problem and 16 seconds to perform a single division, but it was the foundation for the computer empire of IBM.

Howard Aiken, the leader of the Mark I project, hailed it as "Babbage's dream come true." We did not begin this history with Babbage's mathematical "Engines" because they never really worked, but we will hear more about this nineteenth-century genius very shortly.

To get back to the million calculations a second, the first computer that could perform at *that* speed was ENIAC. Completed in 1947, it caused a great stir because it was said to do the work of 20,000 people. While it had some disadvantages over today's computer on a chip—it weighed 30 tons, stood nine feet high, and took up 1,500 square feet—it was the first "solid state" computer, operating with stationary (and silent) vacuum tubes instead of moving mechanical parts.

In a way, ENIAC's state was too solid; its operations were controlled by thousands of wires and soldered connections, most of which had to be rewired to transfer its computing power from one kind of problem to another. In 1948 ENIAC's successor, EDVAC, circumvented this problem by creating a *memory* in which instructions could be stored and changed; we will hear more about memory later.

Three years later, in 1951, the first UNIVAC was completed, with several improvements over ENIAC and EDVAC. UNIVAC weighed only three tons and occupied only 575 square feet. Even more important, it was the first computer able to handle words as well as numbers, making it even more general-purpose. This UNIVAC led to a long, continuous line of computers mass-produced by Sperry Rand for a ready, waiting, and wealthy market.

Commercially produced computers, descendants of giants like Mark I and UNIVAC, continued to evolve, with more power packed into less space at a lower price. In the 1960s, the new technologies of transistors (first developed at Bell Telephone Laboratories), photo-etching, and general miniaturization began a parallel and speedier evolution. At the same time, computers were helping to speed the development of automated mass production and were even being used to plan improvements in their own design.

In short, the Intel 8080 did not happen overnight. The technologies that made it possible had been developing over a long, long time.

Binary: The Language

Although most of us use the decimal system for everyday mathematics, our classroom computer and all its digital cousins carry out their million calculations a second in the binary system. Binary is a natural language for electrical systems. Electric switches (and transistors are nothing more than incredibly tiny switches) can be on (closed) or off (open); current can therefore flow or not flow, and the current can cause other switches to close or open. If *we* say that a closed switch means "1" and an open switch means "0" and we put enough switches together, we can express almost any real number. Then, if *we* say that certain binary combinations are codes for letters and other non-numbers, we can express almost anything at all.

Later on we will explain how ordinary people who rarely, if ever, speak in binary can communicate with computers that understand nothing else. But we have not yet caught up with the tide of history.

Binary is the one feature of our computer that has been with us since ancient times. All over the world, early man found a need to count things — fish, enemies, wives, children. They counted with various combinations of hands, feet, fingers, and toes. Thus some tribes counted up to 4, some to 5, some to 10, some all the way to 20. A few cultures only got to two. If these last had prevailed, instead of the counters-to-ten, computers would very likely have begun by using the binary system, and they would have come of age a great deal sooner.

While the decimal system was adopted more or less officially around the world and incorporated into the earliest calculating aid (the abacus, said to have appeared in 2600 B.C.), the binary system did surface every now and then, mostly as an intellectual plaything. Mathematicians loved its elegant simplicity. The German philosopher Gottfried Wilhelm von Liebniz, in the late 1600s, found a place for it in his view of religion — "1" was God, who made everything in the universe out of "0."

A later fan of the binary system was Lord Byron's daughter, Lady Ada Lovelace, who happened to be a close friend and enthusiastic supporter of Charles Babbage, the one with the dream. Babbage spent more than 30 years of his life (1823 - 1856), British government grants to the tune of £17,000, and £6,000 of his own, trying to make his gigantic mathematical "Engines" prove their value. If Ada Lovelace had thought of binary as a practical system and had seen its potential application for the Analytical Engine, the evolution of computers might have been hurried on its course. As it was, Babbage's machine — and its mechanical and electrical successors for a long while — were based on that cumbersome, comfortable, familiar old standby, the decimal system.

In fact, the tremendous *practical* potential of binary was not fully recognized until 1937, when Claude E. Shannon, an American mathematician at Bell Telephone Laboratories, published his thesis, "A Symbolic Analysis of Relay and Switching Circuits." In this thesis, Shannon showed the similarity of electric circuit elements to the elements of Boolean logic (more about that in a minute) and to the equally simple elements of the binary system. He even coined what is now one of the most frequently used words in computer terminology, *bit*, which is a contraction of BInary digiT. He called a bit "the amount of information needed to remove the uncertainty between yes and no."

EDVAC, which you may recall was the first computer with a memory, was also the first binary computer, and binary computing has prevailed ever since EDVAC's introduction in 1948. One million calculations a second may seem all the more impressive when you think of it being done with 1s and 0s, but that speed actually would not be possible in our classroom computer without binary and its natural affinity for Boolean logic.

Logic: The Governor

Binary is the language in which computers "think," but logic determines *how* they think. With logic, computers can be given variable instructions — do this if thus and so, otherwise do that — even though they may not make decisions in quite the same way as the human mind.

Most of our computer's ancestors, just a few generations back, were built to solve one kind of problem. Blaise Pascal, in the seventeenth century, built a calculator just for accounting (after many hours of performing computations for his father who was the tax commissioner in High Normandy). In 1837, George Scheutz, a Swedish printer, built an improved version of Charles Babbage's device just to solve actuarial problems. Hermann Hollerith was commissioned to build a machine just to tally the 1890 United States census — without his Tabulator the Census Bureau estimated the job would take 12 years and be 2 years out of date before completion. Even the Mark I had a well-defined purpose — producing the voluminous ballistic tables required for modern weapons in World War II. Our modern digital computer, on the other hand, can solve almost any problem or perform any function that can be reduced or converted to numbers. A primary ingredient of this flexibility is logic.

Charles Babbage was the first to apply logic to the business of computing. His second machine, the Analytical Engine, was designed to change its sequence of operations in response to the results of previous operations. Unfortunately, after Babbage the concept of logic control lay dormant for more than half a century. This neglect is surprising when we consider what George Boole was doing in Babbage's own time and country. In 1847, Boole, an "impractical" mathematician, was working out the fundamentals of what we call Boolean logic, and Boolean logic governs the operations of all digital computers today.

Boole determined that, within a given context, even the most complex relationships and situations can be broken down into elements of "truth" and "untruth" on which further truths or untruths can be based. By determining (or assuming) the truth or untruth of a number of carefully specified conditions, conclusions could be drawn. In philosophy, the conclusions might be called rational deductions or logical assumptions. In dealing with applied mathematics, the conclusions could themselves be called truths, leading to further truths.

Here we come to the similarity between the binary system we were discussing just a minute ago and Boolean logic — the similarity noted by Claude Shannon. Both systems use only two terms. Instead of saying "true" or "untrue" we can, with just a little effort, remember to say "one" or "zero." And the microscopic crystal switches in our computer system can, with equal ease, translate "one" into "yes" and "zero" into "no."

By 1948, binary had been known for centuries, Boolean logic for nearly 100 years, electricity for 70 years, and Shannon's correlation between the three for 10 years. In 1948 the three were finally brought together in one computer —

EDVAC. Today, our classroom computer and its brothers and sisters and cousins work all their wonders through binary codes, represented by electric switches and pulses, all under the control of Boolean logic.

Programs: The Orders

Computers are valued for their speed rather than their intelligence. In fact, computers are inherently imbeciles. If a computer's design includes an incorrect assumption, the computer may insist that $2 + 2 = 7$. And unless told what to do, a computer cannot tell you anything at all. When a computer is turned on, even if it is the most advanced model, it must be instructed to "go get some more instructions."

Certain instructions, such as what to do when first turned on, are always the same. But other instructions vary tremendously, according to what the user wants the computer to do. For instance, our classroom computer can be given a general program (a set of related instructions) that allows the teacher to fill in the specifics, instructing the computer to present a different assignment to each student who *logs on*, to make up random problems suitable for the student's level, and to increase the difficulty at a rate which corresponds to the student's demonstrated comprehension.

Thus a single program can include the means to be adapted — and to adapt itself — to the unique needs and responses of each student. This is the important feature that separates computers from calculators. A true computer is a general-purpose tool whose applications are limited only by the skill and imagination of its programmers and users.

Today, many children in the elementary grades are learning to write programs themselves and having a wonderful time. Almost anyone can learn to make computers do almost anything — a fact that provides considerable food for thought.

As we saw before, Charles Babbage's Engine was the first to follow a *program* through which the feedback from one lumbering mechanical operation could select the next. (He did this by means of punched cards, which we will discuss later.) All of the earliest programs were of necessity mechanical in nature — if a gear was turned, a rod shifted, or a lever moved, it caused something else to move, and so on.

The introduction of electricity, and then binary, made things easier for the machine but not for the programmers, the people who had to provide the instructions. It was still a chore to write a program in 1s and 0s, and a monotonous chore at that since most instructions and many groups of instructions were used over and over again. In addition, it would sometimes take weeks, even months, to write, test, and correct a program. The obvious solution was to make the computer help with the programming.

Languages

Our classroom computer system understands a good number of words designed for people — words like IF and THEN and ELSE and NEXT. Some of its more sophisticated relations can understand entire sentences in true people-talk, although they usually insist on correct *syntax*! How did we ever get from the 1s and 0s of binary to this point?

The first new language, developed in the 1950s, was *assembly language*. A single brief instruction could represent a large group (assembly) of binary commands, just the way the command "Look!" can represent "Turn your head this way and see what I am pointing at and keep your eyes open and pay attention." Assembly programs were translated into binary by the computer, following a special program called an *assembler* written in the machine's own binary language.

The development of assembly language certainly helped, but a great many instructions were still required to accomplish anything useful. It also took months to learn the language, even for experienced programmers, since each CPU design has its own language (an important point — more on this later). The continuing pursuit of ease of use led in the 1950s to the evolution of *high level* languages, becoming more and more like English in syntax and vocabulary. There were sporadic efforts to establish standard versions of specific languages, and some of these were successful. However, human beings always want to improve on things, and now there is a Babel of high level languages and variations thereon.

By now, imagining how many hundreds of binary instructions must go into even a small program, you may wonder how our tiny chip copes with a big program. We human beings, after all, have trouble keeping a shopping list in our heads. If a teacher had to stand by our computer and spoon-feed it instruction by instruction, there would not be a computer in the school. Therefore, the computer must have a *memory*.

Memory

Imagine, if you can, what life would be like if you could not remember anything for more than one second. Computers, too, have to remember. Our classroom computer actually has three kinds of memory. They are usually referred to as *RAM, ROM,* and *storage.*

RAM and ROM

The kind of memory most often mentioned in the advertisements is *RAM,* which stands for Random Access Memory. RAM is very like our own active, conscious memory — the kind a teacher uses in the classroom all day long. For example, a teacher uses this kind of memory to recall details for a discourse, to accumulate feedback from the students, and to store questions that must be addressed later.

Every digital computer must have some kind of RAM for storing the data and instructions it is using at the moment or will be using at any microsecond. Our classroom computer has a RAM memory made up of microscopic switches in special chips. In a few square inches of chips, it can hold the equivalent of 32 pages of single-spaced typewritten text. The problem with RAM is that if the power is turned off, everything in RAM is erased; when the power is turned on again the RAM is as empty as a newly-washed blackboard.

For truly permanent memory, our computer uses *ROM* (Read Only Memory). ROM is rather like an instinct or a reflex — it stores instructions in such a way that they cannot be changed. ROM, like RAM, is made up of microscopic crystal switches, but each of these is fixed in one position.

The early evolution of computer memories is not as well documented as that of the CPU, possibly because memories are less exciting — they don't *do* anything. The problem with the early form of ROM was illustrated by the MARK I, in which all instructions were wired, meaning the machine had to be rewired to change the program. As you may remember, the builders of EDVAC solved this problem with a variable memory into which the program could be written electrically. That variable memory was the ancestor of our modern RAM chips. EDVAC could not only read instructions and data from this memory but could also vary both on the basis of results and store these variations. Thus EDVAC, in 1948, became the first electronic computer to work with programs stored in memory, as computers have done ever since.

The earliest form of internal computer memory, incredible in the light of today's techniques, was the column of mercury. Mercury conducts electricity, but more slowly than the copper used for wiring. Binary information coded in electric pulses was fed into one end of a column of mercury, the processor performed several operations, and the stored information was then picked up at the other end of the mercury column. A big jump forward from the mercury column was the development in 1953 of ferrite core memories. These used the special properties of ceramic ferromagnetic compounds discovered by Hilbert back in 1909. Fast, reliable, and still used in some systems today, these do have one drawback — they occupy a great deal of space. Our classroom computer would not be able to fit into its cabinet if it were not for the spatial economy of memory on chips.

Storage

We humans have a third kind of memory where we store such things as how to get to the grocery store. Such information does not have to be in our active consciousness all the time, so we put it away until we need it. But if the store moves or a street is made one-way, we must be able to change those instructions. In a computer this kind of memory is essential for long-term storage of data that will surely be changed with time, and for programs that may need revision. This kind of memory is usually referred to as *storage*.

At present, most storage uses magnetization, electricity's alter ego. Magnetization, like electricity, is a natural for binary because it has two directions, and any location on a magnetic surface can be magnetized in one direction for a "1" and the other for a "0." Our classroom computer stores programs and student records on *disks* that look like small phonograph records. Many computers use *magnetic tape*, which looks (and sometimes is) just the same as audio tape. Some older computers, even though they may be equipped with magnetic storage, still store a great deal of data and programs on *punched cards*.

Charles Babbage, who must seem like an old friend by now, used punched cards for storing his Engine's instructions. He got the idea from Charles Jacquard, a Frenchman who invented the cards to control the looms in his textile mill to produce the complex patterned weave that still bears his name. Hermann Hollerith borrowed the idea again for storing his census data and improved on it by adding a mechanical card sorter.

Punched cards ("Do not fold, spindle, or mutilate.") were the most common form of storage for decades, and they are still used in many quite modern computer centers. Another early storage medium that is still in use is paper tape, the kind used by teletypewriters. In the 1940s the British had code-breaking computers that could read paper tape at 5,000 characters per second.

Today magnetic disk and tape storage have taken over almost everywhere, and technology is always packing more magnetic storage onto smaller surfaces. We can now store well over 2,000 pages of text on one 5¼-inch disk. The latest advance is *bubble memory*, which is already making its contribution in the area of portable computer systems. Bubble memory consists of microscopic bubbles of magnetic charge that flow through a medium at incredible speeds. This technology may soon replace our disks with, naturally, chips.

We seem to have come full circle, having started with the computer on a chip, taken a peek at what it does and how it does it, and ended up with memory on a chip. But all of these marvelous developments are still, in themselves, quite useless. What, after all, can one do with a tiny chip of bubble memory, even if it does contain two volumes of the Encyclopedia Britannica? Only a computer can write to such a memory, and only a computer can read it out again. This is one small example of our increasing dependence, and it may begin to appear as though computers can get along without people better than we can without them. Yet we must remember that computers cannot do anything without instructions and that these instructions have to come from human beings — so far, anyway.

So now let us examine the *input* devices, with which we can feed instructions and information to the computer, and the *output* devices, through which we get information back.

Input and Output

Our classroom computer has one element that has not become smaller with time and technology and probably won't. This is the *keyboard*. It made its appearance in the 1940s and 50s already looking like a typewriter keyboard, and it still looks like a typewriter keyboard. This familiar look helps many first-time users feel comfortable with computers. Thus, even though there are many other input devices available today, the keyboard is the most popular and can be expected to remain so.

The keyboard, however, can only communicate in one direction. To get information out of the computer, we need an output device. There are many types of output devices, but the one providing the most instantaneous feedback is the *video display*. The most common video display device is a cathode ray tube (CRT), which is just like a television tube. In fact, many home computers are designed to be used with a television set.

Like RAM, the CRT goes blank when the power goes off, and its image cannot be captured with a photocopy machine. For output of a more permanent nature, therefore, our classroom computer can also output to a printer, which is rather like a typewriter but usually without a keyboard. Many typewriters have been modified to work as computer printers, and the technology in each field has contributed to the other.

Before integrated keyboards and CRTs, computer users got along for many years with punched cards and paper tape. Sometimes they would have to resort to direct input in binary through manual switches and read the results in banks of little red lights — a time-consuming procedure unforgiving of errors. We've come a long way since those days; in the next chapter we'll see just how far — how some computers can hear and understand our spoken words, output animated pictures in color, and do it all to music!

We could go further and see how computers predict election results, guide spaceships to distant planets, and accept instructions from the eye movements of paralytics, but that would be another book. We should also remember that we are only beginning to explore the possible uses of computers.

Where Do We Go From Here?

As noted before, the first computers were built for large but specific purposes by large organizations with large funding. Today's computer is a tool that can lend itself to anything from spaceship control to arcade entertainment. As its dimensions shrink, its memory expands, its power and speed multiply, and its price falls, its versatility will continue to grow exponentially.

But computers still need input and output. Thus the computer industry continues to spawn a vast array of other industries — software houses and manufacturers of printers, video displays, keyboards, disk drives, disks, printing ribbons, joy sticks, tape cartridges, plotters, voice digitizers, and telephone interfaces. All of these industries are busily inventing new wrinkles to enhance the capabilities of the computer even further.

Finally, we must recognize that the computer revolution has been a major contributor to the information revolution. It is no longer enough for business and government to do their work faster. Just to keep up with the rest of the world, they must now have access to more information than they ever thought of needing a few years ago. In addition, big business and government no longer have exclusive access; today, a $1,000 computer can tap into the resources of the greatest collections of data ever assembled.

Naturally, all of this fuels the demand for more computer power, and that demand is tremendously inspiring to entrepreneurs and inventors. We see more and more new offerings introduced every week, both hardware (equipment) and software (programs). Some truly represent new breakthroughs, but many are merely old products in new wrappings, and all too many come on the market prematurely, without proper testing, documentation, or truth in advertising.

In summary, the shift from a relatively manageable process of evolution has given way to a revolution that has run away with itself. While many experts speak of the need for standardization, only time can show which standards are worthy of adoption. In the meantime, these same standards will be overshadowed by new breakthroughs.

In the interim, the would-be purchaser and user finds few charts to navigate through the oceans of advertising hype. In education particularly, where few if any standard systems have evolved, it is all too easy to buy the "best" of each element and then find it impossible to assemble a system because those elements cannot communicate.

Education, probably for economic reasons, is the last market to be vigorously addressed by the vendors. School systems seeking computers to fit their needs must search through an avalanche of products from an industry that has always focused on the markets of business and recreation. Computers will, inevitably, play an ever greater role in education in the coming years. If the classroom computer revolution is able to develop and maintain a stability of direction and purpose, it will be largely through the careful planning and continuous involvement of well-informed administrators and teachers.

Suggested Reading

Forester, T. (ed.) *The microelectronics revolution: The complete guide to the new technology and its impact on society*. Cambridge, MA: MIT Press, 1981.

Hilton, A.M. *Logic, computing machines, and automation*. Cleveland: World Publishing, 1964.

Rosenberg, J. *The computer prophet*. New York: Macmillan, 1969.

Sippl, C.J. *Microcomputer dictionary* (2nd edition). Indianapolis, IN: Howard W. Sams, 1981.

Zaks, R. *Your first computer: A guide to personal and business computing*. Berkeley, CA: Sybex, 1980.

3

The Computer at Work

Part 1: Systems and Users

In the previous chapter we saw how the major individual parts of a computer system were developed over time. In this chapter we will see how they work together today. Part I includes a few demonstrations of how they work for people in the classroom. Part II focuses on *compatibility*, without which the parts will not work together at all. We will try not to get bogged down in technical details: Avid readers can find those in Appendix 1.

Hardware, Software, and Firmware

The above heading may remind you of boiled eggs, but we are referring to the three categories of "wares" that are needed to make our classroom computer work. The listings below show which parts fall into each category. However, please remember that this is only one of many possible *configurations* — not all computers are put together the same way.

HARDWARE: Central Processing Unit (CPU chip)
                memory:
                    short-term variable (RAM chips)
                    long-term fixed (ROM chip)
                    long-term variable storage (disks on disk drives)
                input and output devices (keyboard, CRT, printer, and so on)
                encoders, decoders, and many other supporting components

The term *hardware* refers to things that have physical dimensions, things you can see and touch and pick up. The hardware components in our computer are mass-produced separately and then assembled and wired together. In our classroom computer all of these parts are built into one cabinet, except for the disks. The disks store software as well as data. They can be taken out of the disk drives and replaced with other disks storing different software. Remember that almost all hardware operations are controlled by the software.

SOFTWARE: Operating System
              application programs
              language interpreter program

Software is the general term for programs that tell the computer what to do. Our programs are rather like how-to books, written in magnetic code on disks instead of in ink on paper. The *Operating System* is a large program and very important — our computer cannot run without it. It tells the CPU how to work with all the other parts of the system no matter what application programs are being run. The Operating System is a very general-purpose piece of software.

The *language interpreter* is also a general-purpose program, but it is not an essential part of the system. The computer can run without it. We use one on our classroom computer system because some teachers and students want to write their own programs, and they are not about to write programs in binary! The interpreter translates their language into binary for the Central Processing Unit (CPU).

An accountant, a plumber, and a lawyer might all use the same Operating System and interpreter. *Application programs*, on the other hand, are specialized; they tell the computer how to do specific tasks for the user. Application programs used in our classroom will be quite different from those used by lawyers or plumbers.

FIRMWARE: software stored in long-term fixed memory (ROM chip)

Read Only Memory (ROM) chips store programs in a form that the computer can read instantly, without having to look on a disk. Our ROM chip stores a program to help the computer get started when it is first turned on. Many programs, even operating systems and interpreters, have been built into ROM chips, but not all computers are built to use them.

Putting the Pieces Together

Now for a look at how all these parts fit together in a computer *system*. Figures 1 and 2 demonstrate working relationships rather than physical layout. For example, the CPU and the bank of RAM chips are actually connected by many inches of finely printed circuitry, but they work so closely together that they are shown in Figure 1 as inseparable.

Figure 1 shows the computer's brain (the CPU) and some of the supporting hardware. The latter includes two disk drives with disks carrying software. There are a multitude of other hardware units in our computer; to avoid technical details, this diagram shows only the primary elements.

In this diagram, the power switch has just been turned on, automatically calling up the program in ROM. This program is called a *bootstrap loader*. It gets its name from the fact that it can run all by itself (it does not need the help of an Operating System) and its sole function is to *load* the Operating System. It tells the CPU to read from certain locations on disk, and to copy the contents into Random Access Memory. What is copied, of course, is the Operating System, and it will stay in RAM until the power is turned off.

We call the system in Figure 1 a self-sufficient system because this configuration is capable of computing without the attention of any human operator. With one special command built into the Operating System it can load an application program automatically. It could perform statistical analyses, seek proofs for mathematical theories, read data from disks and write new data out. In computerese, such operations are sometimes called *batch processing.*

Such an operation might be useful in the laboratory, but classrooms are for people. We need a way for people to get into the act. Figure 2 shows how a computer system becomes *interactive.*

In Figure 2 we have added input and output devices to make the system *interactive.* Most of the time people who want to "talk" to the computer use the keyboard, and most of the time the computer "talks" to people through the

CRT (video display). But, as you can see, there are many other devices that could be substituted or added on. The little boxes marked "I" represent *interfaces*. Usually each device requires its own special interface to let it hear and talk to the computer.

This system has already been busy with the following interactive operations:

1. The Operating System has identified itself to the user via the CRT.
2. The user has used the keyboard to call for an interpreter and an application program, in that order.
3. The Operating System has copied both from disk into RAM.

In fact, even though we cannot show it in this small diagram, the first instructions of the program have been sent to the CPU: The video display has presented you, the user, with a question and is now waiting for your answer!

Figure 1
Self-Sufficient Computer System

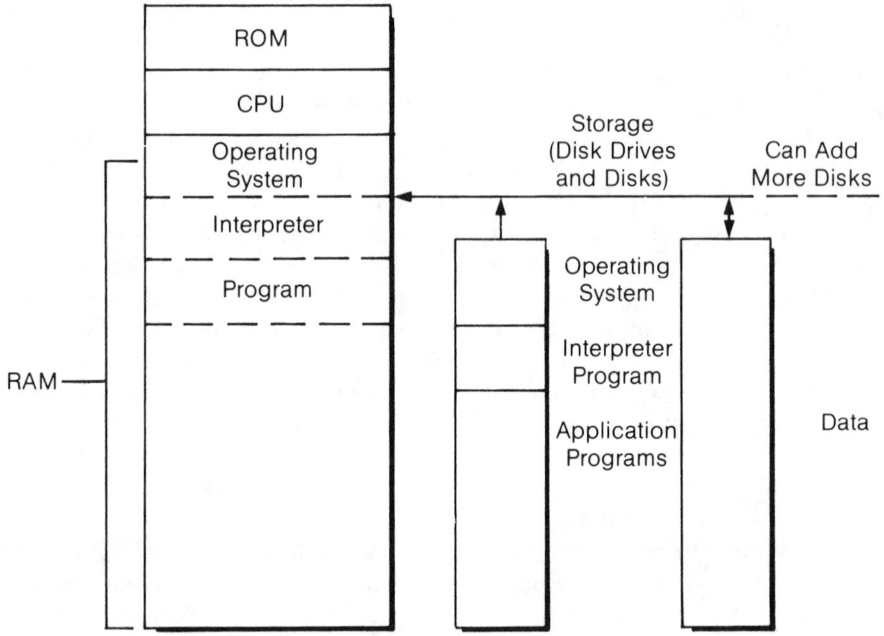

Figure 2
Interactive Computer System

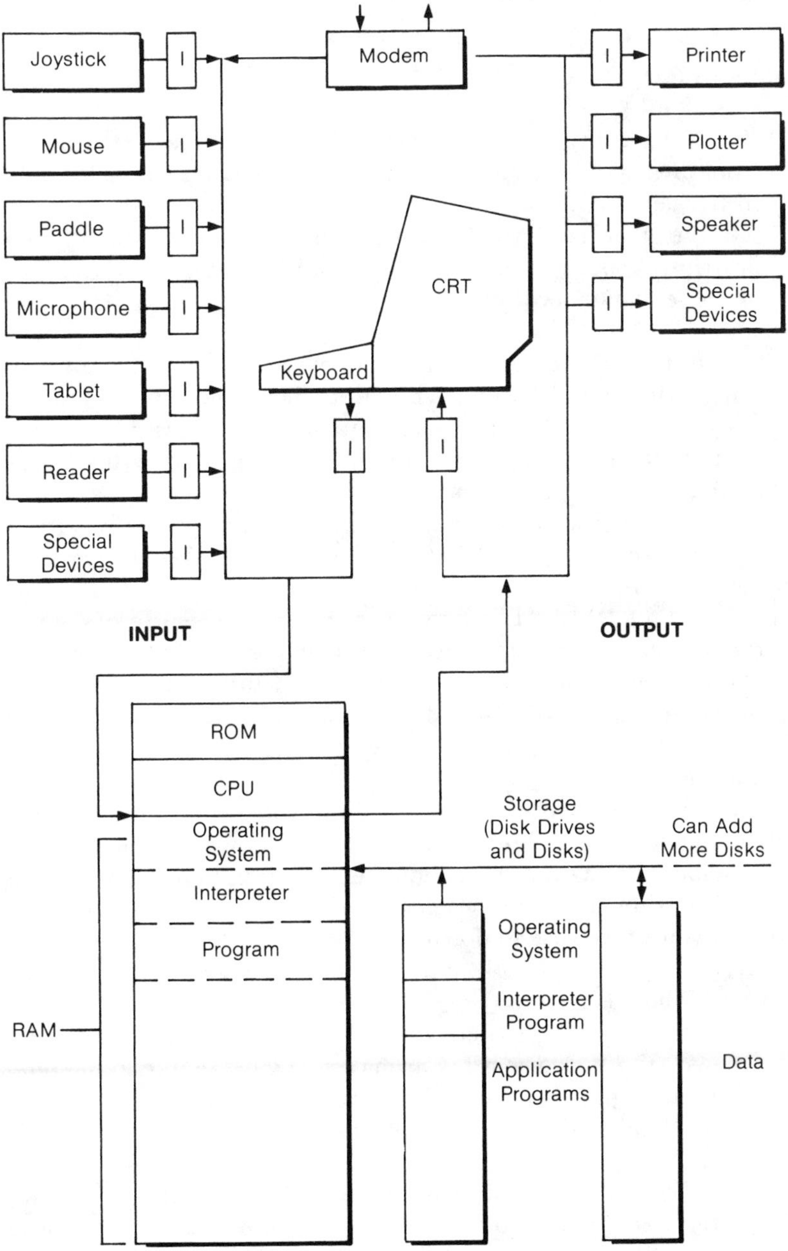

Joystick	I		Modem		I	Printer
Mouse	I				I	Plotter
Paddle	I		CRT		I	Speaker
Microphone	I				I	Special Devices
Tablet	I		Keyboard			
Reader	I		I	I		
Special Devices	I					

INPUT   OUTPUT

| ROM |
| CPU |
| Operating System |
| Interpreter |
| Program |

RAM

Storage
(Disk Drives
and Disks)

Can Add
More Disks

Operating
System

Interpreter
Program

Application
Programs

Data

Using Computers —
Human Reactions and Interactions

Two points to remember:

1. If you have any say in the evaluation, selection, or application of a computer system, some knowledge of how it works will help you make better decisions.
2. On the other hand, you can *use* a computer system without knowing anything about most of the elements or where they are or what they are doing or how they do it.

Children take to computers like honeybees to clover. Children are accustomed to living and working with things they do not wholly understand. They recognize the computer as a machine and take it for granted that they are in control. At the same time, they enjoy being surprised by this machine's occasional display of "intelligence."

Many adults, on the other hand, have been conditioned to be wary of the unknown. The first time they are left alone with a computer, they fear that touching the wrong button will damage the mechanics or set off an alarm. They imagine the DELETE key could erase ten years' worth of data. They think every mistake will be recorded on disk and relayed to the world. When this machine turns out to use human words, the adult novice expects its next words to be "Hey, stupid!" In addition, some adults, even in the teaching profession, fear that computer power will replace them and their human contributions.

For readers who share any of these feelings about computers, these pages will explain a little of how our classroom computer works, and will perhaps alleviate some of these concerns. Along the way, the limitations of computers, even the best of them, should become clear.

Now, if you will please sit down at our classroom computer, you will see that it has two parts that look quite familiar. One looks very much like a typewriter keyboard, even to the QWERTYUIOP. If you press the keys the way you would with a typewriter, you will find that it even feels and sounds like a typewriter. The keyboard, you may remember, is the most common input device, though it is not the only kind by any means.

The other familiar-looking part of our system is very like a television screen. However, this screen is not displaying moving pictures — just words, numbers, and characters. On one part of the screen, you will see a rectangular block, a little larger than a capital letter. On some screens this block flashes or blinks continually and on others it is not a block at all but a flashing

Figure 3

underline. Regardless of its form, it is always called a *cursor*, and it usually shows where the next character will be displayed.

Now, if you press a character key on the keyboard, you will see that whatever you type appears on the screen. It takes the place of the cursor, which moves one space to the right. The screen, of course, is an output device; one of many different output devices available.

What Goes on Between Input and Output

When you press a key on the keyboard, the character seems to appear on the screen instantaneously. It's as if there were a direct link from keyboard to screen. Actually, several other parts of our system are involved.

First, the keyboard encoder chip identifies which key you pressed. Then it sends the binary code for that key to the CPU, which then has to read instructions on what to do with this input. But the instructions are not in binary, so the interpreter is called upon too, to translate the instructions.

The instructions turn out to be two-fold: Store the code in RAM for future use, and also display it on the screen. Eventually, the code is sent to a decoder which tells the CRT to display the appropriate pattern of dots. The Operating System, of course, is always busy in the background, with responsibility for everything that goes on.

Meanwhile, we at the keyboard can type away in blissful ignorance of all this behind-the-scenes activity. In computer jargon, the system is *user-transparent*. If we wanted to enter text, we could actually type faster than with an electric typewriter.

Interactive Programs

So far, you have pressed one key on the keyboard (input) and seen one character displayed on the screen (output). In passing, we mentioned a *program*. The program tells the computer when to accept input, and it is often very particular about what can be entered. Suppose the program asks you to enter a number. You can type all the letters in the alphabet and the computer will refuse to accept them.

The programs used in our classroom computer are *interactive*. They may read information from a disk and write new information out, but most of the time they are interacting with the user. They present *prompts* asking for user input and wait until they get it. Some are compassionate: They understand that people are fallible, they try to catch mistakes, and they give you another chance. Some even stand ready to respond to a user's plea for HELP!

Now let's look at some demonstrations of sample interactive programs from the user's point of view. It is important to remember that the computer itself does not have a point of view or a theory. The same computer can be used with equal ease for any educational approach. The controlling element in classroom computing is the software, the programs that help the computer to interact with students and teachers.

However, it is also important to remember that software for people is created *by* people. Many educational programs purchased off the shelf do have viewpoints — the viewpoints of their authors. Also, some programs are defective, written with good intentions but full of errors or *bugs*. Some are just plain bad. We recall a colorful and attractively designed package that was marketed as a teaching aid in grammar. Our discourse with the program, on a small desktop computer, went something like this:

Computer, on video screen:

A VERB is a word we use for an action. In the sentence "Bill WALKS to school" the word WALKS is a verb. Some other verbs are EAT, GO, and JUMP. Now, you type in a verb.

User, by keyboard:

GHYUOPQ

Computer:

VERY GOOD!

The flaw in this human-computer interaction was a serious one. This so-called teaching tool did not merely fail to catch mistakes, but actually reinforced them. The basic flaw, you will note, was not in the computer hardware. Nor was it a bug in the software, which could be fixed by changing a line or two of coded instructions. The fault in this program was in the basic idea. That small computer could not possibly check whether a verb had been entered. To do that would require comparing it with a stored list of every verb in the language in all forms, persons, and tenses! The storage space required and the time to scan the list would not be justified for this application.

On the other hand, the program could have put the question this way:

YOUR CAT SAT ON MY HAT.
Which is the VERB in this sentence?

If you had already figured out this approach, or a better one, then you are well on your way to being a programmer. But remember, you don't need to be a programmer to work with computers.

Examples of Interactive Programs

We have already mentioned that a program can provide a frame or form in which the teacher fills in the blanks. In this way the program can be tailored to fit the needs of individual students. In the three simulated routines shown in Figures 4, 5, and 6, a teacher uses this kind of software. This demonstration is not drawn from an actual software package, but the programs would not be difficult to write.

The first program (Figure 4) shows how the teacher logs on to the system and calls up the next program. The second (Figure 5) helps the teacher define the assignment (a simple addition drill) with a few instructions. The third (Figure 6) leads a student through the assignment.

None of these programs is especially creative. The student's program does not encourage student creativity — addition, after all, is not exactly the place for innovation. (Software that does help students explore and experiment will be discussed in Chapter 4.) Finally, these programs do not begin to take advantage of sophisticated computer capabilities: They do not use graphics, color, or sound. Still, they are an improvement over some of the software offered for education today.

In Figure 4 we see the interaction between a computer program and a teacher. The program has instructed the computer to display a *prompt* for each item of information required from the teacher. We have underlined the teacher's input for identification. The teacher logs on to the system by responding to the first two prompts and entering name and password. Passwords are supposed to prevent access to the system by unauthorized

Figure 4

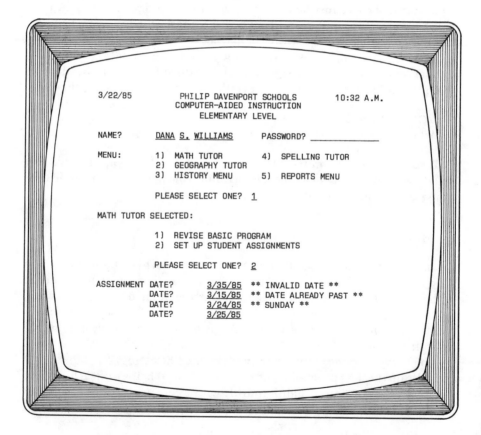

persons. The password is *not* echoed on the screen because that would give it away to anyone watching. However, the computer does read it from the keyboard and also checks it for validity.

The *menu*, like a restaurant menu, presents a list of options from which the user can make a choice. The menu can be controlled by various levels of security. A teaching aide might have a different password and might not be allowed access to #5, the Reports Menu, a set of programs that print out records of each student's progress.

As you can see, this program also checks the assignment date. Our computer uses a battery-operated calendar/clock that runs even when the computer is turned off. Every program can "read" the current date and time (see upper corners of the screen), and the user does not need to enter this information — a good thing, since our teacher seems to have trouble with dates. Dates can be important. For example, this program will store assignment dates for tracking each student's progress over a semester. Checking the validity of dates and other information that can be verified, and providing clear error messages, like those shown in this example, are two of the features that can help you identify good software.

This software demonstrates a degree of logic not always found in packaged programs: Logically, teachers do not prepare assignments for a previous date or a date when there will be no school. This program would even reject today's date if it were already 4:00 in the afternoon.

The program in Figure 5 was loaded into RAM and put into operation by the menu selection that we saw in Figure 4. The teacher's name and the assignment date were passed along. The teacher now enters the specifications of an assignment for Sally Kendall. These "specs" will be stored on disk and used by the assignment program when Sally logs on to the system on 3/25.

This program is *user-friendly*. When the student's initials are entered, the computer looks in the student file, gets the full name, and puts it on the screen for confirmation. Also, when all the *fields* (numbered items of information) have been entered, the user can go back and change any one field by using its field number. Without this convenience, he would need to go through all the questions again from top to bottom.

As you can see, the entire assignment can be set up in 20 keystrokes or less. Since we are designing this program as we go along, we can assure you that the teacher's task is made as easy as possible. Having set up the drill for Sally Kendall, the teacher could assign the same drill for other students by simply entering their initials.

In fact, the need for teacher input could be reduced even further, if we wished: The program could instruct the computer to review Sally's progress over the term and set up assignments automatically. However, as the creators of this program, we have introduced our own viewpoint: As we see it, teacher involvement is essential, even in drill assignments. There are important human qualities that cannot be imparted to a computer, qualities such as intuition, judgment, understanding, and recognition that one student needs to build confidence while another needs to be challenged.

In our final example (Figure 6) Sally is doing the assignment specified by the teacher. The computer is controlled by the program AD2 (Addition Drill, Module 2 in Figure 4), using the specs we saw being entered in Figure 5. The program makes up three-digit addition problems at random and presents them one at a time. As instructed, it does not erase problems and answers but leaves them on the screen for reference. (By the way, the program lets Sally type in numbers from right to left, the way one would do it by hand.)

The program identifies the difficulty with CARRY. It automatically

Figure 5

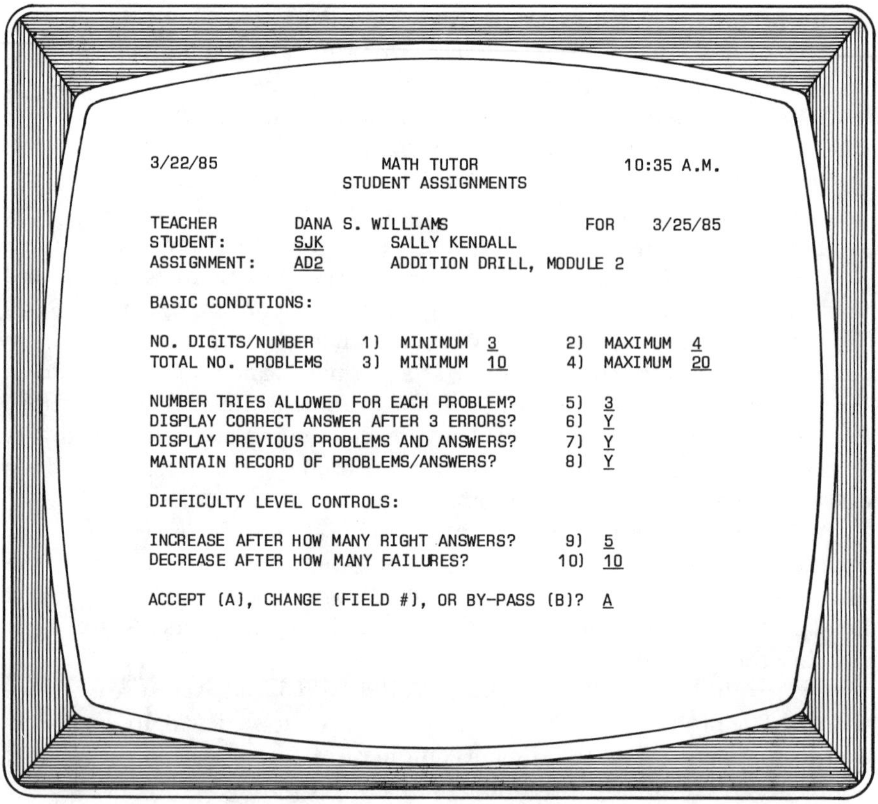

```
3/22/85                MATH TUTOR                10:35 A.M.
                    STUDENT ASSIGNMENTS

TEACHER        DANA S. WILLIAMS           FOR    3/25/85
STUDENT:       SJK         SALLY KENDALL
ASSIGNMENT:    AD2         ADDITION DRILL, MODULE 2

BASIC CONDITIONS:

NO. DIGITS/NUMBER    1)  MINIMUM  3      2)  MAXIMUM   4
TOTAL NO. PROBLEMS   3)  MINIMUM  10     4)  MAXIMUM   20

NUMBER TRIES ALLOWED FOR EACH PROBLEM?   5)  3
DISPLAY CORRECT ANSWER AFTER 3 ERRORS?   6)  Y
DISPLAY PREVIOUS PROBLEMS AND ANSWERS?   7)  Y
MAINTAIN RECORD OF PROBLEMS/ANSWERS?     8)  Y

DIFFICULTY LEVEL CONTROLS:

INCREASE AFTER HOW MANY RIGHT ANSWERS?   9)  5
DECREASE AFTER HOW MANY FAILURES?        10) 10

ACCEPT (A), CHANGE (FIELD #), OR BY-PASS (B)?  A
```

presents five new problems all requiring this operation. The teacher did not need to specify such decisions because they are built into the program.

One aspect of computers that students find appealing is the instant feedback. With this program, Sally knows immediately whether an answer is right or wrong. This program even provides verbal encouragement when deserved. Another popular feature, naturally, is the fact that each student can work at his or her own pace.

Drill programs such as this can be enlivened with many other features if supported by the hardware. They can use color, graphics, and sound (e.g., a fanfare of "trumpets" when a student has done 50 problems without an error). On the other hand, some educators might feel that such embellishments are a distraction and an unnecessary crutch.

But now that we have seen a little of what the computer can do up front, let us see what is going on *inside* our computer.

Figure 6

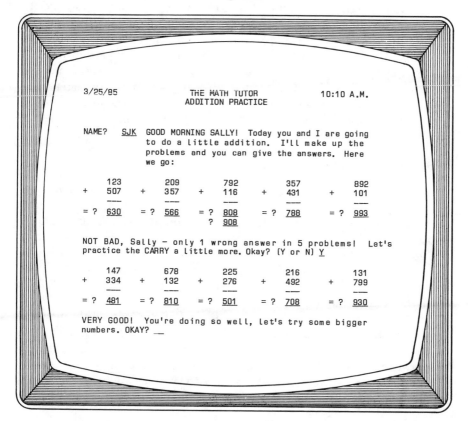

Part II: What Goes on
Behind the Scenes

Invisible Signals at the Speed of Light

The truth is, we cannot actually "see" what goes on inside our classroom computer. If its cover were made of glass, we might be able to see the blades of the cooling fan spinning away. We might glimpse the movement of a rotor or read/write head on a disk drive. But all the other elements just sit silently in their places, seemingly doing nothing at all. This is because all the information going through the computer is in the form of electrical signals. These signals are controlled by switches and the switches are controlled by other electrical signals. Even if these switches were encased in glass, and the printed circuits that carry the electrical current were equally transparent, we still could not see anything happening. The switches are microscopic, the current is invisible, and the signals are transmitted at the speed of light.

Perhaps we can visualize the computer as a very efficient restaurant. After all, we have already seen how a "waiter" (the video screen) can present us with a menu. We can give our orders to another "waiter" (the keyboard). Naturally, our orders are then sent to the "kitchen" (the Central Processing Unit).

Processing in the CPU

There are two cooks in our CPU kitchen. They are called the *Arithmetic Logic Unit*, or ALU, and the *Control Unit*. The head cook, naturally, is the Control Unit. Every instruction, every item of information, that comes into the CPU has to be fetched by the Control Unit and handed on to the ALU. Everything that goes out is dispatched by the Control Unit. The Control Unit is also responsible for ensuring that everything happens in the right sequence. The Control Unit is very powerful, but it has no mathematical ability. This is where the ALU comes in.

The Arithmetic Logic Unit is responsible for all mathematical functions. As you would expect, it can add and subtract, multiply and divide, just like a pocket calculator. But one of the most frequently used functions is that of comparing numbers. Remember that everything in the CPU is in binary. When you type a "Y" you see a "Y" on the screen, but the CPU sees a binary number — in this case 01011001. (In the decimal system, that's 89.) Now suppose you have been asked to answer a question with "Y" or "N." If your coded input is 01011001, the CPU will do one thing; if not, it will do another. Thus the computer can be instructed to make logical decisions based on simple numeric comparisons.

The ALU and Control Unit are constantly talking to each other. For example, consider the running dialogue involved in processing a very small part of Sally's addition drill (Figure 6). Very much simplified, and presented in English instead of in binary, it might be imagined as follows:

CU: Let's see, we need a three-digit integer. Pick a number, please!

ALU: 792 (but in binary).

CU: Okay, I sent that to the video. Now another one.

ALU: 116.

CU: Sent, along with the prompts. Now add those two numbers.

ALU: 908.

CU: Now I'll get SJK's sum from the keyboard. Here it is. Compare that with your sum. Are they the same?

ALU: No. The number you just gave me is 808. That's not the same as 908.

CU: Ooops! Well, it says here we're supposed to store it anyway. I'll put it in RAM and send it out to disk later. Now, do we have three wrong answers for this problem? I do wish I could learn to count!

ALU: No, just one. That's less than three.

CU: Very well then, I'll have to ask for another answer.

The above scenario involves many more steps than suggested here, but it may be completed in two or three seconds. You may be surprised to find that almost all of that time is taken up waiting for Sally's answer. The CPU could be doing at least several thousand other things in those two or three seconds. Computer experts deplore this waiting around, but this is the responsibility of the Operating System (our restaurant manager).

Some Operating Systems can keep the CPU busy with multiple tasks for one user, or even for many users at once. The users will not notice the difference because most users cannot keep up with the CPU anyway. Human beings, and the input devices they must use, are all too subject to human limitations. Actually, all elements of our computer system have some limitations. This point brings us to one of the most important aspects of selecting computer systems — the question of compatibility.

Compatibility means, at a minimum, that two parts working together use the same language of coded instructions. Next, it means that one part doesn't ask for more than another can deliver. Ideally, it also means that all the capabilities of each part can be used. You wouldn't expect our cooks to turn out a 20-course meal on a hot plate. Similarly, you wouldn't furnish them with ten burners, four ovens, and a steamer to prepare hamburgers and french fries. Let's examine how this question of compatibility relates to the various parts of our system.

CPUs Are Not All The Same!

The CPU in our classroom computer is exactly like thousands of other CPUs. Mass production is the reason for its low cost. On the other hand, our CPU is quite different from many more thousands of other CPUs. To name just a few processors in use as of this writing, there are Z-80s, 8080s, 8086s, 8088s, 6502s, 6800s, and 68000s. There are probably many others on the drawing board.

Each CPU design has its own vocabulary of one-word instructions. Software can use these instructions without further explanation. The more limited the vocabulary, the more the software has to explain. Also, different CPUs often use different binary codes for the same instruction.

Another difference between CPUs is in the number and size of the *registers*. Registers are the CPU's work space, rather like the counters and stove top in a kitchen. Until 1983, most microprocessors were *8-bit* systems, meaning that each register had room for eight bits at a time. Eight bits make up a *byte*. Depending on which bits are set to 1 and which set to 0, one byte can represent any one of 255 binary codes; but that is still not very much information. For example, a single letter or punctuation mark uses up the entire 8 bits. Now 16-bit systems are becoming common, and 32-bit systems are being introduced. More work space and larger registers usually mean faster processing — but not always.

There is at least one more important difference between one CPU design and another: Each has its own arrangement for moving information around. Data and instructions, as you know, are sent back and forth in the form of electrical signals. These signals have to flow into the CPU, from register to register, and out to memory. They are carried on *data paths* or *data buses*. A 16-bit data path can move 16 bits of data at once, twice as much as an 8-bit path.

In short, the various CPUs differ in language, vocabulary, work space, and communication speed. No one CPU design is the best. One may be the fastest, another the best suited for handling large numbers. One may be the easiest to use from the programmer's viewpoint. Still another may be the best all around, meaning it handles a variety of tasks well.

Since the CPU is the computer's brain, it would seem to be the most important part. You might well conclude that the first thing to evaluate in a computer system is the CPU. Is that a fact?

CPUs and Memory

Our computer's CPU is always getting data and instructions from its Random Access Memory and putting new information into it. To do this, the location in memory of every byte of information, whether data or instructions, must be remembered or defined or found. The location is called a *memory address*, and it is expressed in binary. When needed, it must be stored, even if only for a microsecond, in the CPU's register space reserved for addresses. Here we come to another difference between 8-bit and 16-bit microprocessors.

In most microprocessors two registers are combined to store an address. Thus an 8-bit CPU can work with 16-bit addresses. The highest number you can express with 16 bits is 65535 (decimal). Thus the maximum amount of RAM supplied with an 8-bit CPU is usually 65535 bytes (commonly referred to as *64K* RAM). Various ways have been found to get around this limit (see *Bank switching* in Appendix 1).

In the same fashion, 16-bit systems can handle 32-bit addresses. In theory, these systems can all access many millions of bytes (*megabytes*) of RAM. Not all systems take full advantage of the fact, but not all systems need to. Our classroom computer, for example, may not need vast amounts of memory. For the programs demonstrated earlier in this chapter, 64K RAM would be more than sufficient. But remember, we were not using all of the computer's capabilities. If we added sound, color, and animation, our program would use more memory. Furthermore, the school system as a whole may have other uses for a computer, such as planning schedules for 700 students, 40 teachers, and 50 courses. For that type of operation, memory capacity is a major consideration. But there are still other factors to consider.

CPUs and Operating Systems

Whatever its relative merits, each CPU design must be recognized by the Operating System that works with it. An Operating System that asks a CPU to do something it wasn't built to do, or asks for it in the wrong language, is quite useless. Sometimes an Operating System designed for one CPU can work with a "new improved" version but cannot use all the new capabilities. An Operating System for an 8-bit CPU cannot use the powers of a 16-bit processor. For example, even though the processor would be ready and able, the Operating System would not ask it to access a large memory or to move data 16 bits at a time.

It may seem at this point that the Operating System should be the major element of choice in choosing a computer system. After all, a powerful Operating System must have a powerful CPU behind it. But there are still other factors to be considered.

Operating Systems and Storage

A major responsibility of our Operating System is to help the CPU find information on disk and write new data out. In order to do this, the Operating

System must know, and perhaps control, the *format* of the disk. The format, in turn, determines the disk's storage capacity. A computer disk is rather like a phonograph record. There is more music on a 33 1/3 RPM record than on a 45 or 78. Depending on the Operating System, a 5¼-inch disk may be formatted to store as little as 80,000 bytes of data or as much as 360,000 bytes.

Our Operating System must also recognize the limitations and capabilities of our disk drives. Some drives have one *head* for reading and writing, and read only one side of the disk. Some have two heads and can read both sides.

What this all adds up to is a great potential for incompatibility. All too often, you cannot write data or programs on a disk with one Operating System and read them off with a different one. This is one area where manufacturers might be expected to adopt universal standards, just as record publishers have. So far, this has not happened.

At this point, perhaps you believe that the best Operating System is the one that lets you store the most data on a disk. But we have just begun to scratch the surface.

Operating Systems, Interpreters, and Compilers

We already mentioned that the Operating System manages just about everything that goes on in the computer. One of its duties is seeing that instructions given by other software are carried out correctly. Other software includes application programs and translators.

Application programs, such as those used for our demonstrations, are usually written in a *high level* language. High level means that the language is closer to human speech than to binary. Since the CPU understands only binary, programs in a high level language must be translated. This translation is done by special programs (more software).

There are two kinds of translators. One kind runs along with the high level program in memory and translates each instruction as it is called on. This is called an *interpreter*. If you are writing your own programs, interpreters are convenient; you can change the program, try it out, and see immediately if your change was for better or worse.

The other kind of translator is a *compiler*. A compiler translates your whole program and produces a new program on disk, in binary. When your program is perfect, you don't need the compiler any more. The compiled program runs by itself. Compiled programs usually run faster and take up less space in RAM. Of course, they also use less RAM because they do not require an interpreter to be there.

Whether you use an interpreter or compiler, the end result is the same. Instructions are given to the CPU in binary, and they are both given and carried out under the close control of the Operating System. So — you guessed it — these elements must be *compatible*.

Now you probably think that a computer shopper should find the best translator and go backward from there. Well, you're getting closer. Programmers who have used many compilers will tell you there are major differences. For instance, programs are very rarely written perfectly the first time. Translators pick up and identify all the mistakes they can, but some do it more nicely than others. Some announce "Punctuation Error on Line 1320" while others may simply say "Error #54" or just "Error." Thus the choice of translator may affect ease of programming and ultimately the quality of programs. However, there is still the matter of what language is to be translated.

Interpreters, Compilers, and Languages

Any translator has to understand two languages, the original (source) and the final (destination). A person may be fluent in Spanish and English, and still not be much help to a Frenchman. Just so, an interpreter or compiler for one language may communicate perfectly with your Operating System but be unable to translate the language or version you want to write in. There are many high level languages, such as *BASIC, COBOL, LOGO, LISP, PL/1, C, FORTRAN*, and for many of these a number of different versions have evolved.

In the next chapter we will concentrate on some of the popular high level languages and their respective merits. The choice of language is an important matter when you or your students will be writing programs. But for many applications, such as the type of drill demonstrated earlier (Figures 4 - 6), you may want to purchase ready-made packages.

Languages and Software

You have probably gotten the picture by now: From CPU to Operating System to translator to language, there is a need for compatibility, for two-way communication. Each "middle-man" must understand a higher level, and be understood by a lower level. Now we have reached the level at which we, the users, become involved. We are the ones who will find the computer a tool or a nuisance. We, after all, are the ones the computer is supposed to serve. For us, the most important parts of our computer system are those we work with directly:

1. The hardware through which we talk to the computer.
2. The software that tells the computer to listen and respond.
3. The hardware that delivers that response.

But as you know, the hardware cannot do anything without software.

Packaged Programs, Producers, and Users

In the early days of computing, there were no packaged programs. Those who needed software learned how to program. The users were the producers. They knew what they wanted to do, and they learned how to do it themselves. Today, a great deal of software is written by nonusers. Some of it is based on the producer's notion (often fuzzy) of what the users want. Some is produced by contract programmers, at great expense, to user specifications. The problem here is similar to the compatibility problems already discussed. Producers and users do not always speak the same language.

It is not the intention of this book to evaluate specific application packages for education, partly because we could not do justice to such a rapidly evolving field, and partly because only the user can decide what software is best for the purpose at hand. Chapter 9 discusses a few of the features to look for in packaged software as well as in programming languages and hardware. The point we want to emphasize is that *software and languages should be your first priority*. The choices made in this area will simplify the choices of Operating System and hardware.

This brings us back to the last of the hardware elements, the input and output devices that serve as our personal and physical links to the computer. You will be happy to hear that almost any input or output device can be *interfaced* to almost any computer system. (Sometimes it does require a bit of wizardry.) But, once again, we must consider the software.

Programs and Input Devices

The program used by teacher Dana Williams in our first demonstration program (Figure 4) presents a menu. Using that menu, Dana has only to type in a "1" to call up the next program (MATH TUTOR). Without the menu, Dana would have to type in "RUN MATH TUTOR." The program gives meaning to an otherwise meaningless "1." A simple step in the program saves the teacher twelve keystrokes.

In theory, an entire program for any application could be written this way: All possible options could be presented on the screen in sequence, with yes/no questions. The user would not need any input device except for a two-way switch. You may recall that many instructions for the earliest computers were indeed entered with banks of two-way switches.

Today there are many variations on the input theme. The fundamental problems of input have been solved. Any kind of input that can be measured — electrically, magnetically, mechanically, or optically — can be converted to binary codes for the CPU. It is the responsibility of the program to make sense out of the codes. Input devices in common use today include joy sticks, paddles, mice, touch screens, light pens, digitizer tablets, and voice digitizers. (For more information, see *Input Devices* in Appendix 1.)

As of this writing, special input devices for the handicapped have not been widely publicized. This is partly because their existence is due more to humanitarian than commercial motives. However, a number of individuals and organizations have developed systems and system enhancements that allow handicapped persons to use and control computer operations.

One of the simplest of these special input devices is the keyboard with key tops embossed in braille for the blind. More complex is the voice digitizer with which one can literally talk to the computer without using eyes or hands. Even more elaborate devices have been designed that can detect the flexing of one muscle — or even the eye movements — of paralytics incapable of other movement. Depending on the software support, single muscles and eye movements can exert as much control as joy sticks.

There may already be more ways for people to talk to computers than ways for people to talk to each other. The kinds of information that can be conveyed are still limited — computers cannot as yet read "body English." On the other hand, they may learn to. Some day your computer screen may display the message "Good morning! What are YOU so cheerful about?"

Programs and Output Devices

We saw above that input such as motion, pressure, rotation, and sound can be converted into digital signals to be read by the computer. In the same way, binary codes from the computer can be converted into output that can be recognized by humans. The output through our video display uses light in patterns of tiny dots, most commonly bright dots on a dark background.

Other computers, many of them in classrooms, use color displays. Color is very appealing and can be used effectively for emphasis and for clarification. But as you can probably imagine, the software has to be written for color! It is not enough to just tell the CRT how to put an "A" on the screen. The instructions and the language and the interpreter must allow for codes defining the background and foreground colors.

Color is especially valuable for graphics. But remember, you still need the right software or the right language to take advantage of any graphics capability. Graphics software may permit the intrusion of text, but its focus is on lines, angles, mathematical curves, shapes, and filling in shapes. Once you have shapes, you may want "animation," which lets you change the shapes and move them around the screen. This, too, requires software support.

There are video displays that can project their images onto a large screen to be seen by the whole classroom at once, but even the most sophisticated video display has its limitations. The output cannot be passed around the room or sent home with the students. Perhaps we need a printer.

Printers range from very inexpensive models (under $200) to laser printers (many thousands of dollars). Generally, higher prices are justified by such factors as printing speed, visual quality of the image, precision of control (especially for graphics), and multicolor capabilitiy. Some printers let the user define the shape and even the size of characters. On the other hand, you might have more need for graphics than for text. In that case, a preferred choice might be a *plotter* which actually draws with pens.

Once again, the wonders of printing technology will do you no good unless your programs can address them. Special features are turned on and off by special codes. If the program doesn't know the code or won't allow you to send it, the special feature is a wasted investment. Experienced users always try the software with the hardware before buying either.

Video displays and printers may satisfy all the needs of the office but in the classroom there is an increasing demand for output devices using sound. Inexpensive home computers can already produce a variety of sounds — musical tones, chords, and unearthly special effects. Some computers provide for synchronizing standard audio tape with a program. This allows the teacher to add oral instructions or comments to the material displayed on the screen.

Finally, there is the *voice synthesizer*. For human beings, the voice is one of the earliest teachers. We learn to understand language by ear long before we learn to read it. A vocal computer can communicate with the preliterate, the illiterate, the blind, and those who cannot sit in front of a CRT for long periods.

Because of its great potential, intensive research and development effort is going into the *synthesis* of human speech. Synthesis should not be confused with prerecording speech on tape. With synthesis, the choice of words to be "spoken" is controlled by programs, in the same way as the prompts and other variable output displayed on the screen.

Before leaving this brief discussion of devices for input and output, we should mention *communications hardware* and *videotext*. The first combines input and output, letting your computer talk to and hear from other computers and peripherals in the next room, the next town (by telephone), or the next continent (with satellite assistance). The second combines features of computers and television.

As computers become more powerful and less costly, related technology is helping more people to access that power. Appendix 1 furnishes more details on many input and output devices as well as other hardware now in common use. The pace of development is such that the list may already be obsolete before this book is printed.

Computers and Values

The modern computer has devices for simple, direct, and personal input and for output in easily recognizable media. Many modern devices can compensate for a human being's physical handicaps. When the computer and all its extensions can be seen as a single comfortable tool, we can forget about how it works and concentrate on using it, even using it to overcome other kinds of handicaps. When we can do that, perhaps we will no longer question the value of computers for human beings.

In this chapter we have focused on the essential building blocks of a computer system and examined the fundamental relationship between hardware and software. Hardware furnishes the computer's power, but programs and languages are at the controls. Thus software provides the direction and the values. In the next chapter we will look at the building blocks of software — languages.

Suggested Reading

Bradbeer, R., & DeBono, P. *The beginner's guide to computers: Everything you need to know about the new technology*. Reading, MA: Addison-Wesley, 1982.

Heller, R., & Martin, C.D. *Bits 'n bytes about computing: A computer literacy primer*. Rockville, MD: Computer Science Press, 1982.

Zaks, R. *Don't (or how to care for your computer)*. Berkeley, CA: Sybex, 1981.

4
Languages and Packaged Software

Chapter 2 traced the evolution of computers, emphasizing the hardware. In Chapter 3, we saw how the hardware and software elements of a computer system work together, emphasizing the fact that these elements must be compatible or they will not work together at all, and also that software is a major factor in all computer operations. In this chapter we will look more closely at the building blocks of software—computer languages—and examine the status of ready-made software.

You may not plan to write a single computer program ever, but an understanding of computer languages will help you understand the differences between the rigid limitations of computer hardware and the almost infinite flexibility of software. At the same time you might conclude, as many others have, that learning a programming language and writing programs, for or with your students, can add a new dimension to the teaching experience.

At the beginning of the computer evolution there was no software at all. Instruction sets for the computer were hard wired. To change the program you had to change the wiring. The development of variable memory and stored programs made it practical to have many programs on tap at once: To change from one program to another, one only had to "read" the new program from storage into memory. Now a computer could run any program at any time.

As a result, more and more programmers were hired to produce volumes of software for myriads of applications. At first everything was written in binary, the only language the machine could understand. The development of assembly language made programming easier, but the development of application software was still a laborious task. Increasing demand inspired the creation of high level languages to make programming easier.

Since then, languages have been created, revised, and cross-bred. While some of these were created to solve special problems efficiently, a major motivation in language evolution has been to make life easier for the user/programmer.

Features of High Level Languages

Modern high level computer languages are easier to learn than human languages:

1. They are always written, so there is no need to worry about pronunciation.

Figure 1
2+2 in Twelve Languages

```
BASIC         FORTRAN   PASCAL          COBOL
10 PRINT 2+2  N=2+2     PROGRAM HARRY;  IDENTIFICATION DIVISION.
              PRINT *, N BEGIN;          DATA DIVISION.
              END       WRITELN(2+2);   WORKING-STORAGE SECTION.
                        END.            01      N PIC 9.
                                        PROCEDURE DIVISION.
                                        MAIN-ROUTINE.
                                            ADD 2 2 GIVING N.
                                            DISPLAY N.
                                            STOP RUN.

ALGOL                   ADA              PL/I
BEGIN    PRINT(2+2);    PROCEDURE HARRY IS  HARRY:  PROCEDURE OPTIONS(MAIN);
END                     BEGIN                       PUT LIST(2+2);
                            PUT(2+2);               END;
                        END;

C                                 SNOBOL              PILOT     APL  LOGO
MAIN()                            OUTPUT = 2 + 2      C:#K=2    2+2  PRINT 2+2
{                                 END                 C:#N=#K+2
         PRINTF("%D\N",2+2);                          T:#N
}

LISP        FORTH   VISICALC  EASY
(PLUS 2 2)  2 2 + .  +2+2     SAY 2+2
```

From *The Eleventh Edition of the Secret Guide to Computers* by Russ Walter, 1984. Reprinted with permission. (*The Secret Guide to Computers* consists of two volumes — Volume I: The Main Secrets, Volume II: Deep Secrets. Both are available from Russ Walter, 92 St. Botolph Street, Boston, MA 02116, Tel: 617 266-8128)

2. They have a relatively small vocabulary.

3. There are no conjugations, tenses, persons, or participles.

On the other hand, most of these languages impose very strict rules about syntax, Figure 1 is Russ Walter's (1984) synopsis of the addition operation for 2 + 2 in 12 languages.

Later on we will discuss some of these languages in more detail. For now, let's see what major factors differentiate one language from another.

The following features determine the *power* of a language, its efficiency in solving widely varied and complex problems:

> VOCABULARY: the number of commands, functions, and descriptors provided
>
> VARIABLE TYPES: how many kinds of data the language can cope with
>
> FUNCTIONS: predefined and called upon with one-word terms
>
> ARRAYS: groups of similar elements given a common name and identified by an index or subscript.
>
> MATRICES: arrays on which mathematical operations can be performed across the board.

Other features determine the *ease of use* — the ease with which a language can be learned; the ease of actual programming; and the ease with which programs can be read, understood, revised, or used.

> SYNTAX: the required order of terms and punctuation in a line of code
>
> FORMAT: indentation, line numbers, free form vs. rigid layout
>
> VARIABLE NAMES: user-assigned, but length limitations affect clarity
>
> EDITOR: a built-in editor is a boon to the programmer
>
> PORTABILITY: permits running same program on different makes of computer
>
> STRUCTURE: may be restrictive but ensures logical thinking

PROCEDURAL ORGANIZATION: small program units can call
upon each other
EXTENSIBILITY: the user can define new terms
and add them to vocabulary

Here are two features that may be important in the classroom but are not available with the majority of computer languages today:

GRAPHICS: some languages have built in
graphics capabilities
COLOR: some languages include codes
to control colors

On the following pages we will examine some of these features more closely.

Vocabulary

In high level languages, the smaller the vocabulary the easier it is to learn. The first *BASIC* (Beginners All-purpose Symbolic Instruction Code), designed for computer novices, had only 15 terms, and 8 of these were bonded in functional pairs such as IF...THEN. On the other hand, the larger the vocabulary the greater the user's control. A modern *BASIC* has a vocabulary of nearly 100 terms. There are computer languages with so many terms that most are hardly ever used. One of these is *PL/1*. Its vocabulary is so enormous, in fact, that many computers are not big enough to handle it. To solve that problem, a number of smaller versions of *PL/1* have evolved.

For writing simple programs, most high level languages use terms whose meaning can be understood at once or figured out without too much difficulty, as in the following examples:

PLUS, ADD, or +   BEGIN, END
IF...THEN...ELSE   READ or GET, WRITE or PUT
FOR...NEXT   GOTO (sometimes GO TO)
PRINT or DISPLAY (on video screen), LPRINT (on printer)

The more powerful the language, the more likely it is to have a large vocabulary, including terms that are not self-explanatory. For example,"MKI$" in *BASIC* and "getc" and "struct" in the language *C*.

Most high level language vocabularies include terms for the following:

- giving direct commands (e.g., **GET, PRINT**)
- defining conditions for executing commands (**IF** so-and-so...**THEN**)
- assigning names and values to data items (**LET** A = B + C, or A = 2.5)
- defining data item types (**INT** for integer)
- defining one data item as a function of another (B = TAN(A))
- formatting statements for video display or printouts (TAB(20))
- defining where to read or write data in a storage file

The terms in each language's vocabulary are *reserved words* and cannot be used for any other purpose. However, each language allows the user to make up almost any number of words for naming *variables*.

Variable Types

A variable is like a box or entry space in a preprinted work sheet. The same box always has the same label, such as STUDENT NAME or DATE or ANSWER. The contents of the box, however, can vary from student to student or day to day.

Just as the earliest computers could deal only with numbers, so the earliest languages only allowed *numeric* variables. Most languages today can cope with *string* variables — strings of characters that can include letters, numbers, spaces, and special characters. Without string variables a program cannot handle names or addresses, let alone text. Some languages offer great flexibility with many forms of string manipulation.

Languages also differ in the types of numeric variables allowed and in the ways they are identified. Common types of numeric variables for microcomputer languages include:

INTEGER: five digits, ranging from –32767 to +32768, with no decimal places (these are the largest decimal numbers that can be expressed in binary with 2 bytes or 16 bits)

SINGLE PRECISION: up to six digits with a floating decimal point whose location can be specified in the program

DOUBLE PRECISION: up to sixteen digits with floating decimal point.

Some languages only allow single precision numeric variables. Some allow all three types. Some allow more digits in a given type. *FORTRAN*, created to solve scientific problems, also allows complex numbers, arrived at by combining real and imaginary numbers.

Functions

All languages let you add, multiply, subtract, and divide with simple terms. More powerful languages also have built-in functions that quickly find the square root, tangent, sine, cosine, or natural logarithm of a given value. *FORTH* and *FORTRAN* let you specify other trigonometric functions, such as arctangents and hyperbolic cosines; *APL* includes several esoteric functions, such as factorials and binomials.

Most languages let you define functions of your own, with an instruction like:

DEF FNA(X) = SQR(X) + 2.375

Having defined the function once you can use it anywhere in the program, substituting any variable for X. For example:

Z = FNA(HUP)...if HUP is 2, Z will be 6.375

Arrays

An *array* is a group of data elements, usually all of the same type, such as JAN, FEB, MAR...NOV, DEC. Any one element in the array can be identified by using its *index* or *subscript*. Thus, in the array MONTHS, MAY would be MONTHS(5). However, some versions of some languages insist that the first element be 0; then MAY would be MONTHS(4).

Some languages insist that all arrays be made of numbers. Some also permit string arrays. *LOGO* allows an all-inclusive array called a *list* that allows numbers and words to be mixed indiscriminately.

For many applications, the use of arrays is a tremendous convenience. Some languages allow *multidimensional arrays*. For example, a student's progress record might include a three-dimensional array of grade by skill by month.

Matrices

For even greater convenience, some languages let you treat an array as a *matrix* and perform an operation on all elements with one instruction. For example, multiply every element by two or calculate the sum of all elements or add the elements of one matrix to the corresponding elements of another. Using matrix averaging, you could easily average a student's progress in each subject over three years.

Syntax

Syntax means about the same thing in a programming language that it does in human language. It refers to the order in which terms appear in an instruction, and to the punctuation used. Most high level languages are highly unforgiving about syntax. In fact, the syntax is sometimes a good deal harder to learn than the terminology, because it is peculiar to the language. For example, in most languages, arithmetic operations are performed in the order they appear, from left to right. Thus, 3 x 7 + 8 will result in 21 + 8, or 29. But *APL* does it backward: 3 x 7 + 8 will result in 3 x 15, or 45.

Format

Format refers to the way instructions are arranged on the video screen or on paper when printed out. Languages vary widely in their format requirements: *RPG* allocates specific columns for everything; *COBOL* and a few others require indentation for detailed instruction lines; *BASIC* is pretty much free form, except that every line starts with a number. In *BASIC* one can give an instruction in line 50 to GOTO 620. Languages that do not use line numbers may let the user assign a *label* to a sub-set of instructions and then say GOTO GETANS or GOTO WRITEREC.

The requirement for a specific format imposes a discipline on the programmer, and makes it easier for an experienced programmer to read the creation of another. On the other hand, it means another set of rules to remember. Even if a program is correct logically, the computer will not accept it if the format is wrong.

Variable Names

One feature that can make a big difference in ease of programming is the length of the "name" you can give a variable. *ALGOL* allows names of up to 64 characters; one *BASIC* sets the limit at 2, while another allows 40. Still another allows 40 but only pays attention to the first two; if you name one variable NAME and another NATIONALITY this language reserves one box called NA, with unpredictable results.

Editor

Writing and revising a program can usually be done with any text editor or word processor. If functions such as Change, Delete, Append, Renumber, etc. are built into a language it saves a great deal of time, especially if one is developing programs on a trial and error basis and making a great many revisions.

Portability

Many languages vary according to the computer being used. *LOGO* is one of these; if you start out with *LOGO* on one computer, and later want to acquire hardware from another manufacturer, you may need to purchase a new version of *LOGO*. A major reason for the rapidly growing popularity of the language *C* is the promise that a program written in *C* will run on many different makes of computers. This promise, coupled with the inherent power and flexibility of *C*, is expected to outweigh one disadvantage: *C* is not an easy language to learn or to use, certainly not as easy to use as *BASIC*.

Example of a Basic Program

To illustrate some of the features we have been discussing so far, let's look at a small part of the addition drill in Chapter 3, as it might be programmed in *BASIC*. *BASIC* is one of the most popular general-purpose microcomputer languages, and it is available in several versions for different CPUs and Operating Systems. In this example, the computer is told to:

1. pick two three-digit numbers;
2. determine their sum;
3. display the numbers on the screen;
4. give the user up to three chances to find the right sum;
5. present another problem; and
6. keep doing this until five problems have been completed.

One part of this program segment may seem a bit obscure — the part that tells the computer to pick a three-digit number at random. This operation is explained later on. The rest of the steps in our program segment are straightforward. To make the segment even easier to follow, we have omitted the instructions needed to display date, time, prompts, "?," "—," etc., and to define where everything appears on the screen. As with all programs in all languages, the computer reads this program line by line unless it is told to do otherwise.

Figure 2
Segment of *BASIC* Program for Additional Drill

TASK IN ENGLISH	LINE	INSTRUCTION IN BASIC
Set up for five problems	10	FOR P = 1 TO 5
Pick a three-digit integer and call it "A" (for further explanation see Note below)	20	A = INT(RND * 899 + 100)
Pick another and call it "B"	30	B = INT(RND * 899 + 100)
Add A and B and call result "C"	40	C = A + B
Display the value of A	50	PRINT A
Display the value of B	60	PRINT B
Ask for user's sum, get it from keyboard, call it "ANS"	70	INPUT ANS
If answer is right, go get ready for next problem	80	IF ANS = C GOTO 110
If we have reached this line the answer must be wrong; so add one to count of wrong answers	90	WRNG = WRNG + 1
If third wrong answer, display right answer. If not, go back (to line 70) for another answer	100	IF WRNG = 3 THEN PRINT C ELSE 70
If we're here we must be ready for a new problem, so we have to start counting wrong answers all over again from zero.	110	WRNG = 0
If we are here it is time for another problem (if we have done five problems already, on to line 130)	120	NEXT P

Lines 10 and 120 define a FOR-NEXT LOOP: The task within the loop is to be performed five times.

Lines 20, 30, 40, 70, 90 assign VARIABLE NAMES (A, B, C, ANS, WRNG) to values.

Lines 40 and 90 call for ARITHMETIC functions.

Lines 50, 60, 100 send OUTPUT to the video display (using instruction PRINT).

Line 70 asks for, waits for, and reads user INPUT of user's ANSwer.

Lines 80-120 demonstrate LOGIC control: IF so-and-so, THEN do this; otherwise do something else. Line 90 is reached by implicit logic — if the condition for going to 110 has not been met, then 90 is read by default.

Explanation of Lines 20 and 30

1. The teacher had specified that this addition drill should use three-digit numbers, meaning numbers from 100 to 999.
2. The term RND instructs the computer to select a random number between zero and one (a decimal fraction, such as .822347).
3. When this value is multiplied by 899, it yields a number between 0 and 899. (We use "*" to indicate multiplication since "x" often means the letter x.)
4. Now we have a number between 0 and 899. Adding 100, we get a value from 100 to 999. (In *BASIC*, as in most languages, arithmetic operations are performed in the order they are read, from left to right.)
5. Since it is very likely that we still have a fraction, INT rounds the result to the nearest integer. The parentheses tell the computer to make an integer of everything within the parentheses.
6. Thus INT(RND * 899 + 100) is all we need to obtain a random three digit number. The "A =" assigns that value to a variable called "A."

Structure and Structured Programming

We could write this program in any of several other modern languages, and some will say we should. Purists criticize *BASIC* for its lack of structure. The proponents of structured programming insist that all instructions should be read from the top down. *BASIC* allows forward jumps, as in the above example, where line 80 instructs the computer to GOTO line 110; but it also allows backward jumps, as from 100 to 70.

Long programs in *BASIC*, especially as improvements are made, are apt to sprout GOTOs all over the place. The result can be thoroughly confusing to the human reader. Corrections and improvements become both difficult and hazardous. Programmer jargon for this kind of program is "spaghetti code."

Structured programming, its proponents claim, forces the programmer to think logically. The programmer must learn to:

1. analyze all the tasks to be performed,
2. consider the logical sequence of operations, and
3. plan ahead.

Some languages favor, or even require, the programmer to follow the rules of structured programming. *RPG*, for example, is a strict disciplinarian. All input, files, tables, and arrays must be defined at the beginning of a program; these are followed by instructions for processing and for user interaction; output to disk storage or to a printer must be defined at the end. It is nearly impossible to write an *RPG* program without preliminary analysis and planning.

Structured languages have another advantage: They tend to be *self-documenting*: *COBOL*, as used today, is very structured indeed. Anyone who knows *COBOL* can pick up a *COBOL* program and easily see what is going on, and how to modify it if necessary. Thus *COBOL* is a favored language in large corporations with many programmers and high turnover.

Procedural Languages

Another approach to structure is found in the *procedural languages*. These let you define one procedure (set of instructions), perhaps with just a few lines of code; call up that procedure from another one; and so on. With a procedural language, even a large and complex task can be seen as a sequence of discrete operations.

Among procedural languages, *LOGO* and its variations are claimed by many to be the most flexible. *LOGO* is especially popular in the classroom, where it is often used by five- and six-year olds. When we say "used" we mean the students actually learn the language while writing their own procedures. They may have a specific goal in mind, or they may just try something new and see what happens.

LOGO was developed at MIT as a computer language for children. At that time there were no video display screens, and *LOGO* proved almost as boring as any other language. To make things more interesting, the computer was hooked up to a mechanical *turtle*; the turtle moved around the floor under the control of a *LOGO* program. The turtle was equipped with a pen, and *LOGO* had instructions for **PEN DOWN** or **PEN UP**. Finally, the floor was covered with paper; when the pen was down, it drew a line wherever the turtle moved.

When video display screens came along, the turtle was converted to a small triangle (in place of the standard cursor). As before, a *LOGO* procedure could move the turtle and draw a line wherever it moved. Short programs, or *procedures*, could produce surprisingly interesting pictures.

Example of *LOGO* In Use
In the following excerpt from Papert's *Mindstorms* (1980), we see a hypothetical but typical example of two students carrying out an experiment

with turtle graphics *LOGO*. Their initial goal is to draw a flower (see Figures 3-8*).

They begin with the procedure, already defined, that draws a quarter circle using a given radius (Figure 3).

Using QCIRCLE twice, this procedure draws a petal. The "RIGHT 90" means turn to the right 90 degrees (Figure 4).

Figure 3   **Figure 4**

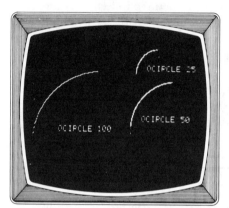   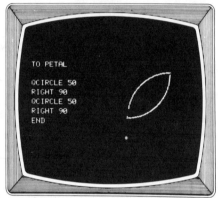

Figure 5   **Figure 6**

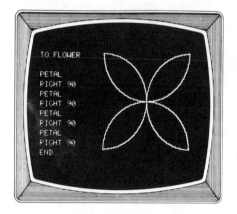   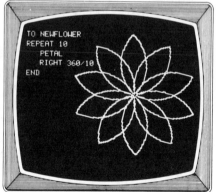

To make a four-petal flower, the students use PETAL four times, turning right 90 degrees between each petal. However, as one student says, it looks "more like a propeller." They decide they need more petals, maybe ten (Figure 5).

---

*From *MINDSTORMS: Children, Computers, and Powerful Ideas* by Seymour Papert. ©1980 by Basic Books, Inc., Publishers. Reprinted by permission of the publisher.

They don't want to type the PETAL and RIGHT instructions ten times, so they try the REPEAT function. (This REPEAT is rather like the FOR...NEXT loop in BASIC.) Now they have a flower, but it's too big (Figure 6).

Here the PETAL size has been changed to 25, and a stem and a leaf have been added (Figure 7). Presto, a PLANT!

Now truly inspired, our two artists call upon a SLIDE procedure that moves the turtle without drawing a line, and they use RANDOM to get various sizes and numbers of petals. Some of the plants have no leaves, but who needs them in such a GARDEN (Figure 8)?

Figure 7   **Figure 8**

Extensibility

LOGO is also known as an *extensible* language, because its own vocabulary can be extended. Procedures such as QCIRCLE, PETAL, NEWFLOWER, and PLANT, once defined, become functions that can be used in any other procedures, simply by referring to them by name.

Proponents say that *LOGO*, without imposing its own rigid structure on users, leads to discovery of structure. In the process, they assure us, the students learn something about the process of thinking itself. They discover that a seemingly complex procedure consists of a series of small steps that must usually be taken in a particular order. With guidance, students learn that analysis and planning skills used in *LOGO* can be applied to other kinds of problems.

As noted earlier, *LOGO* comes in different versions for different computers. Some versions do not include turtle graphics; some go beyond line drawings and permit the user to create shapes (cars, people, animals, clouds, trees) in color, to assign several levels of viewer distance (foregound and background), and to move the shapes around individually on the screen, with the foreground shapes always passing in front of (obscuring) the background. In short, the user can develop most of the effects seen in video games.

Graphics

The *LOGO* language was developed with graphics as its focal point. In most other languages, the ability to define graphic elements is either nonexistent or is only included as an extension. Languages with built-in graphics permit the user to define points, lines, vectors, angles, circles, arcs, shapes, bars, and so on. The graphics feature is especially valuable for work with learning-disabled students because it provides an additional and very appealing means of communication.

Color

If graphics add a new dimension to communication, color adds still another. Some monochrome screens substitute texture for color; in general, however, controls for determining color are of no value unless the program is used with a color monitor.

Is There a Best Language?

For any computer and any purpose there will always be one or two languages more suitable than others. Vendor offerings and user priorities change rapidly, but as of 1984 some popular languages for specific purposes are as follows:

- Instruction and drill programs written by teachers: *PILOT* or *BASIC*
- Student programming: *LOGO, GraFORTH, BASIC, LISP*
- Scientific work and "number crunching": *FORTRAN*
- Accounting and office records: *COBOL* or *RPG* for mainframes, *BASIC* for microcomputers
- Statistical analysis, as in evaluating student body profiles and educational programs: *SPSS*
- General-purpose: *C* for dedicated programmers, *BASIC* for the less experienced.

It is not for this author to say which is the best language for use in any school. It would be possible for a school to use *COBOL* for accounting; *BASIC* for drill type programs; *LOGO* for student programming; and other languages for word processing, scheduling, or statistical analysis. It might be possible to use one language, such as *BASIC*, for all of these, but the results would leave something to be desired in each area.

In general, acquiring a large number of languages requires a considerable investment. In addition, many software vendors require that one unit of a package — whether program, language interpreter, or compiler — be purchased for each computer on which it might be used. Thus a school system purchasing *LOGO* for use on 20 computers might have to buy 20 *LOGO* disks at the outset.

At this point, the fundamental question of educational purpose deserves some attention. Is the goal to use the computer as a teaching aid in a traditional curriculum? Is it to prepare students to live in a computer-dominated society? Is it to begin preparation for eventual employment in the computer field? Is it to develop general problem-solving skills? Is it to open the students' minds to new ways of thought through a new medium of communication and expression? If the educational goals include all of the above, where are priorities to be assigned?

Perhaps an equally fundamental question is: How much of a commitment is the individual teacher prepared to make? How willing is she to explore a new technology and a new direction? If the teacher is going to write programs, she must understand programming logic and develop familiarity with the language. If the students will be writing programs, the teacher must not only know the language but must also understand the many ways it can be used.

If programs are to be purchased off the shelf, the teacher must be prepared to evaluate available packages. Published reviews, recommendations of other educators, and even advertising material can be of some help, especially in weeding out totally unsuitable programs. However, no software should be purchased solely on the basis of other people's opinions. The teacher must still decide whether a candidate program will fit into the particular learning situation in the classroom, and whether it will meet the highly individualized needs of the students.

Packaged Software

Software written specifically for education represents a small fraction of the volume of packaged software available today. One reason for this is that the business and home markets have always been viewed as larger and more lucrative. Another is that few programmers have been trained in education; similarly, few educators have learned programming. As of 1983, there were well over 7,000 producers of microcomputer software. Of these, only a few dozen were producing programs that offered, intentionally or fortuitously, educational value for the elementary level. And of such programs, many were intended not for classroom education but for home entertainment.

Game Programs

An early example of such fortuitous educational value is the computer game *Lemonade.* Two or more players compete to see who can achieve the most profit (or smallest loss). The price of ingredients and supplies is given, and each player decides on the quantity of lemonade to be prepared, as well as the size and sale price of a glassful. The computer chooses the day's weather at random — sunny but cool, rainy and cool, cloudy and hot, etc. As you can see, playing this game develops some understanding of business as well as skill in planning and arithmetic.

Micro-worlds and Simulation Software

Lemonade could be categorized as a *simulation program,* a type which is gaining favor among educators. A simulation program represents a real-life or perhaps a fantasy situation in which the user/player/student is given a set of parameters and expected to draw conclusions or make decisions, or both. Sophisticated programs offer many levels of difficulty involving more and more parameters. Many allow the competent user to move through the program at a faster pace, perhaps even taking shortcuts. The more ambitious packages are sometimes called *micro-worlds* because they offer a more or less complete definition of a unique environment.

Educators whose students have worked successfully with simulation programs say that their primary benefit is the development of general analysis and problem-solving skills — drawing inferences, making associations, recognizing cause-and-effect relationships, planning, and evaluating results.

Microlaboratories and Discovery Programs

Some simulation programs are exploratory rather than goal oriented. They might be classified as what-if software. One type of simulation software is the MBL, or Microcomputer-Based Laboratory. *Catlab* displays a number of graphic felines with genetic color traits, and some information about which traits are dominant and which recessive. The user selects pairs for breeding and the results are displayed — immediately instead of six weeks later. Good microlaboratory programs, incidentally, do not try to duplicate experiments that could be carried on in the classroom just as well without a computer.

Discovery Programs

Catlab could be called a *discovery* program in that the user can find out governing principles on his own, which is often more effective than being spoon-fed the same information. In this case the field has a narrow focus, but some discovery programs deal with broad areas of such subjects as geometry, music, or language. The latter type of program may require considerable guidance from the teacher to help the students assimilate their discoveries. Alternatively, it may require considerable restraint, giving the students time for true *discovering* rather than just being shown.

Strategy Software

Strategy programs are goal oriented and involve some way of measuring success. A strategy program, like a board game of chess or bridge, develops skills in analysis, weighing alternatives, and planning. It does not have to be a competition between two or more individuals; it may be a race against the clock or just the challenge of doing better than last time. Some strategy programs are abstract, some are simulations of real-life situations, some are adventures in fantasy land.

Computer Literacy Software

A small number of packages are intended primarily to develop an understanding of how computers work. One example is *GraFORTH*. *GraFORTH* is sometimes called a language; it is easier to learn than *BASIC* or *LOGO*. Like turtle *LOGO*, it emphasizes the creation of graphics. The student is introduced to the fundamentals of programming and logic, and the graphics provide a visual image of the results.

While *GraFORTH* focuses on software, the popular package *Rocky's Boots* is an introduction to the elemental hardware components and their functions. It includes six sections: The first three sections are tutorials on the various hardware components, and the last three allow the user to assemble units in various configurations to see if and how they work.

Tutorial Software

Tutorial software conveys information directly, rather than leading the user to discover it for himself. Although inherently less exciting, it may use graphics and sound to reinforce the instruction — two balloons with a large word "TWO," a large number "2," and a voice saying "TWO balloons." Unlike a textbook, tutorial programs should be interactive, asking for input to test the user's comprehension and providing immediate feedback as to the correctness of the input. Some programs may track the student's progress and vary the pace of the tutorial accordingly. Unless every student has the full-time use of a computer, this type of software is often less cost effective than teacher presentations and textbooks.

Drill, Practice, and Quiz Software

Drill, practice, and quiz programs, whatever the subject, work rather like the sample addition drill we saw in Chapter 3. Their intention is not to teach but to provide practice and measure progress in such cut-and-dried areas as arithmetic, spelling, and grammar.

At the very least, computer drill programs offer the psychological reinforcement of immediate feedback. Some go much further, trying to make practice sessions fun with animated color graphics and perhaps sound. Some go too far in this direction: A student who has difficulty concentrating may do better with a program that focuses all of his attention on the problem at hand.

We recall seeing a simple but highly effective — and very popular — program written by a special education teacher in Lexington, Mass. The program allowed the teacher to enter a group of words. For each word, the program created a long scrambled string using the letters of the word, and then embedded the word at a random location in the string. Thus, beginning with the word "child," the program might produce "dlcihichdildhlidchild-lcihdic." The student's task is to move the cursor to the beginning of the actual word.

Drill programs should always allow the teacher to tailor the program to the needs of individual students. Another important feature of drill and practice programs is to capture and store information so that the teacher and others can evaluate each student's progress.

Administrative Software

A number of packages are available for tracking student progress, performing statistical analysis, and doing other administrative tasks. Unless such a package is designed to work with instructional programs and capture the data accumulated in their use, all data will have to be entered by the teacher.

Finding Educational Software

Although the volume of software packages for education is far less than that for business, it is still large enough to intimidate the casual investigator. Advertising only shows the tip of the iceberg; advertising is so expensive that few in the educational field can afford it. A number of directories are being published on an annual or monthly basis. Those that list many programs can only offer scanty information on each. Those that provide detailed descriptions of each package cannot cover much of the field. Many directories list only commercial software, while the very package you are seeking may have been written last year by an imaginative teacher in the town next to yours.

Probably one of the first priorities of a school system interested in purchasing software is to become familiar with sources of information — dealing with private as well as commercial software, and on levels ranging from local to international.

Evaluating Software Packages

A small but growing number of organizations are taking responsibility for evaluating software. Some establish a rating method and give each package a score. A really thorough evaluation of a complex program may require months, to determine the instructional effectiveness of a program in diverse situations and the long-term retention of information or concepts conveyed. Thus it be may never be possible to apply this evaluation method to all the packages available.

Ideally, no software should be purchased until the teacher who will be using it can evaluate it personally to determine its suitability for the particular students in the specific learning environment. Regardless of its approach or application, any software package for the classroom should be carefully studied and tried before purchase. The following is a discussion of a few of the features that should be considered.

Documentation

Does the package include a user's manual? Is the manual clear and complete? Does it tell you about potential difficulties that might be encountered and how to cope with them?

Accuracy

Is the educational information conveyed (factual and conceptual) valid and accurate? Does the program always reject incorrect answers? Does it ever reject correct answers? If the program is complex, with multiple branches and levels, it may be necessary to spend some time with the program to check its accuracy in all areas.

Simplicity

Do razzle-dazzle special effects dominate the program? Animated color graphics may be very exciting on first inspection, but may quickly lose their appeal, be distracting, and actually mask a lack of real content. Sound effects that are acceptable in the home may not be appreciated in a classroom where several students are working on computers at once.

Flexibility

Can the program vary dynamically in response to the user's comprehension? At the very least, it should permit the teacher to predetermine the level of difficulty and the user response speed required.

Suitability

Are all the parts of a program written for the same level of comprehension? Or does it, for example, use text at a fourth-grade reading level to explain arithmetic operations to second graders?

Integration

Is the program designed as part of a series so that skills and concepts can build in a logical continuum? If not, will it at least make a substantial contribution to the current or planned curriculum? It is surprisingly easy to accumulate a hodgepodge of unrelated software.

User Interaction

Is there immediate feedback? Can the user see the effects of his input right away? Can this feature be bypassed, reducing the amount of hand-holding, and allowing a substantial block of user input before feedback?

Convenience, Forgiveness, and Help For Users

Can the user enter commands and responses with a minimum of keystrokes? Does the program go to pieces if the user hits a special key or several keys at once? Is there a way for the student to get additional help from the program, or at least get out of a particular part of the program if he — or the program — gets confused? Advertisements for one program boast that "the student is never abandoned."

Social Concepts

Does the program foster socially acceptable concepts? Many game programs are based on violence and destruction via missiles and bombs; many cling to outdated stereotypes of male/female roles. Some educators criticize computer games for their almost universal portrayal of extraterrestrial beings as monstrous and hostile.

Efficiency

Does the program carry out its internal operations quickly, or does it use too much time presenting prompts, changing from one screen to another, and providing feedback? If it is a discovery program, does it go to more fuss and bother than necessary to convey a simple idea?

Graphics Quality

If the program uses graphics, are the images clear and unambiguous? If it uses color, is the color used to help get the message across? Will it be effective even with a monochrome monitor? (Graphics programs should be tried with the type of monitor you intend to use or with a number of different monitors.)

Source Code Availability

If you want to make your own revisions, some vendors will provide software in source code form (its form before being translated into binary), sometimes for a higher price. To make your own revisions, of course, you will need an interpreter or compiler.

Vendor Reliability

Does the software house or other vendor have an established reputation, or offer a guarantee, or promise to provide updates as the program is improved? If the program is copy protected, can worn out disks or tapes be replaced at little or no charge?

Hardware

If you already own or plan to purchase a particular hardware and Operating System, does the program run on it without special adaptation? Do not take anybody's word on this, but insist on seeing it run. The program may have been created for an earlier or newer model or a different version.

Conclusion

In this chapter we have seen that purchasing a computer system and using it are two very different matters. There is a growing consensus that use should be the primary consideration, from which the selection of hardware and operating systems and languages should follow logically.

For those readers without previous knowledge of computers, we hope that Chapters 2, 3, and 4 have provided a degree of understanding of the computer as a tool. For those with experience, we hope these chapters have served as a review and an overview of the many and diverse factors that must be considered by teachers and administrators in planning hardware and software acquisitions. Now, it is time to turn to the major theme of this book, how microcomputers are actually used and how they might be used in the special needs classroom.

Suggested Reading

Chantler, A. *Programming techniques and practice.* New York: International Publications Service, 1981.

Moursand, D. *Basic programming for computer literacy.* New York: McGraw-Hill, 1978.

Papert, S. *Mindstorms: Children, computers, and powerful ideas.* New York: Basic Books, 1980.

Walter, R. *The eleventh edition of the secret guide to computers,* 1984. (Available from Russ Walter, 92 St. Botolph Street, Boston, MA 02116; Tel: 617/266-8128.)

Section II
Microcomputers:
Applications to the
Instructional Process

5

Computer Assisted Instruction in Special Education

Computers can be useful with special education students because instructional techniques demonstrated to be effective for teaching mildly handicapped students can be easily incorporated into computer assisted instruction (CAI). The computer's advantages for special education students include:

1. Individualization and self-pacing: With well-programmed CAI, special education students work at their own pace with material that meets their specific needs. In addition, rate of presentation and response may be regulated for each student.
2. Immediate feedback: Students receive immediate feedback about their performance.
3. Consistent correction procedures: Special education students are often confused by corrections that are too wordy. CAI can provide specific, consistent correction for errors.
4. Repetition without pressure: Since the computer is emotionless and infinitely patient, repetitive tasks may not be aversive or embarrassing for the student, but indicative of mastery. This is particularly important for slow-learning students who do not experience success in academic tasks frequently or easily.
5. Immediate reinforcement for correct responses: The software provides

immediate positive reinforcement for correct answers, which motivates students.

6. Well-sequenced instruction: A task may be analyzed, broken down into manageable steps, and then programmed. Special education teachers often do not have the training or time to construct the consistent, well-sequenced instruction that most special education students need, and that good software can provide.

7. High frequency of student response: If the interactive features of the computer are put to full use, students get more practice solving problems than they do working in large groups or with work sheets.

8. Repeated demonstration of mastery of academic subject matter: A sense of mastery of subject matter, especially academic subject matter, is very important to students who have experienced and continue to experience failure in instruction. The computer allows them to review their earlier attainments and recall them. The students can demonstrate to themselves and others their competence in academic subjects. These ego boosts can be critical at times of frustration. The special education student can be "in control of" his learning.

9. Peer response: Computer use by students in the special education setting may be viewed positively by other students who do not have computers in their classrooms.

10. Motivation: This can be described at two levels. Many special education students are excited by working on a computer, even doing class work. For others, it is an excellent motivator to allow time for computer games as a reward for work completed. Earning computer time may result in more focused and concentrated work by easily-frustrated students who produce slowly or not at all in their usual assignments.

   Many teachers feel that this reward system is out of place in schools. However, if games generate work from students who are very poor producers, then the student benefits. The practical benefit for the child is more critical than moralizing about "proper" avenues for school learning. Restricting the student's selection of the computer game may make this reward system more palatable to teachers since some games reinforce academic skills, social skills, and eye-hand coordination.

11. Improvement of motor skills and visual motor coordination: Playing computer games with a paddle or joystick improves a student's gross and fine motor skills and visual-motor coordination. Learning and practice of these skills are embedded in more naturalistic settings than the often artificial exercises offered in individual or small-group therapies. It is easy to imagine a child with limited control over his wrist or arm movements willing and motivated to play a game against

the computer or another child that will "force" him to exert more conscious control over his movements.

12. Minimize disabilities: The computer enables the poor or inefficient learner to minimize or circumvent significant barriers to learning. Students who are able to understand basic math concepts but unable to do error-free calculations (due to poor memory, visual, perceptual, or other problems) can manipulate numbers and letters with greater ease and accuracy in an interactive mode. Their reasoning abilities can be expressed without interference from their problems in producing output. Using the computer as a word processor may help a special education student bypass writing, spelling, and language arts problems by allowing the student to edit and revise work easily. The time and energy formerly spent on laborious rewriting of rough drafts can be spent developing ideas in a legible and acceptable form. The ready availability of spelling- or punctuation-checking programs can pit the child against himself. The computer motivates him to reduce spelling or other writing errors, since he can chart his errors after each attempt to reduce them. Most important, the child unable to produce acceptable work can demonstrate his productivity to himself and others.

A Brief Contrast Between
Micros and Mainframes for CAI Delivery

CAI was traditionally delivered by a mainframe computer, which provided a great deal of flexibility. Recent developments in technology have made computers more readily available in schools and homes by dramatically reducing their price and size, increasing their ease of use, and providing a wide array of applications software. However, the limitations of microcomputers have also imposed limitations on the elegance of instructional programming.

Mainframe computers of the past decades provided large memory and storage capabilities that allowed elaborate instructional formats, monitored performance of the learner, and permitted some elegant forms of feedback (i.e., interweaving failed items in subsequent arrays of problems). However, mainframes were at a considerable distance from the classroom and had to be accessed by telephone hookups that were expensive, required a skilled person to manage, and often broke down. By 1975, the close of the period in which mainframe computers were dominant in CAI, some sophisticated programming had been developed. This programming is exemplified by *PLATO*, developed and marketed by Control Data Corporation.

The earliest educational software—designed mainly for the first Apple microcomputers which had a 16K memory capacity—consisted of simple drill and practice programs that presented problems in a rote order, much like flash cards or workbook pages. Drill and practice remained the dominant approach of educational software for microcomputers, even when 64K memory became a common feature of micros for personal or home use. Machines with 64K memory are still limited since the microcomputer's active memory (its capacity to handle data at one time) is limited by the machine's built-in memory. One can access a large data base by connecting the system to larger, passive memory storage (such as a hard disk and expansion boards) which may add millions of bits of memory. However, the system remains limited by the capacity of the computer's central processor.

It is likely that these limitations will remain until the internal active memory of the microcomputer is vastly increased or programming requirements become more efficient and diminish the need for internal memory. These limitations become critical when considering the possibilities for instructional software—the current state being universally described as woeful. However, this situation is only due in part to the limitations of the microcomputer. Interesting educational software can be written within these limits but it is only beginning to appear. Small, independent software developers write for the machines being sold at a high volume to recoup their investment quickly since the software may become obsolete or be pirated. The school market, referred to as "the sleeping giant," has lagged behind in acceptance of the microcomputer and was not seen as a large purchaser of software until recently; so less interest has been generated in educational software than in business or home applications.

As the hardware technology dramatically changes, the software inevitably lags behind since software products cannot be written until the machines are available. More recent practice by hardware manufacturers has been to minimize this lag by making later machines compatible with earlier models, by adopting operating systems that allow the new models to utilize widely-available software, and by making specifications for new machines available to software developers prior to introduction.

Modes of Computer Assisted Instruction

Six modes of instructional software commonly used in computer assisted instruction are:

1. drill and practice
2. tutorial
3. educational games
4. demonstrations
5. simulations
6. problem solving.

Other computer applications that provide additional compelling instructional advantages include word processing to stimulate and improve writing, spelling and language-arts programs to monitor accuracy of the written output, computer programs developed by the child, data analysis programs, and games developed by the child.

Drill and Practice

Drill and practice is currently the most commonly used mode of CAI in schools. It is designed to help integrate and consolidate previously learned material through practice on the computer. Drill and practice software provides immediate feedback, appropriate individualization, repetition, immediate reinforcement, and self-pacing. It serves as a supplement to other forms of instruction. The common model for drill and practice software is the workbook. More sophisticated software can exceed the workbook by noting the items the child has failed, inserting them in the next series of items to be learned, and *fading* them as they are learned.

While drill and practice programs have been criticized for demonstrating few advantages over much less expensive workbooks, they do provide distinct advantages for special education children who have experienced extended periods of failure. Working with the computer can be exciting and motivating because successful interaction with the computer can generate a sense of potency. This sense of power or competence in learning is infrequently experienced by many special education students. Given positive learning experiences, they work longer at the computer than at their workbooks. Further, when they experience failure, the previously successful computer interaction beckons as an ego boost: They can return to that program and repeat their successful learning, showing themselves, if not others, that they *can* perform well.

Other aspects of drill and practice software are valuable. With work sheets, the child may repeat the same incorrect response over and over again. On the computer, the immediate feedback and reinforcement for correct and incorrect answers guides the student's subsequent responses.

One of Hartley Courseware's drill and practice programs, *Clock*, presents four different exercises to show the student how to convert from digital time to clock time. Modes 1 and 2 have the student move the hands of a clock to correspond to the time shown in digital form, and vice versa. Mode 3 gives a written expression of time in 15-minute increments, and the student sets the clock hands to the correct positions. Mode 4 allows the student to move the hands of the clock, and the corresponding digital time is synchronized with the hand movements. This helps the student understand the relationship between digital and analog time. *Clock* may be used for drill and practice of specific skills needed to tell time. If drill and practice programs such as *Clock* are used appropriately, students feel competent.

This sense of competence, however, can be undercut by poorly designed drill and practice programs or by a mismatch between the child's skill level and the software selected. Many programs do not present multiple versions when teaching a skill or content. Parallel forms of information presentation are needed for special education students because repetition of the same task is needed to master the materials. Without parallel forms, the student ends up repeating the same items with the same content; suffers a decrease in motivation, which induces boredom; and may eventually resist working on the computer.

If a program is too hard or if the student is unable to read the directions and has not become familiar with the idiosyncrasies of the program, drill and practice is unproductive and the student becomes discouraged. The teacher should create the conditions for the student to be successful by knowing both the software and the student's capabilities, and making the appropriate match.

Tutorial

A tutorial program places the computer in the role of teacher. Material is presented and the computer interacts with the child by questioning him on the material and responding to his responses. The student's response can be provided in several ways: Usually it is typed, but it may be indicated with a pointer (a mouse) or his finger if the screen is touch-sensitive. Depending on the nature of the response, the computer offers new information, repeats the question, or recycles the student through that section of the tutorial. The student moves through the program in sequenced steps by answering questions, and may be branched to remedial or review segments as well as continue to more advanced levels. The software must understand and respond to a range of responses, correct and incorrect. Different incorrect responses might trigger different levels of instruction from the program. A response that indicates a lack of understanding of the materials might produce a branch to a segment that explains the information further or a segment that teaches more basic information. Some misspelling while typing responses should be tolerated by the software, but it should then provide the correctly-spelled response.

There is little software presently available in this mode. However, tutorial CAI programs offer four attractive features for special education students. First, tutorials can provide a number of task repetitions. Repetition is necessary for many handicapped students to learn a task completely (Engelmann & Carnine, 1982). Often, time constraints do not allow the teacher to provide enough individualized instruction or repetition and lead to frustration for the teacher and student. An interactive tutorial CAI program can provide continuous repetition of a given task, which may lead to enhanced student performance.

Second, tutorial CAI can be structured by a basic teaching tactic that is particularly important to teaching special education students. That is, a tutorial CAI program provides consistent instruction that does not change according to the mood or training of the teacher. Students who are instructed with a variety of teaching methods may be left confused. Since a tutorial CAI program remains consistent in wording and approach, students may learn specific skills more rapidly.

Third, the CAI program presents material in an instructional sequence: It does not forget important steps in the learning sequence. The student has to go through every step of the task to produce the desired outcome. However, as the student progresses, some steps in the learning sequence may be systematically faded. On the other hand, if a student is not yet prepared for some of the steps or demonstrates unevenness in understanding, branching may be used to have the student practice unlearned steps.

Fourth, the student must respond correctly to each segment of a given problem, and he receives immediate feedback for both correct and incorrect responses for all parts of the task. This immediate feedback may be contrasted with what a teacher typically does: After reviewing the child's final product, the teacher may have to reteach the entire procedure because the final product may not give clear clues as to the exact place at which the student experienced difficulty. Tutorial CAI may circumvent this problem by systematically recording the child's responses in a carefully sequenced program.

A sound tutorial CAI program adheres to the guidelines listed below.

1. Set objectives are required, sequenced by subskills or component parts.
2. Rules that teach learning strategies to the student should be demonstrated and repeated, first through simple applications with consistent content and settings. Subsequent applications of the strategy should use materials similar to those in which the learning first occurred and then vary the task content to which the strategy is applied, the specific task, and the setting in which the learning occurs.

The intent is not only to solidify the child's grasp of the strategy's use but also to help him see that it can be used with different contents, different tasks, and in various types of problem-solving settings. Having mastered a strategy for solving a problem, special education students often experience difficulty using that set of solutions in other settings. The goal of teaching strategies for problem solving is for the student to generalize the strategy for other situations, and to understand when the strategy is not applicable (the negative case). However, these features are not yet present in tutorial programs.

3. There should be a high rate of response and constant feedback as to the correctness of the response. If an incorrect response is given, the student should be corrected immediately using consistent correction procedures.

4. Teaching should be done in modules and clusters with periodic review of previously learned concepts (Carnine & Silbert, 1979; Becker & Carnine, 1980).

Educational Games

Educational games can develop problem-solving strategies within a highly motivating context. For example, the "Hangman" spelling game can lead to an increased understanding of the relative probability of the occurrence of vowels and consonants in English words, teach spelling, and induce strategies that enable the child to solve the problem.

The use of games in the classroom is a controversial issue. If chosen wisely, games can be used as a powerful motivator in teaching skills. Students find games challenging and non-threatening. Games can foster cooperation and teamwork, and facilitate cross-age grouping and productive social and learning interactions with nonhandicapped students. Games provide many students an incentive to produce work with more focus and output, and, if demanded, greater accuracy and thought when game time is offered as the reward. Students do seem to work harder and produce more if a computer game is provided as a reward for completed classroom work. The teacher might also want to demand high quality work since the student may try to rush through a task in order to use the computer. Games may also teach specific skills unobtrusively in a natural setting, including fine motor control and improved eye-hand coordination, via the need for quick, focused response using the joystick or a game paddle. If fine motor coordination or basic mathematics skills are practiced with a computer game, the student will typically perform with greater accuracy.

Many educators may dismiss games as time wasting; however, carefully selected games provide important avenues for motivating children who have been difficult to motivate. They provide opportunties to build and consolidate skills in natural settings, rather than the more artificial contexts of the academic lesson and occupational and physical therapy.

Demonstrations

Demonstrations are traditionally used in teaching science and mathematics concepts. The laboratory demonstration demands equipment — which is either old with parts missing or newer and expensive — and a knowledgeable teacher who requires considerable set-up time. Mathematics and physics teachers try to illustrate the impacts of different variables on a chalkboard or by using transparencies. The computer is a potential solution to these problems: It provides a failure-proof medium replete with color, graphics, and sound; and allows students and teachers to manipulate relationships among variables merely by pressing a key. Imagine a teacher or student manipulating one variable and observing its effects on other variables in a visual representation. The student can examine these relationships working alone on the computer and complete a laboratory report in response to structured laboratory exercise sheets.

The possibilities are immense, using the color, sound, and graphics capabilities built into many small microcomputers, even inexpensive home computers. The software, while a distinct advance over transparencies and blackboards, still has not tapped the possibilities offered by the hardware. Even with the current software, though, the advantages are considerable. It is likely that the demonstration will work, that teachers do not need to be science specialists to convey the information or produce the experiemental results, and that students can work through the demonstration themselves with a laboratory instruction sheet.

For example, one demonstration uses a thermister, a 6-inch wand-like instrument with a tip that serves as a thermometer, which is attached to the computer. The thermister may be moved around or placed in contact with elements that vary in temperature (e.g., ice cubes, coffee, alcohol, radiator). The software has the computer record the temperature, graphing the time it takes for the temperature to rise or fall as the thermister is moved from one heat range to another. The software reproduces and manipulates the data, graphs the different temperature curves, and presents a table that compares temperature values for different materials and environments. A laboratory sheet can be developed to instruct the child to perform certain tasks sequentially, and write a laboratory report of his findings and conclusions. What does the student learn? The student may wish to demonstrate the difference in temperature between ice and ice water or that heat rises because it's colder on the floor than near the ceiling.

Instruments used as extensions of the computer, such as the thermister, allow the student to go beyond the usually constrained laboratory demonstration and observe many phenomena through the computer program. The student can systematically interact with the environment, through experiments developed by the teacher to illustrate some physical phenomenon, or use the instrument's capabilities to develop experiments. The demonstration mode of CAI permits, ultimately, learning science by discovery.

Simulations

Simulations offer students a chance to make decisions about hypothetical problems. Many simulations approximate commonplace problems found in daily living. Simulations may incorporate many features of games, but they are often intended to model some reality. These exercises can be highly entertaining. Students are motivated to use many academically-related skills, such as mathematics, and develop strategies to solve a problem or series of problems presented in the simulation. Simulations also offer the opportunity to be in control, to develop and use problem-solving strategies, and to feel the power of being totally responsible for discovering a solution and achieving success.

Lemonade, originally produced by the Minnesota Educational Computer Consortium (MECC), is a well-known simulation that has been successfully used with many special education students. The student's goal is to make money selling lemonade. Variables such as weather, cost of the original goods, and advertising costs are presented. The student must read directions, decide on the price of the lemonade, complete arithmetic computations, and learn to make allowances for potentially-changing variables. At one point in the program, "Mother" decides to charge for sugar needed to make the lemonade instead of providing it free to her entrepreneur. This change must be taken into account if the student is to succeed in the lemonade business. *Lemonade* is a program that demands reading and arithmetic as well as reasoning skills in a highly-motivating environment.

Problem Solving

Problem-solving skills can be taught using the computer, and the computer can be used to help students apply these skills in other situations. Papert (1980) proposed using the microcomputer to allow the child to generate problems and then solve them using a programming language called *LOGO*, which was developed by a group of computer scientists and educators at MIT. With *LOGO*, the more common computer-student roles are reversed: The student "teaches" the computer. The student begins by using simple English commands to make an object, a sprite or turtle, move on the screen. As the student becomes more proficient, he designs more complex sets of commands, or routines, to which he assigns a name. He can then recall the entire routine or program segment by typing in the name. The program can be made more complex as the student develops more complex routines. The language is structured to encourage the use of these routines and debugging procedures. These routines enable the student to generate more general rules and create designs of varying complexity, some quite exciting. The student learns to generate on the computer. Programming with *LOGO* is said to teach problem-solving skills.

The potential of this approach for many special needs children is considerable. A major problem for many of these children is a disordered approach to problems or an inability to make something happen — to achieve a sense of power or mastery over their learning attempts. Since the student must enter precise information in a very specific format, he must follow directions, give directions, organize, and use short- and long-term memory skill. Training in accuracy, attention to detail, receiving nonthreatening feedback about mistakes, and problem solving are provided by *LOGO*. The student may gain an understanding of geometry, including knowledge of angles, symmetry, geometric shapes, and spatial relationships. Other basic skills, such as reading, spelling, estimation, measurement, and directionality, may be exercised. Developing and testing their own theories can help to strengthen analytical thinking skills and can be highly motivating because students can be in total control of their experiment.

As we shall see, however, Papert's (1980) stress on discovery learning may not be desirable unless it is embedded within a structured learning setting. (Chapter 4 presents more information about the *LOGO* language.)

Preliminary research with cerebral palsied, autistic, orthopedically handicapped, and learning disabled students indicates that *LOGO* does provide a rich learning environment for special education students (Goldenberg, 1979; Weir, Russell, & Valente, 1982). It is most dramatically effective in engaging students who have difficulty producing work. Weir et al. (1981) describe experiences with severely physically handicapped students who have had extreme difficulty communicating or expressing themselves creating complex displays on the computer screen.

To determine whether *LOGO* would be beneficial for special education students, the teacher should first experiment with it, becoming familiar with the language and defining what it offers students. The teacher must also grapple with a philosophical question: After the student is taught basic commands, Papert (1980) advises that he be allowed to work with *LOGO* independently, following his own interests and learning strengths. This learning-by-discovery approach can be extremely successful for many students, and the teacher may want the student to use *LOGO* in an unstructured situation. However, the teacher must monitor the special education student's response to make sure he doesn't end up with an unfruitful, confusing experience.

For many special education students, a more structured application of *LOGO* may be desirable until the student has a firm grasp of the programming language. Then the teacher may allow the students to develop and work on their own projects. This introduction to *LOGO* is suggested because many special education students are unable to organize their learning situation. The unstructured introduction may exacerbate a disorganized problem-solving approach: Lacking the controlled exploration facility of other children, the students simply may not know what to do or how to find out what to do. A structured introduction uses the highly-motivating medium, but within an organized context that is meant to orient and build confidence rather than control or limit. When the student shows the ability to proceed independently without frustration, he may then explore on his own. Regardless of the approach (structured or unstructured) chosen to introduce *LOGO*, the teacher should have clear objectives for the student and an understanding of what students may gain by using the language.

It appears that while *LOGO* may help special education students apply many needed skills, these skills may not spontaneously generalize to other environments. This is a common occurrence with problem learners, and generalizing learned skills cannot be taken for granted. The teacher may want to develop additional practice for skills in different settings. For example, exercises on following and giving directions or estimating lengths or directionality may be presented to the student, citing the *LOGO* procedures he used to communicate this request to the computer.

Many children find *LOGO* an exciting experience. However, if it does not help strengthen a child's skills or motivation and interest in school, one should have second thoughts about devoting a great deal of time to *LOGO*.

Word Processing

A new, powerful, and spreading use of the microcomputer is for word processing. This is an exciting application that allows everyone, including the many special education students who have difficulty expressing themselves on paper, to write correctly and easily. Word processing software can free the student to write with much greater ease because the task of editing and rewriting is handled by the computer in tandem with a printer. Misspelling, bad grammar, and poor sentence construction no longer require recopying the entire paper. They can be corrected on the screen, rememorized on the disk, and printed in the revised version. The student can learn to write without penalty once he learns to format the composition and use some simple commands to enter new prose and correct what is already written.

Many times a student knows something is incorrect but will not change it because it will either make the paper look messy or require rewriting the entire text. Being able to change spelling and wording, move whole paragraphs, and insert and delete words and phrases encourages editing until written material is nearly perfect. The result is that the student can produce a neat paper with minimal errors — something he can be proud of.

Output can be increased and clarity improved in all areas, including creative writing, report writing, poetry, essays, and letters. Accuracy of the written word can also be attained more readily. Correct spelling, capitalization, punctuation, writing in complete sentences, and general grammar rules can be applied without risking additional errors while correcting recognized mistakes.

The skill of proofreading is absolutely essential for most special education students, and word processing provides a natural environment in which to develop proofreading skills. For example, after a student has written a paper on the word processor, the teacher can transform the proofreading task into a game or challenge in which the student can win and be successful. The teacher can tell the student that there are "X" number of misspelled words, "X" punctuation marks missing, and so on. The student's job is to find these errors and correct them. Students may also read other students' papers or teacher-prepared papers on the word processor and correct errors. Receiving and accepting feedback on written work can be turned into a pleasant experience and can help the student produce more accurate assignments.

This discussion has focused primarily on the amount, clarity, and accuracy of written expression, but another aspect of word processing involves quantity of output. Because of fine motor coordination problems, a special education student might avoid writing at all or write only very short assignments. Typing courses are usually not available until junior or senior high school and, even if touch typing is learned, the process of erasing and correcting errors on typewriters can be very frustrating. (Tutorial software to teach typing is also readily available.) A suggested instructional scenario for improving writing, spelling, and language arts is presented in Chapter 7.

Word processing on the microcomputer can help the student change his relationship to the act of writing.

Availability

The above six modes of computer assisted instruction present a broad array of options for the teacher and the student. Some options are immediately available; others will require patience before interesting software becomes available.

Suggested Reading

Beckerman, J. You don't have to know the language. *The Computing Teacher*, 1983, *10*(6), 23-25.

Bitzer, D. Uses of CBE for the handicapped. *American Annals of the Deaf*, 1979, *124*, 553-558.

Budoff, M., & Hutton, L. Microcomputers in special education: Promises and pitfalls. *Exceptional Children*, 1982, *49*, 123-128.

Computer Assisted Instruction for Handicapped Children and Youth (No. 506). CEC/ERIC Computer search reprints. (CEC Publications Sales, 1920 Association Drive, Reston, Virginia 22091.)

Fisher, G. Lemonade (and other simulations) for sale. *Electronic Learning*, 1983, *2*(5), 78-82.

Geoffrion, L.D., & Goldenberg, E.P. Computer-based exploratory learning systems for communication-handicapped children. *Journal of Special Education*, 1981, *15*, 325-332.

Muller, J. The million dollar smile. *The Computing Teacher*, 1983, *10*(6), 20-22.

Proceedings of the Johns Hopkins First National Search for Applications of Personal Computing to Aid the Handicapped. The Institute of Electrical and Electronics Engineers, Inc., 1981. (Order from IEEE Computer Society, P.O. Box 80452, Worldwide Postal Center, Los Angeles, CA 90080.)

Ragan, A.L. The miracle worker: How computers help handicapped students. *Electronic Learning*, 1982, *1*(3), 57-83.

Sandals, L.H. *Computer assisted applications for learning with special needs children*. Paper presented at the Amercian Educational Research Association, San Franciso, April 1979. (ERIC Document Reproduction Service No. ED 173 983.)

Schwartz, L. The computer as tutor, tool, and tutee in composition. *The Computing Teacher*, 1983, *11*(3), 60-62.

Thorkildsen, R.J., & Allard, K.E. *Microcomputer/videodisc CAI development considerations*. Paper presented at the National Education Computing Conference, Norfolk, VA, June 1980.

Weir, S. Logo and the exceptional child. *Microcomputing*, 1981, *5*(9), 76-83.

Weir, S., Russell, S.J., & Valente, J.A. LOGO: An approach to educating disabled children. *Byte*, 1982, *7*(9), 342-360.

6
Authoring Languages: Promises and Pitfalls

A major problem for special education teachers is having computers serve the particular instructional needs of a student in a timely manner. The teacher may know how to structure a task for a particular child and want to use materials familiar to the child or materials that are likely to evoke a response. However, the teacher's choice of software is limited by the small amount available and, usually, the budget. If a program is found that sounds useful, it is likely not to be available in the school building or district and must be ordered. This is a painstaking procedure: The order must go through the district's purchasing department and, if funds are available, the courseware may arrive six months later. By that time the student may no longer need the program. Most often, software that meets the specifications is unavailable.

The computer's instructional offerings can indeed be tailored to the instructional needs of a child, but one must know how to write instructional software—a skill of few teachers. *Authoring languages* seem to provide an alternate route. Authoring languages allow the teacher to develop software that meets a specific instructional need.

91

What Is an Authoring Language?

The Ideal Authoring System

An authoring language allows a user to develop customized, computer assisted instruction without computer programming experience or instructional programming knowledge. The authoring system provides a structure for the lesson. A teacher tailors programs to the needs of a student. The authoring language provides the teacher with an "intelligent" structure that allows great flexibility in writing lessons with a minimum of training (perhaps a training diskette or a manual). The language provides a preprogrammed set of options, and the teacher responds to prompts as she develops the lesson. Prompts in the authoring phase, in which lessons are written, and in lesson presentation should use ordinary English rather than programming terms; they should be *user-friendly*. The lesson writer can create courseware without learning a programming language. Authoring languages make sophisticated programming skills available to novice computer users without the need to learn a programming language.

Courseware is developed by following an interactive step-by-step process with the computer. Steps are prompted on the computer screen and, at times, referenced in the accompanying manual. During the authoring or lesson-writing session, the microcomputer asks the instructor for the information it needs to create and present the student's lesson. If the lesson is teaching new material or repeating materials previously learned, the computer asks the instructor to type in the information to be learned. Then the microcomputer asks for questions the writer wishes to ask the student. For each question, specifications include the correct answers, as well as the latitude with which incorrectly spelled words will be accepted as correct; the hints for students if they pause in responding or give incorrect answers; the encouragement or responses for correct and incorrect answers; and the consequences of being wrong for subsequent sections of the learning process. For example, two incorrect responses of a particular type can branch the student to a sequence that covers prerequisite materials that the student does not understand. Other incorrect answers may branch the student to a different sequence because they may reflect a different misunderstanding. Sophisticated branching and graphics can be incorporated by the lesson writer without having to learn programming. All interaction prescribed by the teacher for the learner can be accomplished by specifying instructions to the computer.

Four levels of branching can be identified: direct, linear, prescriptive, and dynamic. *Direct branching* and *linear branching* route the learner to preset sequences when he fails and do not allow for learner-performance contingencies; that is, the learning moves through the cycle of the branch.

Prescriptive branching examines the learner's performance over a wide range of lessons. The responses are reviewed and new lessons are developed as required by the learner to master the given task(s). Alternatively, based on the results of a pretest in the task domain, the program indicates the lessons the learner should be assigned next. *Dynamic branching* considers the quality of the child's performance within an instructional unit and indicates the next level the learner should undertake. For example, if the criterion for mastery is preset at 75%, the program indicates the next level of difficulty if the criterion was met or repeats the lesson if the criterion was not met.

Each authoring or lesson-writing session may continue for as long as the writer desires and be as detailed and complex as the writer desires, or can write, and the language permits. The instructor may leave the microcomputer during an authoring session, recording the partial lesson on a disk or tape, and return at another time to develop the lesson further. When the instructor is satisfied with the lesson(s), the authoring session is ended and the lesson(s) stored on the microcomputer disk for later use by the student.

During the student instruction session, the lesson is presented to the student patiently and repeatedly in the exact form specified by the writer. In the ensuing interchange, the microcomputer asks questions and responds to the student's responses. During the student's instructional session, detailed records of the student's progress are kept by the computer. Responses are recorded in an answer file so the teacher can follow the child's progress through the lesson on a video display or printed copy (if a printer is available). Automatic grading and lesson analysis can provide quality control and immediate validation.

Ideally, the lesson(s) can be constructed to be sensitive to each student's style of learning, with a modifiable rate of presentation and speed of response. If designed so, a student can receive individualized instructions designed to maximize his response. Rate of presentation and response can be tailored to the student. Lessons can easily be updated or adapted to the needs of other children. A word processing system built into the authoring system allows the lesson writer to change words, sentences, or items within lessons.

The microcomputer can interact with videodisk or videotape equipment by accessing selected frames or sequences. This permits interaction with pictorial or graphic materials as stimuli rather than restriction to print materials. As the capacity of the microcomputer systems available in schools increases, computer-generated graphics can also be included in instructional materials. In addition, as a greater variety of response systems becomes available, the lesson writer can allow a variety of acceptable response modes. The student who has difficulty keyboarding the correct response (e.g., typing a word) can instead point to the correct response on a touch-sensitive screen, use a light pen, or write on a graphics writing pad which is separate from the video display but shows on the display. A *mouse*, an independent device that allows a person to point to the correct response on the video screen, can also be used. The Apple MacIntosh has a mouse input device.

The following table compares the promise of authoring languages with ordinary programming, such as in *BASIC*:

Authoring	*Programming*
● Prompts or questions writer as the writer works through the predefined authoring (lesson writing) format	● Blank slate for programming; can program any lesson structure
	● Can program any lesson configurations
● Includes preformatted instructions for writing branching elements, recording student scores, and keeping student achievement records	● Each lesson requires writing format for branching, student achievement scores, records
● Preset structures allow writing within the structure	● Must develop a structure to write in
● Requires relatively less production time	● Requires extended production time

The Reality of Authoring Systems

The promise of authoring languages, then, is to provide vehicles for computer novices to write lessons on an as-needed basis, a situation that adds dramatically to the promise of microcomputer technology and is particularly important for the special educator working to individualize learning. Since the capabilities of microcomputers are increasing rapidly and dramatically, the potential utility of authoring languages or systems is considerable. The promise, however, is not met by the reality. The currently available authoring languages that are relatively easy to use primarily permit drill-and-practice lessons to be written. Such a use requires considerable experience with the authoring language before the lesson can be written by a teacher during a free school period.

Users must understand the intricacies of the authoring language in order to write lessons. Authoring languages require considerable learning and practice, more than the spare period or two typically available to the classroom teacher. Becoming familiar with the programming requirements and constraints of the authoring system in order to set the initial parameters of a lesson requires a considerable investment of time and experience.

The promise of authoring systems can seem illusory. The authoring language is indeed easier for writing lessons than a usual programming language, since there is an underlying intelligent structure—many parameters have been specified. However, it does require a specialist, someone who has spent considerable time becoming familiar with the system. It is likely that unless and until school systems that invest in the currently available authoring systems also invest in an in-house writing capability, authoring languages will not represent an easily-accessible option. The reality is that currently-marketed authoring languages will not provide the special education classroom teacher with the means to respond to the prescriptive needs of individual students.

An Authoring Language Alternative

Most authoring languages allow the intelligent structure of the program to help lesson writers write lessons. However, unless the writer develops the lesson as a format—the step-by-step progression which requests the content of the lesson — he must start afresh each time, formatting the lesson and filling in the content. We suggest there is an intermediate step which can be supplied to teachers: lessons that are formatted on the disk and only require the addition of content. An increasing number of software developers are now including this intermediate step as a program option that allows the teacher to input materials into preset formats. The software developer has already formatted the lesson but left the content and answer boxes empty. The teacher may fill in the boxes with materials to be learned, questions, specifications of acceptable and unacceptable answers, prompts, reinforcers, feedback options, and so forth. The resulting preformatted lessons utilize the authoring language but are tailored to the specific task requirements of students. This preset-format program option allows variations of the same lesson format with different teacher-determined lesson contents. An array of preformatted lessons, available on disk, provides the teacher with lesson-writing options that can be as easily accessible to a novice computer user as any good applications software.

This alternative, then, is to use the intelligent structure of the authoring languages as a tool to preformat lessons or develop *templates* — specific preset structures for different types of lessons. Teachers can generate lessons from these templates, or structured lesson formats. The preprogrammed formats allow teachers to insert learning materials appropriate to the student at a point when the lesson or material is needed.

As the preset-format option is more often incorporated into educational software, the special education teacher will be better equipped to take advantage of computer assisted instruction. Hartley software has offered this option for some time. Most Hartley programs also have a teacher file in which student performance is recorded by simply entering the student's name. Listed with each incorrect answer is the correct response. This allows the teacher to see immediately what the student missed and what the correct answer should have been.

Clearly, this is a direction that educational software will go, especially as the market shows signs of expanding. It reflects the realization that most users of microcomputers do not want to become programmers but do want the applications to be useful and easily accessible with flexibility incorporated into the design. These are the same market forces that are beginning to result in software for business applications that can be easily used with minimal knowledge but also be adapted to the user's specific needs.

The next section describes an authoring language, based on the description given by its developers. *PILOT*, an acronym for Programmed Instruction, Learning, or Teaching, was developed by Dr. John Starkweather at the University of California Medical School. Available on the Apple and, more recently, the Commodore 64, it illustrates the capabilities and claims of an authoring language.

PILOT

PILOT is a powerful, easy to use system designed to support program development for computer assisted instruction (CAI). Color graphics, sound effects, and a character set editor allow lessons to be presented in words, pictures, and sounds.

PILOT may be learned quickly because it is menu-driven; provides help screens; significantly heightens students' interest and retention through its graphics, animation, and sound effects capabilities; and gives instructors access to large libraries of material. It allows educators to share material to create new and different lessons because libraries of pictures, sounds, character sets, and *PILOT* routines can be saved on diskettes. It can record both student lessons and grades on the same diskette because the author can programmatically create files for general-purpose record keeping. It places no restrictions on lesson length since a single lesson may span many files or diskettes. It helps evaluate student performance by timing individual student responses. It assists in foreign language instruction because character sets in different languages can be developed easily. It allows educators to make hard-copy files of lesson text through a built-in print routine.

PILOT operates in two modes — author and lesson. In author mode, the instructor/designer creates lessons and stores them on a lesson diskette. The student then uses that diskette to take a lesson; that is, to interact with the computer as specified by the teacher.

In the author mode, menus and help screens direct and assist lesson creation. The main menu provides the following options:

1. Initialize a Diskette. A diskette can be automatically formatted and certain required systems programs and files can be copied from the author diskette.
2. Create/Edit *PILOT* Lesson Text. *PILOT* is a high level language particularly geared to the needs of courseware developers. It is the heart of the system. Using simple commands, the author defines the flow and logic of a lesson and generates any previously defined graphics, sound effects, and special characters related to that lesson. The lesson can also be tested by using the run option.
3. Create/Edit Graphics. The author can create high-resolution color graphics to include anywhere in the lesson(s). Simple keyboard commands draw lines, circles, and rectangles; or the control paddles can be used to sketch free-form designs. Text may be written anywhere on the graphic screen. Graphics are stored on diskette.
4. Create/Edit Sound Effects. Music/sounds can be created dynamically and played back using simple menus and keyboard commands. The sounds are stored on diskette for inclusion in any lesson.
5. Create/Edit Character Sets. User-defined characters are simply "drawn" on a grid using keyboard commands or control paddles. These special characters can be associated with any Apple or Commodore keyboard characters.
6. Copy a Lesson Diskette. The author can make multiple copies of a lesson diskette for wide distribtion or concurrent use by students.

In the lesson mode, the student merely inserts a lesson diskette into a disk drive and is presented with the material as specified by the author/teacher.

Apple *PILOT* requires the following system components:

1. Apple II or Apple II Plus, each with 48K of memory.
2. One Apple Disk II drive with controller for lesson mode; or two Disk II drives, one with controller, for both author and lesson modes. No more than two drives are supported.

3. DOS 3.3 or the Apple Language System, each with 16 sector state and boost PROMS.
4. Video monitor or television. Optionally, if lessons are to be printed, a compatible printer and control card are required.

Commodore *PILOT* on the Commodore 64 runs with similar requirements.

Suggested Reading

Chiang, A. *Demonstration of the use of computer assisted instruction with handicapped children: Final report.* Arlington, VA: RMC Research Corp., 1978. (ERIC Document Reproduction Service No. ED 166 913.)

Kleiman, G., & Humphrey, M. Writing your own software: Authoring tools make it easy. *Electronic Learning*, 1982, *1*(5), 36-41.

Thorkildsen, R. *Microcomputer/videodisc authoring system for instructional programming.* Paper presented at the annual meeting of the American Educational Research Association, New York, March 1982.

7
Integrating Computer Assisted Instruction into Instructional Scenarios

This chapter discusses the logic of instructional scenarios and provides illustrative examples for the reader to consider and apply. *Instructional scenario* is a term used to describe the instructional program for the special needs child — the sequence of instructional procedures planned for the student. The teacher considers the instructional objectives for the child and constructs an instructional program based in part on the child's past successful learning experiences. The sequence of instructional events in that instructional program is the instructional scenario. Conceptually, this multifaceted plan, using different instructional media at different points in the instructional sequence, represents the realities of teaching. By contrast, research with instructional procedures usually compares the effectiveness of two instructional procedures as if they are always offered in isolation, which rarely occurs given the learning styles of special education students.

We use the term "scenario" to emphasize the constructive aspect of building a plan because the teacher must think through or design a script for each child's learning. The teacher actively puts together the sequence of activities, identifying the milestones in the process as the student's learning proceeds as well as the unique capabilities of each medium to teach skills or knowledge, enrich the learning experience, or engage the student in learning. The selection of these activities takes into account the student's personal style of response and learning. Developing a scenario involves thinking about how one integrates various instructional modes successively for the student so he will learn the precursor skills, practice them, and learn to apply them more broadly in increasingly complex learning settings.

The question often asked when examining the instructional power of the computer is: "Will the computer be better or worse than workbooks or a regular book in enabling students to learn?" This need to "prove" the superiority of the computer is a posture that reflects the past failures of mainframe computers to impact significantly on learning and teaching in schools. This question is inappropriate because:

1. It suggests an approach to programming and research which translates the workbook to the computer so a direct comparison of effectiveness can be made.
2. It overlooks the expansive learning and teaching possibilities the computer can offer, such as simulations, word processing, and programming.
3. It does not recognize that our thinking about instruction has progressed. Current thinking seeks to integrate the implications of the most common finding — when there is any merit in the instructional procedures being compared, combined treatments are more powerful than single treatments in isolation.
4. It views instruction too simply and unrealistically. Teachers use multiple ways to teach skills and knowledge, especially with students who have experienced difficulty in learning.

Computers — like tape recorders, slide or movie projectors, language labs, science equipment, books, games, work sheets, and workbooks — are instructional tools that can be used strategically to teach children particular materials or skills. Although the computer is expensive to purchase, maintain, train people to use, and supply with software, the challenge, as with any other instructional tool, is to find the computer's distinctive and unique applications. Future research should specify these unique instructional capabilities and the conditions which tap them so that students can become more familiar with the technology.

It is our belief that technology has generally failed to become integrated into schools' instructional practices because it is placed in an either/or paradigm as a miracle worker without emphasizing the distinctive role the technology can play in accomplishing learning goals. Usually as part of faddist hype, the technology is attributed magical powers to achieve dramatic improvements. Often teachers do not understand how to use the technology in the instructional process, children and teachers become disinterested, and the technology "fails."

This consistent failure to integrate innovation generally, and technology more specifically, into instructional programs in classrooms leads to our putting forward the concept of instructional scenarios. Special education students in particular need various instructional procedures to engage and pace learning. Used concurrently and successively, the elements in an instructional scenario reinforce the acquisition of skills and knowledge, and augment each other. Collectively, they are superior to teaching in one single instructional medium. The instructional scenario concept describes the multifaceted teaching that is required with students who find learning difficult. The proper (but very difficult) approach to evaluating the utility of computer assisted instruction, then, is to examine instructional scenarios in which the computer is embedded in a skill- or knowledge-learning sequence.

In constructing scenarios, teachers can deal with the technology at several levels, depending on their familiarity, comfort, and sophistication. In their first contacts, they may use it to achieve limited ends, as with games that motivate or drill and practice. As teachers become more familiar with a computer's capabilities, they may start to think more complexly about the potential contributions of this technology to their instructional efforts.

Workbooks are effective for students who use them well, especially in the absence of unlimited computer time for all children in the classroom. Workbooks are obviously cheaper, and it is more cost-effective to have the student acquire the basic understanding of material in a workbook and then do his learning on the computer. We know there are students who will not work in workbooks. For them, the order of work may have to be reversed: The student learns the basics on the computer, then moves to other instructional media to develop and expand his competence.

Teachers will use the computer differently with different students. If sustained productivity and output are the issues, the first and most salient use of the computer may be simply as a motivator. That is, for noncomputer completed work — whether written, work sheets, a book read, or an assignment completed — the student earns time on the computer. The time may be offered when the work is completed or may be accumulated and used that day or during the week by agreement with the student. It may be reasonable for the teacher to reserve the right to choose the computer use the student can earn so that indirect educational value may accrue, even with game-like tasks.

A child who produces or completes little or no work with the usual work sheets or assignments and has a wandering attention and a wandering body might be entranced enough by the computer to attend to assigned tasks. The intent is to use the novelty of the computer to engage the student's attention so that he can work independently.

The teacher may use an aide, another child in the room or a peer volunteer to show a student how to use the computer, and perhaps work with him. If the child cannot read the text, the person working with him can read it.

These are two different strategies for managing a child's time on the computer. Each is appropriate for different children. Clearly, there are other scenarios for computer use to pace the learning of children with problems. Different children clearly need different types of facilitating conditions. Most important, as the child develops in his performance during learning activities, his instructional scenario and the role of the computer will change.

The student who comes to treasure learning on the computer may develop a sense that he can only learn on the computer, much as some special education students come to see themselves only learning with their personal aide. The restriction to a single mode of teaching places this marginal student in a situation in which he feels he can only learn in that particular setting. One must be aware of this situation because students with an extended history of failure tend to develop an early sense of the conditions under which they learn, and then stop trying to learn under conditions that have proven difficult in the past. It may be a blessing that students do not have unlimited access to a computer in school, since they cannot then restrict their learning to computer time.

Instructional scenarios also vary for children with extended histories of difficulty learning mathematics, spelling, or reading as opposed to children who progress independently with little more than instruction to focus their efforts or explain materials. For easy learners, books clearly are efficient and allow a good student to pursue his learning independently. The computer may be a major element for these students when challenging software is available and heavy doses of drill and practice are appropriate. It can also be a major element for problem learners who will work on computer drill and practice with enthusiasm. However, the computer should not be the primary learning medium for any learner unless computer technology, such as programming and various computer applications, is the subject of study.

For the child who does not function well with academics but has become entranced by the computer, the technology can serve many different purposes. Imagine a sample scenario in which a student may be challenged to learn arithmetic operations by programming them, and so develop his own understanding; he may learn long division by programming the operation. He undoubtedly could then be engaged in creating problems for other children.

Instructional scenarios can be as varied as the teacher's imagination and capability with the computer. It is necessary to develop a familiarity and ease of use with the computer and its possible applications in order to integrate the computer into the instructional program of the classroom. Without this familiarity, the computer is most often grafted on as another unrelated program element. To achieve this goal of integrating the computer, it is crucial that active in-service training programs be held and, more important, that teachers have the opportunity to share their experiences in groups that meet regularly in the school, the district, or the region. The teacher who encourages a child to program long division problems must be ready to help him with the programming when, and if, he gets stuck. Or, alternatively, the teacher must have someone in the wings who can do so. The computer has the potential to be harnessed to a broad range of the unique learning and motivational problems that special education students evidence: It is as powerful an instructional tool as the practitioner and software writer are capable of generating.

Examples of Instructional Scenarios

Following are examples of instructional scenarios drawn from classroom practices, including sample scenarios in mathematics and language arts. The last scenario discusses what we think of as the most powerful single application currently available — word processing — with suggestions for using it to encourage writing and improve the quantity and quality of written expression.

Scenarios for Mathematics

The student learns the basic format of a long division problem by direct teaching as part of a small-class grouping and solves simple instances of long division with other children on the chalkboard. He may then shift to a workbook to practice long division problems of the same complexity until he demonstrates understanding of how to solve these problems. This prepares him for computer drill on the segment(s) of work he has completed. In this scenario, the computer serves as the drillmaster, assuring that the child has mastered the relevant concepts.

Alternatively, the child may work on the computer at the start of an instructional sequence in long division, especially if he has been exposed to the computer previously. The programs test the child for his understanding of the various components and indicate, diagnostically, what the child does and does not understand. The teacher then selects appropriate instructional materials — whether manipulative materials, workbook problems, chalkboard presentations, or appropriate software — for additional practice individually, in small groups, or on the computer. Once the child has been so exposed, the teacher might use work sheets or software to have the student demonstrate his understanding and to track the student's solution process. The computer could then again serve as drillmaster, checking and solidifying proficiency with long division problems.

A Special Education Teacher Talks About Her Mathematics Scenarios

I also use it [the computer] for math drill. I had a machine for many years called a math computer, which was a very unsophisticated version. It was really like "Little Professor." I have "Little Professor" also. And we have a number of programs that do just that kind of drill, which many kids need. But I don't tend to use the computer for that any more. Now I use the "Little Professor." I mean that's good enough. And I just have a record sheet and they do that. They like to work against the machine. If you put them into the workbook and put exactly the same problems in the workbook, they do more against the computer, even for drill and practice. They'll work much longer and more accurately. Especially with the programs that give feedback. Some of the programs, like the plural, are hard — when you type the word and this face lights up flashing; it says "Right."

***

This is a little bit better than just drill. Fractions it actually teaches and it teaches in a pretty good way. You can't...it's not one that you can let the kids do on their own. You have to sit with them on the fractions one. This one, once you've taught them how to do this, they can do this on their own. They really, really like to do this. And this is another of those kinds that if you gave them in a workbook they would hate it.

***

I have performance objective exams that I had made by the computer. There's a big manual and you tell them what you want, and I have it for whole numbers through decimals. And this is like a whole number. And I just told the master computer at the high school to run me one problem of every type of a specified kind, and I use these as three versions of the same types but different. So I can do pre- and post-testing. This is whole numbers through decimals, which is what I basically focus on. Whole number, fractions, and decimals. In a sense, the pre-algebra stuff that's most commonly needed to move on. And that I primarily use, that's not the practice stuff. That's the pre-/post-testing stuff. So the rule book is in conjunction with the initial lesson and then is a reference tool. And then we do drill in workbooks.

I do the diagnostic and that gives you some leads as to where the kid's weak and strong and then we focus on the weak spots. We start with the lowest skill and we move up and we put the rule in [his rule] book. We put a model problem, we discuss it, we drill in here, and the workbook or the computer have test materials. I have a million different things I might pull in. The computer comes in on a routine basis around a particular skill. In other words, if we're working on a particular thing like long division, then I would pull the computer in to reinforce that skill at that time for more drill, out of the workbook drill. Then I might pull it in as a kind of review. Most of my students need continuous review and practice to keep it as part of their repertoire. And that's how I do often use it in the math area. I don't know if I ever teach to mastery. With my students that's kind of a rarity. I wouldn't call it mastery in the truest sense of the word. Mastery for the moment, but not in the endurance sense.

Scenarios for Language Arts

Spelling

Last year, well, the last four years, I've been able to get the computer any time I needed it, and basically I used it every period. My style as an educator is to work in stations. And each student is doing something different and the computer fits right into it.

What I use it for mostly, it's a very big piece of my spelling program. [I do] a diagnostic at the beginning of the year. I use the *Spellmaster* diagnostic. Identify the patterns, the word patterns, the homonyms, the irregular words, etc. And then I do one of a variety of things.

There's a tape which a [local] teacher wrote, it's called *Word Flash*. *Word Flash* flashes a word in a box. And you can program how long you want it to flash and how long you want the students to wait before they can begin to type it back in. And then they type it back in and it will not allow them to type an error. They have three chances. If they make three mistakes, it gives them the correct letter to put into the word. It does not actually type the mistake. The newer version gives them a drill on the words.

What I did from his program is I then made it a master of all the spelling words we've had, and it's based on the *Spellmaster* diagnostic test, mainly from students I had several years ago. And so what I do, based on the *Spellmaster*, is identify the rules they should be doing.

There's a sequence to it. I mean, first they study the rules in a workbook. We go over the rules. I use about 10, 15 different spelling books to give them rules. We go over them. First we go over the rules, we discuss the rules. We do some written work based on the rules. We do dictations based on the written rules. [Then] we drill on the machine for the drill part [on the different rules]. And we do the post-test and that kind of thing. It's just part of the larger program.

Well, [the computer is used] for sight drill. It's very boring, spelling is very boring. How many times can you write a word nine million times? It's only a visual kind of thing. They still may have to do the writing because they're multi-dimensional learners. It's motivating in and of itself. The kids enjoy it. It strengthens the visual skills anyway. It's good for a variety of purposes. But it's not the only component in any of them.

We do this program with two separate things. We do it with words we missed in our own written work. We keep track of words we miss in our written work and we indicate what program we use. Now this is *Letter Zap*. *Letter Zap* is like *Space Invaders* and it gives you the word, it disappears, there's a little box up here and one letter at a time appears in the box and you're shooting, the machine is shooting, or you can play a partner and the partner can shoot, and you want to hit the letter when the right letter shows up. And the score is being tallied. So it's sort of like a *Space Invaders* for spelling, and that's wonderful. You do that with words you've missed in written work. We also do it based on lessons we've covered in the workbook.

Now for example, the kids today did this particular unit. This is an eighth grade kid who happens to just be doing very nicely. He's just really motivated to move this year. We went over the rule, we discussed it, we discussed the exceptions and how bizarre the exceptions to this rule really are. We then did some written work in the workbook. Then we stopped, we didn't go on with the written work. We will go back to the written work. We programmed in the words we wanted; we did the plurals, not the originals. Okay, now he had nine words. Now he can pick which of the words he wants to do now.

Proofreading, Programming, and Improved Language Arts

I have on the *Word Flash* tape all the spelling words we have and all the homonyms from A through Z, every homonym in the world. Because that's like a big issue. And we do that in connection with a lot of other things, like *Homonym Tales*. *Homonym Tales* are just stories where they use a lot of homonyms. It's by Curriculum Associates. You do a lot of proofreading along with it. A lot of different exercises. I make up stories and spell every word wrong and they have to find it.

They are all taking programming but I'd like to teach a little programming. I'm trying to think of a way to integrate some programming into the resource room as a content area in a sense, because it's so precise and I spend so much time teaching proofreading. I mean, we're up to our ears in proofreading. We proofread everything we ever do and nothing can be more perfect for attention to detail and proofreading than the programming. Because if it's not done exactly the way it's supposed to be, it will not happen.

For example, I left the room for a second to get something and one of these kids, they're very impulsive, he pushed a button and he erased all my words, nine spelling words. And he said, "Well, why don't I put them in?" And I said, "That's a good idea." Well, that's very important, and I said to him, "Well, you have to proofread your word before you press return, because if it's incorrect you have to start all over again." Well, that's a fantastic exercise. Doing that, he didn't have to do the problems as far as I'm concerned. He got already half the work. He got more. So it's a very good tool for that kind of thing because the computer is very demanding. It's dumb, which makes it a very hard taskmaster. I love it for that part.

Word Processing: A Scenario for Improving Writing and Language Arts Skills

The most powerful single application of the microcomputer and one that is attractive to a large proportion of computer users is word processing. The power of the word processing application is illustrated by the fact that Arthur C. Clarke, the well-known science fiction writer, wrote his most recent novel on a word processor in Sri Lanka and then transmitted the text by satellite to his publisher in New York. This book was written on a word processor and transmitted by telephone from our computer, a Commodore PET, to a typesetter.

The two major functions of a word processing program are editing, which adds, deletes, and rearranges typed materials; and formatting, which deals with the characteristics of text when it is printed. The writer can set column margins, number of lines per page, spacing between lines, tables, and so forth. The more complex the program, the more formatting functions available; such as putting a heading on each page with a page number. The basic functions permit the writer to type directly into the computer and use the computer as an electronic writing pad—a typewriter that allows one's mistakes to be corrected. After typing text into the computer and viewing the characters on the screen, the writer can make any desired alterations in the text. Letters, words, lines, or entire paragraphs and pages can be deleted. Many programs allow the user to view the product as it will look on the printed page. By recording the file on a cassette or disk, and having a provision in the software to link files so they can print or be viewed sequentially, one can write documents of essentially unlimited length.

The application to student writing is evident. The student can make errors and correct them easily without having to rewrite or retype the entire paper, letter, composition, report, or book. The student, whether a facile and diligent writer or one who writes with great difficulty, can work on the keyboard, see the product as he types it, and—with a printer available—have a copy that he and the teacher can correct. When one adds the availability of programs that check spelling accuracy, the student can correct his work on the screen, use a spelling-checking program, or correct the printed copy and revise it on the computer. To correct his essay, he can retrieve the recorded file rather than having to retype it. Word processing at this time may be the most important single application of the computer for regular or special education students, with direct benefits for a critical skill.

Examples of how practice on the computer helped schoolwork follow.

Margaret was a student who had a particularly painful time writing reports. Yet she seemed to enjoy a game entitled *Science Fiction Story Writer*, in which the computer assisted the student in creating a story by offering parts of the plot for her to choose from in various possible combinations. After Margaret's computer time was up (during which she had created several "stories" in this manner), she then sat down and wrote a three-page report that had been assigned as a California History project. In this case the computer had worked in a way that other "motivators" did not.

Another teacher talks about word processing for stimulating writing and improved language usage:

Now Bob, who is my colleague, he's doing *Apple Writer* in his room right now. I think it's in there right now. He's doing a lot of word processing. What he does is give an assignment. The kid has to look up the information, or Bob shows them where to look, and the kid reads it. If he can't, we try not to have the kid's poor reading interfere with his other learning or his writing. So we make sure the kid can read the materials he is working with by having it tape recorded or having someone read it to him. Then the kid decides what he wants to write; takes the notes out of the book, puts them in his notebook, and begins writing extended notes for his essay in his notebook. Then, when he pretty much has his writing figured out, he can work on the computer by having Bob schedule time for him. Bob gives him a more open-ended time than he would get if he were doing drill.

He then types his composition into the computer and checks it out for errors to make sure it reads like he wants it to, puts a name on the file, and memorizes it so we make sure he has it and can't wipe it out by mistake by pressing the wrong button. Then he checks it for spelling, punctuation, and capitalization errors. When he is pretty sure it is OK he makes a copy on the printer. Then he loads the spelling-checking program. The program lights up all the words that don't agree with the dictionary in the spelling program. He counts the number lit up, copies them into his notebook, and leaves the computer. He has to look each of them up in the dictionary and correct them on his printed copy. Then when he has corrected them, Bob checks the corrected words in his notebook. Then he can go back, recall his file from the disk, and put in the corrections for each word. Then he checks again for punctuation, capitalization, and spelling errors. When he decides it is OK, he prints it, saves it to disk, and checks the spelling program again. Again, if any words are lit up, he writes them in his notebook, looks them up in the dictionary, Bob checks the list, and then he corrects the errors, and so on until Bob and the kid agree the essay is OK.

Obviously Bob is the only one who can correct errors of word usage, punctuation, and capitalization. The kid then makes a chart and records the number of errors for each version he printed. They love it and it has increased their writing dramatically. Some of them had written almost nothing, except with a lot of prodding.

He and I worked out this sequence. I'm waiting to get the Apple some periods of the week, with the printer and the word processing software and the spelling-checker program. Then we'll be using it here. I've been looking forward to that for a long time, because they really need that kind of a thing to do. Plus it reinforces the typing skills; for most of these kids that's very important as well. None of them take typing until the ninth grade. We used to be able to give it to kids in seventh and eighth grade but we haven't for the last couple of years, so this will be very helpful.

Bob started it by bringing in his own Apple and word processing software. He had trouble getting a printer for them. And finally they bought the spelling-checker program.

***

[Kevin was a second grader, a skinny, frustrated mischief-maker who could barely read or write, and who was in danger of being held back.]... No one knew what to do with Kevin. When I met him, I found he was incredibly interested in machines, so the first day he came in we opened the computer lid and talked about interface cards and how impulses went to the printer.

It was pretty tough for him to use the keyboard. It was hard for him to coordinate what his hand was doing with his eyes, and to scan the lines of print. But we started talking about dirt bikes, which he just loved. I told him I thought other kids would be interested in what he knew about dirt bikes.

The next session Kevin came in with his title "All About Dirt Bikes," and started writing: "There are many ways that you can start a dirt bike. You can turn on the key, kick the peg, or hotwire it. Dirt bikes come in many sizes. They have many chain lengths. Some chains are 23 inches long and some chains are 48 inches long." It was his first story on the word processor. It grew to eight sentences, and took him five days. Hearing what he typed helped him stay with it. [The teacher used a speech synthesizer, activated by the student, which read aloud what was typed on the screen.]

When it was printed, Kevin carried the story away with delight, only to return three days later looking exasperated. "When you write books, you don't put the whole thing on one page.... I can't make a book out of one page!"

[The teacher] sat him down at the computer. "I'll show you the next level of word processing.... You decide what is page one and I'll show you how to move the rest down to page two." Kevin was awed. He figured out where to break up the story, printed three pages and left happy.

Five minutes later he came back. "The title should be on its own page," he said. The chastised educator watched her budding author create a title page.

As his motor coordination and confidence improved, Kevin started teaching other second graders how to use the word processor. But he doesn't get to use it himself anymore. Now in third grade, he is no longer regarded as learning disabled (Trachtman, 1984).

The teachers' comments illustrate how instructional scenarios provide a constructive manner in which teachers can think about individual educational programs for their special education students. By considering the complexity of the instructional program as an instructional scenario, a teacher should be better able to view the role(s) the computer might play in the student's learning program.

Suggested Reading

Carman, G., & Kosberg, B. Educational technology research: Computer technology and the education of emotionally handicapped children. *Educational Technology*, 1981, *22*(2), 26-30.

Dugdale, S., & Vogel, P. Computer-based instruction for hearing impaired in the classroom. *American Annals of the Deaf*, 1978, *123*, 730-743.

Goldenberg, E.P. *Special technology for special children: Computers to serve communication and autonomy in the education of handicapped children.* Baltimore: University Park Press, 1979.

Haberman, E.L. Effectiveness of computer assisted instruction with socially/ emotionally disturbed children. Doctoral dissertation, University of Pittsburgh, 1977. *Dissertation Abstracts International*, 1977, *38*, 1998A-1999A. (University Microfilms No. 77-21, 221.)

Hart, B., & Staples, I. Microcomputers in special schools. Special education: Forward trends. *British Journal of Special Education*, 1980, 7(4), 22-25.

Heller, N. Computers in an urban library media center. *The Computing Teacher*, 1983, *10*(6), 51-55.

Lally, M. Computer-assisted teaching of sight-word recognition for mentally retarded school children. *American Journal of Mental Deficiency*, 1981, *85*, 383-388.

Pennell, D. The light in Brian's face. *The Computing Teacher*, 1983, *10*(8), 16-18.

Pollard, J. Adaptive devices for special education. *Electronic Learning*, 1984, *3*(5), 44-46.

Vitello, S.J., & Bruce, P. Computer-assisted educational programs to facilitate mathematical learning among the handicapped. *Journal of Computer-Based Instruction*, 1977, *4*(2), 26-29.

Watkins, M.W., & Webb, C. Computer assisted instruction with learning disabled students. *Educational Computer Magazine*, 1981, *1*(3), 24-27.

8

How
Special Education Teachers
Use Computers for Instruction

Thormann (1982) conducted a study of how special education teachers in Oregon use computers. She polled 208 special education coordinators by questionnaire and received 174 responses (84%); and interviewed a sample of special education teachers (N=28) and coordinators (N=26) by telephone. This chapter presents and discusses the respondents' use of microcomputers in special education settings, focusing on the more detailed statements of the practitioners who were interviewed. This is a selective report, necessarily, and the interested reader should refer to Thormann's work.

Which Special Education Students Use the Computer

Teachers interviewed used computers with students with all types of handicapping conditions except visual impairment. This includes learning disabled students, educable mentally retarded students, and severely emotionally disturbed students. A few teachers reported they also worked with trainable mentally retarded, other health impaired, and hearing impaired students. Not all students in the special education classrooms necessarily used the computer. While half the teachers reported most of their students used the computer, some teachers restricted its use.

Factors that help the teacher decide which students should use computers vary according to hardware and software availability, teacher training, and classroom needs. The primary factors appear to be the ways in which teachers actually decide to use the computer and the availability of software which matches students' capabilities and needs. If the teacher used the computer as a reward for work completed, some software could usually be found (i.e., a game or drill and practice). Teachers who used the computer for academic purposes only were unable to allow as many students to use it because software matching every student's needs was not available. In general, teachers said they did not use the computer indiscriminantly with students but weighed the pros and cons carefully. They tried to justify its use as part of the objectives they were pursuing with the child rather than using it to fill time.

The amount of time students spent at the computer each day was carefully monitored. For most students, the average time spent at the computer at one sitting was 10-20 minutes. The teachers (72%) estimated their students spent about 30-90 minutes each week at the computer.

Teachers understood the computer could be a powerful motivator but also realized that too much of a good thing can turn students off. As a result, they limited the time spent at the computer. In part, this may have been due to limited access to hardware and the shortcomings of the available software. Research to determine the most effective amount of time to use the computer and for what purposes is badly needed. However, until this type of research is conducted, it is fair to say that 10-20 minutes at one sitting would allow students to improve some skills and gain computer experience. However, if the student is writing at the computer, or programming, he could spend more than 20 minutes productively, and still be working on the task.

How Students were Introduced to the Computer

Some teachers may be concerned that it takes a lot of time to introduce students to computers and then more time to supervise their use. The survey showed these concerns should not stand in the way of allowing special education students to use computers.

Students were introduced to computers in three ways: individually (36%), in small groups (19%), and in a combination of small-group and one-to-one instruction (27%). Three teachers reported their students learned through a variety of methods, such as peer instruction or by reading instructions. Some students were already familar with the computer's use.

One elementary school teacher described a creative way she introduced the computer to the school which familiarized the nonhandicapped students with the resource room and enhanced the social status of the resource room students.

> I wanted to introduce it to the total school, so after a few days of using it with the [special education] students and doing it one on one, just showing them how to press the buttons and responses and so forth, I set up a schedule with the teachers for them to come and bring their entire class at the times the students from their class would normally be in the resource room. And then I used the [special education] students from their class to help me demonstrate it. It was really neat because again these kids were spotlighted as something special for a change and the teachers got a chance to see it [the computer].
>
> I had previously offered times for the teachers to come out and let me show them all about it and I just wasn't getting any teachers out here. They were just really busy after school. As long as they could bring their whole class, on class time, they came and it sparked their interest as well as the students'. That worked out really well. I had each teacher come with their class, and the counselor and I gave a little talk about what this room was and how it was different than other rooms to kind of take the mystery out of it.

How Much Supervision is Needed?

About 50% of the teachers reported that students needed "a great deal" of supervision at first, but the majority (73%) indicated that not much supervision was necessary once the student learned how to use the machine. Some teachers stated that the amount of supervision required depended on the age and ability of each student. A comment made by one elementary teacher stated the views of many teachers regarding the amount of supervision special education students needed when using the computer:

> Like with all students, our goal is to have them be individual learners — that they do not need supervision. That's a goal for most teachers — to celebrate learning! My goals with the computer and with the special ed students is to see that they can go in and sign their own number, do their work, and report "I only missed one out of ten today!" and see that they are improving.

Clearly, the time and effort invested in training and supervising students was felt to be well spent.

Where the Computer is Located

Location of the computer is not always under teacher control. Most teachers indicated that the computer was located in the special education classroom, and generally preferred this location. Two teachers commented that having the computer in the classroom provided motivation for students since computer time was used as a reward. Two teachers mentioned that the special education classroom location for computers helped encourage interaction between handicapped and nonhandicapped students: Nonhandicapped students had the opportunity to relate to special education students. Two teachers felt that by having the computer in the classroom they could make sure it was secure. The following excerpt from one elementary school teacher illustrates some specific advantages of having the computer located in the special education classroom.

> It's really handy for us. I have an aide. We have found that we can put one or two children on the computer for a few minutes while we work individually with another. We have the child we're working with have his back to the computer so that we can see what's going on with the computer as well as the child we're working with. If it was in another room it would be impossible to monitor that [work at the computer] while we're working with another [student].

Some of these teachers recognized some disadvantages of classroom location—noise, disruptions, not enough access for all students, and difficulties monitoring computer use. However, these same teachers reported that the advantages outweighed the disadvantages.

Scheduling Use of the Computer

Because teachers do not always have control over location, number of machines, and software, scheduling practices varied. Some assigned student use, some had a rotating schedule, and some had student sign up for use. Many teachers (38%) used computers as a reward for students when other work was completed. The teachers reported they did not change curriculum goals or IEPs as a result of using the computer but scheduled use and chose software to fit individual student needs.

Teachers' Reports of Instructional Use

Instructional use clearly is dictated by software availability and teacher training. Furthermore, the definitions of drill and practice, academic games, and extracurricular games are somewhat subjective since teachers sometimes consider game-type software as drill and practice, and vice versa. The software most commonly used consisted of drill and practice in math (88%), drill and practice in language arts (64%), academic games (56%), extracurricular games

(48%), and simulations (32%). Other types of instructional applications such as tutorials in math (24%) and language arts (16%), drill and practice in reading (8%), and programming (4%) were used less frequently. This teacher interview data matches data from the coordinators' questionnaires that indicated drill and practice and games were used most frequently with students. Teachers comment:

> In math I have drill and practice and in English they are fun activities. I wouldn't call them games because there's reading involved. There are skills involved. For example, *Mad Libs* is one — I have several of those for spelling programs. In social studies one of the great favorites is called *Oregon Trail* and that involves many different skills. I have mainly activities that give them practice. There are some games but I really sit on them because unless I see a definite learning skill involved, one that child particularly needs, I really don't want them used.

***

> I have a lot of the MECC (Minnesota Educational Computing Consortium) products. All that are appropriate to my classroom needs, so I have the language arts and simulations. I have a clock program through Hartley and two other programs — *Word Families* is one of them. I don't use them much.

Very few teachers had considered teaching special education students how to program. One high school teacher's comment is representative of attitudes of most interviewed teachers toward teaching programming.

> We can do a simple loop like "PRINT GO TO PRINT," and that's about it, where you can get the same phrase coming up. Now with special students, we have not had that intent at all to teach them that [programming].

Another teacher reported that cooperative efforts between special education and regular education teachers occurred with the use of the computer.

> We had social studies and science teachers develop some programs around test materials...[For example,] a science teacher was teaching the metric system in the classroom. He came in and developed a programmed game on the computer that gave the students drill and practice on conversion from the metric system. What this did was enable our lower level students some practice time on the computer and then they went into the testing situation and were much more successful.

The same teacher observed that instructional use of computers can have a positive influence on communication between special and regular education staff.

We're trying to develop that area now, that is, finding teachers who would be willing to spend some time in putting their tests or their instructional materials on a program so that we can use it here in the resource center. I think that is a way we are developing a better understanding between mainstreaming staff and special ed staff.

Problems with Software

Ten of the 28 teachers (36%) reported that the software is generally inflexible. For example, programs do not allow the teacher to regulate presentation rate or student response rate. Some teachers would have liked to use their own spelling lists, but not all software permitted this. Some teachers (29%) indicated that the teaching formats are poor and software documentation is often very inadequate. As a result, even if poor teaching formats or inflexibility could be changed, it might not be possible to alter the software substantially due to poor software documentation. Some teachers (14%) stated that the commercial software's readability level tended to be too high for their students.

Teachers identified many specific weaknesses of current software. Examples of some of these weaknesses are described in the following excerpts, indicating that these teachers were critical consumers of instructional software.

> I think that our graphics are somewhat limited. We have students with visual perceptual problems and a lot of the software is done in tight formations. We would rather spread it on the machine and get a little more spacing.

***

> A common problem is in repetition and correction procedures. The reinforcement and correction procedures are the biggest problem — when you get an answer right it may not consequate the way I would like it to consequate. When you get an answer wrong it doesn't consequate or go back. Another problem we've run into in software is the basic task analysis. As for the rate of response, there's not much variability that we've found in most programs. We can't adjust programs and have the students go at their own speed versus a standard speed.

***

> The commercially purchased ones have worked out beautifully. The teacher-made materials don't always work out as well (and the teachers realized this themselves). Some teachers set up programs that might have been slightly

different than the way they taught a skill in the classroom. One program comes to mind, a metrics program — on the computer he used fractions but in the classroom he was teaching decimals and the carry over. The transition was not possible for the low-level students. So he reprogrammed using decimals, the way he was teaching in the classroom, and it was much more effective.

***

Too many words on the screen. Some of them get upset when they see all those words and they don't have a marker. They tend to need a teacher anytime there's something new. They have to spend a long time to go through it — a couple of times. Once they know what to do — what buttons to push to get past the reading parts, since they already know what it says — then they're fine. But that takes time out during the day because they'll go back and say "What is this?"

***

Getting out of programs is a problem, or if the machine is not working right. We get in/out errors a lot. They get upset and want my help immediately because I have learned how to get around that problem most of the time — not always. I can usually get the program back but that takes 4 or 5 minutes. They go bananas.

***

The selection of practice items is not always on the same level. I couldn't see them [computers] being independent instructors. There isn't enough of a sequence of skills from one difficulty to another. There's always a dry period before we get to another program that is appropriate for the kids. We've got some stuff for low kids and high kids but not much middle range.

***

I made one bad purchase. From the descriptions I read, it sounded good. When I got it, it was not at all usable. The documentation, surprisingly, was adequate enough for me to adjust it as much as I could but it was still too high level for my kids. I know that one of the recommendations often made is adapting commercial software. I don't think that's a viable solution. It's certainly not for me. I don't have the expertise to do it firstly, and secondly I don't have the time. If there were any adaptations to be made what I would like to do is to bring it to a computer programmer and say, "This is not working and this is why. This is what I want done" and just have them solve it. But I wouldn't have a lot of time to mess around with it. My goal is to buy commerical materials that immediately serve the needs without any modification.

Dangers or Inappropriate Instructional Use

Overuse in general was mentioned by 48% of the teachers and coordinators interviewed, unmonitored use by 41%, and 28% cited overuse of games. Of the interviewed teachers, 21% were concerned that computers might be regarded as a panacea rather than as a helpful educational tool. The concerns expressed by coordinators were different. Of the coordinators interviewed, 19% expressed a fear of dehumanization, 15% were wary of overuse of computers as a reward, 12% were concerned with cost effectiveness, and 8% were wary that untrained teachers would use computers inappropriately. Several additional dangers or inappropriate uses were mentioned.

> [There is] a danger in misrepresenting the data by folks who have access to it for a report. They may not represent the data accurately.... We could get so programmed that we would lose sight of the student. It would be easy to pull, for example, an IEP goal out of the computer and say it fits the kid and in fact it didn't really fit the kid at all.

***

> It's very, very expensive. I think new computers coming out are going to be much smaller. They're probably going to be more effective to use. I think if we buy too much of the hardware and software at this time, we're going to have some dinosaurs on our hands in a year or so.

***

> The teacher who is going to misuse the computer is going to misuse other types of curriculum materials or systems. I can see teachers depending on computers to do their thinking for them, for selecting objectives and materials and not looking at the computer critically. I wouldn't just put computers in the classroom; I would try to supervise the teachers more effectively.

***

> We have some kids — and it isn't really within our special ed program. Kids are sophisticated enough. They are able to get into programs, change them and put in four-letter words. That's one of the drawbacks. And then they're able to lock it up so the teacher can't get into it. We had to get the experts in to unlock it for us.

***

Analyzing testing data, writing IEP goals. I think you find out things when you test a kid that you wouldn't find when they work on a computer — body language, just different signs, just what's going on and how they're relating, how they're functioning. I would be fearful that people would think that we have these tests that the computer can give and they'll just give us these numbers or grade equivalents and we'll just plug them [students] in.

***

The biggest danger is that it is easy and it does not necessarily relate to actual living situations that you're going to run into — that the computer is a substitute for going out into a store and making purchases and doing the type of things that need to be done to assure that you are getting a community referenced total curriculum. It can be a crutch. It takes all your data. It makes everything look real good for accountability, but it may not necessarily be accomplishing anything as far as real life influence on the individual.

Effects of Computer Use
on Special Education Students

What did the teachers say were the effects of computer use on special education students? They reported it was a good motivator for students, boosted self-esteem, and increased attentiveness. The following quotes are characteristic of teacher enthusiasm.

It kept them on task a lot better. There are some cooperative things they do well on it, like when it's a game between two people. They are really willing to work on things that if I gave them a work sheet they'd have a fit. You put a kid down with 20 problems to do and 20 minutes later they're still on number one and you say get back on task; the same kid in that amount of time on the computer would probably have 50 problems done. It just really keeps them on task — keeps them moving on things academically. I think they accomplish a lot more.

***

I've got a girl who is learning long division. She's never tried before this year. I think the amount of time it has taken her has been radically shortened by the computer program because she sits there. Sometimes she spends the entire period at the computer on that long-division program and she wants desperately to conquer it. And she keeps working. She doesn't have to raise her hand to ask for help every time she gets it wrong. The computer shows her what she did wrong. I think the computer has just really decreased the amount of time it takes her to learn the skill. She's really getting it.

***

The supplementary practice that the machine allows will allow us to move ahead more quickly in presenting the material because we won't have to take so much time for practice during the primary instructional session. We can give them the practice on the machine.

***

They respond very well to the use of the computer, especially because so many of them have problems in various modalities, either hearing, visual, or auditory. The use of a tactile machine such as a computer is generally very successful for special education students. A lot of our kids don't get this opportunity outside of the resource center. They don't have that individualized attention. Affectively, it reinforces positive behavior to know that they have the opportunity to use something special because computers are not used in other classrooms except for the math unit.

***

I think they can definitely see the carryover of what they do with the teachers and the computer. They're taking it very seriously. So much of what we are doing would go back to paper and pencil type of things that have bogged them down for years and years. This is a different approach to learning and it's very exciting to these kids. Most of them have writing problems, spelling problems, language problems. They are very turned off by pencil and paper type of things.

***

It's a machine that they can learn to manipulate, and it's not critical of them. They learn that they have to be precise with it, and they can't get frustrated and just hit everything. They have to be careful in what they feed into the computer, since what they put in is exactly what they get back. While a regular child may need 35 repetitions, a special ed kid may need 150 and that takes patience, and the computer has got it. There's no judgment and no frowning at them.

Why Use Computers?

Since computers in special education are being used by few districts, from a practical point of view it would be helpful to know what motivates individuals to use computers. If we know the reasons people started to use computers, we will have some idea how to motivate others to use them.

Among the user districts, 69% reported that computer availability was "a primary reason" for computer use in special education and 11% cited it as "a secondary reason." The availability of in-district computer expertise was cited as "a primary reason" for computer use by 65% and secondary by 17%.

The primary factors contributing to limited computer use in special education mentioned by everyone (N=174) were:

1. lack of hardware (61%)
2. lack of appropriate software (60%)
3. lack of trained staff (56%).

A number of coordinators included lack of money as an additional factor. Overall lack of staff interest seemed to have the least influence on limiting use of computers (14%).

The coordinators were asked if they felt computers might contribute to the progress of special education students. About 60% responded yes, 25% had mixed views, 11% responded no, and 4% had no response. The most frequent comments of nonusers were that computers were good instructional and administrative tools, motivating for students, and beneficial to all students. Some nonusers indicated that more information was needed. Users stated that computers were valuable for paperwork, instruction, and motivation, but that more software was needed.

Coordinators (69%) felt the majority of teachers were very positive or somewhat positive about use of computers in special education, whether or not they had used computers. These comments indicated that teachers need more knowledge or exposure but were positive about use. A few coordinators remarked that teachers needed more exposure, were intimidated, or didn't have time to learn about computers.

While it is difficult to implement innovations in the public school environment, if over half of the special educators feel computers would contribute to the special education students' progress, many teachers might be interested in introducing them. Some realistic barriers do exist. The use of computers in special education can be encouraged if computers are made available, appropriate software is provided, and teachers are trained through district in-service or university courses. Most important, teachers' expectations of the technology must be tempered — they should have a realistic view of what their students can reasonably expect to accomplish with computers.

Training in Computer Use

Training is critical! Almost all of the coordinators who used computers and most of the 28 teachers reported that they learned about computers themselves. Eleven teachers and only one coordinator had attended district in-service training. Friends or colleagues also contributed to teachers' (21%) and coordinators' (27%) understanding. Few had learned about computer use in college, especially about the use of computers in education. Twenty-three teachers said they met with colleagues on an informal basis; 82% met with teachers in their building to share information. Of the coordinators, 58% said that they met with colleagues to discuss computer use in special education.

What Hardware is Used

Deciding what hardware to purchase is becoming more complex as prices decrease, companies go out of business, the technology changes, and large companies such as IBM enter the personal computer market. When this research was conducted, purchasing was decentralized, and little information about the advantages and disadvantages of specific brands of microcomputers was known. This situation is still common.

For instructional purposes, such microcomputers as Apples, PETs, and TRS-80s are being used. Coordinators reported that the decision to buy hardware was made by district-wide committees or personnel in individual buildings. Teachers and coordinators had few comments regarding advantages or disadvantages of specific hardware, since most teachers had used only one brand of microcomputer. Some teachers (29%) mentioned ease of use as a main advantage of hardware. Such disadvantages as inaccurate loading of programs, excessive time needed to load programs on machines with tape drives as opposed to disks, and mechanical problems were mentioned. Most coordinators did not have direct access to computers and apparently had not received complaints from teachers.

What Uses for the Computer in the Future

A major question is "Where are we going?" This section presents concerns about training, priorities for the future, and advice from current users: all valuable to a view of future uses for computers in special education instruction.

Interest in Training and Information

Most respondents (73%) indicated they were interested in further training or information (users 81%; nonusers 69%). The staff was interested in workshops and demonstrations, regardless of their current familiarity, on such topics as special education computer literacy, available software, programming, and instructional strategies.

Priorities for Future Computer Use in Special Education

Current nonusers of computers were more interested than users in storage and retrieval of student information (nonusers 65%; users 45%), as well as drill and practice (nonusers 70%; users 52%). This may be because users already employ computers in these areas. Both groups saw the validity of using computers for tasks that are repetitive and time-consuming. They realized a machine could help accomplish some tasks more efficiently and perhaps more effectively.

Future Instructional Use

Both coordinators and teachers felt that computers should be used for instruction, not only computer-managed instruction and career applications but also instruction on daily living skills and development of thinking skills. Teacher comments concerning future instructional use follow.

> The area of vocational training of children, that could really open up a large area for them. I haven't even touched the area of reading. I haven't come across any programs in reading for them because they're mainly commercial and too expensive. Really, all areas need to be explored. The business area, setting up business problems for them — banking and so on.

***

We're underutilizing computers in their functional academic applications. I don't think the good programs are there yet. The reinforcing capabilities, we are probably underutilizing that also. We've got half a dozen games and they're probably tired of them now.

***

I'd like to have about ten computers so that I could plug kids into different programs. I'd like to see a larger use of it overall.

One coordinator's comments illustrate a view of the computer's far-reaching effects.

I even see art as entering into this. It's pretty far out for a lot of art teachers to accept this but I think it's very conducive to art. About the only thing it's not going to cover is physical education. I think it's unlimited as far as its usage. That does not eliminate the teacher though. I see the possibility of reducing aide time with this budget crunch where something's got to give.

Many coordinators had very specific ideas about future administrative applications.

I'd like to see it cut down on the noninstructional responsibilities that teachers have in terms of writing IEPs, writing lesson plans, taking care of assessment information, locating materials. I'd like to see everything cross-referenced to everything else so that based on assessment information, here are suggested objectives and here are suggested lesson plans and here are suggested materials. I think that teachers could use that and adapt it as they see fit and really be able to concentrate on actual instruction. I can see it being used for computer aided instruction. I don't know how reasonable that is with the money being cut back. I don't see computers being in every classroom in the near future unless they become much less expensive or money picks up. I don't believe there are many programs written for special ed students outside of maybe some borderline kids like LD [learning disability] kids or high EMR [educable mentally retarded].

***

We are trying to get into the annual review and the re-evaluation so that we could provide printouts for staff by month when their students are going to need to be re-evaluated. The annual review is another area where I'd like to be able to provide information. One side benefit is that we are able to provide information to building principals as well, and that seems to be of benefit. They get a little clearer understanding of who their staff is working with.

***

My long range goal is to be able to do the whole ball of wax to the extent that we want to; all the way from feeding evaluation information in to getting recommendations for what the IEP goals and objectives should be. I'd like to see us being able to log the amount of direct instruction time, logging progress on a very short turnaround. Knowing immediately where a youngster is. We don't have the hardware at this time to do that and I'm not sure we'd create the software without the hardware being in place.

Advice to Potential Users

Interviewees were asked what advice they would give to special educators who want to use computers. Both coordinators and teachers suggested that potential users should receive training and should plan and make careful preparations for use. Planning should include coping with novice teachers' potential fears. Potential users should talk with users to learn how computers in other sites are best used and what problems might be encountered. Teachers recommended reviewing available software, then making or trying to influence hardware purchasing decisions that will allow them to share software throughout the district. Comments from coordinators include:

Get the equipment now, with the idea that you're going to provide your staff with a lot of inservice till they all feel comfortable. So when you do go into use of computers in the district everyone really makes effective use of computers. Teach the teachers first before the students.

***

Really decide where the sites for the computer should be and who is going to program them. Have the whole plan of doing it. Make a decision of how much space they need on a computer. Also, if they have two different computers, the languages are so different there is no way of them talking to each other. So they should have a plan either to have the same computer throughout the district or to have some kind of procedure for talking between computers.

***

Take a look at what exists. Don't spend a lot of money reinventing the wheel if it's already there. Decide if what's there can be changed if it's not exactly right.... Do an awful lot of research before they commit time and money to the actual product. Don't use data processing or word processing just for the sake of using them but rather make sure they do cut down on work....I've talked to some administrators who see it as a panacea for everything.... They have to be practical. If it's easier for the teacher to do it in the classroom or the way the teacher has been doing it in the past, then don't try to force computers on them. They'll only resent it.

***

Administratively, some time has to go into determining what you really want. Don't make it a wish list. There's some kind of "mechanical voyeurism" about everybody wanting all the information you can get. A little bit of time has to be spent with building staff, identifying those things that are needed and how those things might be reported. Then take that to computer people and see how it can fit in. It saves going back to the drawing board later on and spending more time than you need to.

***

On instructional purposes, I think a lot can be done there. The uses — maybe something on the uses and abuses of computers in the classroom. The dos and don'ts of it. First, a generalized workshop about different kinds of computers. What they can do and what they can't do. What's available to put into them. How programs can be developed. The amount of time it would take; I think you can go down the primrose path thinking that it's going to save a lot of time.

***

You need to look at the initial time to develop programs. How different people are using them effectively and how they're using them with volunteers. How they can fit into the IEP process. How you can plug in some criterion-referenced tests to do the probes. How to control the computer to keep the dog from wagging the tail, so to speak.

Advice to special educators from the teacher's perspective:

Find somebody who knows what they're doing. Be persistent, hang in there.... We have kids who wouldn't normally walk into resource rooms — "Oh, yuck, resource room" — that will get lured in because of the computer.

***

Get some basic training right off. Know your equipment, know your language, and then use it. Don't be afraid to use it, get in there.... If you do not use it, you're missing a great opportunity. Don't be too dependent on it. Know your friend and enemy, so to speak, because it can be both.

These last comments summarize the excitement and promise of computer use in instruction. To enjoy this excitement and promise, teachers must learn about computers so as not to be intimidated by the technology. It is helpful to view mastering the technology as a challenging opportunity to broaden the range of teaching options for special needs students.

Suggested Reading

Gerzanich, R., Tanoya, C., & Nolan, R. Microcomputer remedial instruction. *The Computing Teacher*, 1982, *10*(2), 50-52.

Loebl, D., & Kantrow, I. Microcomputers in the special education classroom. *Electronic Learning*, 1984, *3*(5).

Ragan, A. The miracle worker: How computers help handicapped students. *Electronic Learning*, 1982, *1*(3), 56-59.

Sheingold, K., Kane, J.H., & Endreweit, M.E. Microcomputer use in schools: Developing a research agenda. *Harvard Educational Review*, 1983, 412-432.

Weir, S. Logo and the exceptional child. *Microcomputing*, 1981, *5*(9), 76-83.

9
Evaluating and Selecting Software

Software selection and planning are the keys to successful use of computers with special education students. Microcomputers can assist the instructional process effectively only to the extent that quality software is available. School districts must attend to developing resources for evaluating software prior to purchase. One avenue is to become aware of the software evaluation services that are available. For example, most personal computer magazines evaluate software and hardware, though not as instructional software. Educational computer magazines feature these reviews. One must clip and index the reviews regularly so they are available for easy reference. The presence of Federal- and state-funded centers that support computers in educational use is increasing and one should inquire locally as to their location. In addition, a national group announced recently an arrangement with *Consumer Reports* to evaluate software for use by schools and children at home. These services will increase as interest builds in instructional computing. Appendix 3 indicates other relevant resources.

In this chapter, we provide some criteria for examining software, and indicate the concerns that special educators must consider. Although evaluations of software done by others are most useful in reviewing the technical characteristics or quality of the software, it must be remembered that evaluations are necessarily very subjective. For example, most magazine reviewers judge "ease of use." Is it reasonable to assume an experienced computer software reviewer would have the same difficulties in learning how to use software as will a computer-naive teacher or a child, much less a child with learning difficulties?

The factors that relate to instructional uses must be carefully thought through when determining suitability for special needs students (as discussed later in this chapter). To ensure suitability for the student and compatibility with their own teaching style, teachers should preview software themselves or use the evaluations of their special education colleagues. Hence, the importance that special education teachers *write down* and *have opportunities to discuss with colleagues* the results of their reviews. This allows a sharing of each teacher's reactions to the software. It can sharpen the staff's sense of the software available and when and how it can be used with special needs students.

Appendix 2 presents a software evaluation form which can be modified to meet specific needs and different levels of sophistication.

How Does One Evaluate Software for Instructional Purposes?

Wager (1981) indicates criteria with which to evaluate the claims of software manuals and CAI software advertisements.

Technical Quality

The first set of criteria relates to technical quality. Technical quality most often refers to the adequacy of the program (Does it run?), the efficiency of the program (How is it organized?), and the demands of the program (What skills, facts, etc. does it focus on? What about the quality or comprehensibility of the manuals accompanying the program?).

From a programmer's point of view, these criteria are as necessary for writing good programs as criteria of good writing are to authors. A publisher would not allow a writer to ignore rules against run-on sentences unless it served a specific stylistic effect. Publishers of computer software also have specific rules. In the evolving world of software writing for an audience that is naive to the inner world of computers, these rules are critical in formulating and operating the program and when communicating the structure of the program in written manuals. The evolution of this practice is summarized by the commonly used term *user-friendly* — easily used by naive users.

Content Concerns

A second set of criteria addresses content concerns. The criteria deal with such issues as validity of the facts, models, rules, and concepts being taught; whether the materials are at the appropriate difficulty level for the intended audience; and the relevance of the program to the subject matter. Wager (1981) indicates that these issues are generally addressed by having subject-matter experts review the program or its documentation to evaluate accuracy. These criteria assume that the subject-matter experts can agree on the content and its relevance. It is likely the experts will never agree!

Instructional Quality

The third set of criteria relates to instructional quality, which has to do with the "process concerns" of the program. Typical criteria deal with the inclusion of instructional objectives; the degree to which a program is *interactive*; the appropriate use of computer graphics; the degree of control given to the learner; and the appropriate use of computer capabilities.

> While at first these criteria might look fairly objective, the truth is that most are not. For instance, how does one judge whether the author has "made an appropriate use of computer capabilities?" This type of criterion implies that we know what an appropriate use of the computer capabilities is. When queried further on this issue, most authors (or computer instruction advocates) would reply that it means that the computer is used as more than a page turner. But page turning might be appropriate in some circumstances and inappropriate in others. How has the nature of the learners, and the nature of the learning task, been taken into consideration? On what basis was "interactive programming" given value? (Wager, 1981)

Theory Base

Wade (1980) advocates the derivation of standards for evaluation from relevant principles of learning. Wade concludes:

> Computer instructional programs are never intended as completely self-contained units to provide all the elements of a good learning situation. Judgment should be made on the basis of what is expected of the program itself relative to the quality of the total learning environment. (p. 34)

Without a theory base, the design and evaluation of computer assisted instruction lack the foundation needed for judgments regarding the appropriateness of certain criteria of different types of learning tasks. Evaluation instruments generally lack a theory base, tending to treat all learning tasks as if they are alike and subject to the same criteria.

Wade describes some considerations that are derived from the application of principles of instructional design as described by Gagne and Briggs (1979). The underlying premise of these theorists is that new learning is facilitated by a series of external events in the environment of the learner. These "events of instruction" are:

1. providing for attention and motivation
2. providing the learner with the program's objectives
3. providing for the recall and rehearsal of prerequisite skills
4. providing the new information to be learned
5. indicating how one may learn the new materials, if this is necessary
6. eliciting performance, providing feedback, so the learning is interactive
7. assessing performance
8. providing for retention and transfer

The Gagne and Briggs (1979) "events" give us some guidance as to what basic components an instructional environment should contain. The functions of these events are clearly tied to a consistent learning theory. Based on this theory, one can design instruction or evaluate the program. One can also identify what is wrong with instruction if it does not work.

Evaluating Software for Special Needs Students

Software selection and planning for use, then, are the keys to successful use of computers with special education students. As indicated, the selection and planning processes are more complex than just looking through catalogues or reading evaluations. As with print materials, software specifically designed for special education is not easily found. When looking for software to use with special education students, the teacher may feel frustrated and sense that the clock has been turned back ten years. Much of the software advertised for special education, and there is not much, does not meet a teacher's specific requirements. Although this view may appear grim, it is not as bad as one might suspect; primarily because special education teachers are accustomed to adapting regular education materials as well as special education materials to meet individual needs. Adapting the software lets the student participate in opportunities not otherwise possible, making available new learning challenges that can be shared with nonhandicapped peers. There is no rule requiring that software be used the way the documentation or program prescribes, and special education teachers frequently deviate from "normal" procedures as they adapt teaching materials to the student's skills.

Finding appropriate software involves:

1. evaluating the software with special education needs in mind
2. determining if it is compatible with the teacher's teaching philosophy and methodology
3. deciding how the selected software might be used successfully in the instructional program for the student (Phrased in the terms used in an earlier chapter, how it can be integrated into an instructional scenario for the student.)

The software needs should parallel the teacher's goals and instructional objectives, and should, realistically, be compatible with her teaching style. It should reflect how she has come to teach the skill or knowledge, so she is comfortable with it. Teachers should not have to adapt curriculum to software unless the software provides a new and possibly better approach to teaching specific skills. The software needs to meet some clear objectives the teacher has in mind, or meet objectives stated in the documentation. It is necessary to make sure student needs and skill levels match the software; if they do not, lessons that allow the student to use the software successfully need to be developed.

One of the major barriers to using most software for special education students is the reading level required. This problem may be circumvented in a variety of ways. For example, the teacher may have peers work together, one reading and the other making input decisions. Alternatively, the teacher may teach unknown or difficult vocabulary before the student uses the software. Peers may be in the special education room or may be nonhandicapped students brought in as helpers.

There are a number of ways to view use of the computer and a view may be determined by individual student needs, teaching philosophy, and the software selected. The computer may be used for several different purposes: as a motivational device to reward students for completing classroom tasks and perhaps to provide additional learning or practice of relevant skills by careful choice of the game, to provide drill and practice after a specific skill has been taught, or as the focus of a tutorial lesson. When the computer is the focus of a lesson, the teacher should have clear objectives in mind and, as with any lesson, students need to be prepared and given structure.

Special education students typically have difficulty focusing and organizing their academic situations. Although the computer is highly motivating, the teacher must be certain the special education student understands how the program works and what he or she is required to do. Exploration and learning by discovery can be encouraged and fostered, but only after the student has shown he understands the response requirements of the program. As in any learning situation, the teacher should not rely on the magical motivating powers of the computer, instead being sure the student knows what to do. Otherwise the student may feel discouraged by lack of success, as in other learning situations.

Computer use, whether for motivational purposes or as the focus of a lesson, should be part of a larger scheme. Almost anything a student learns with the computer should be transferable to other learning or functioning in the student's environment. This is unlikely unless the teacher develops a plan to help the student relate computer learned skills to other situations so that he can appreciate the more general applications of the skills. That is, the computer should not be the sole avenue for learning a specific skill; rather, the experience must be embedded in other work with the same skill. If the student uses drill and practice software to strengthen computation skills, he should also practice those skills in other learning settings: with flash cards, work sheets, and, even better, checkbooks and shopping lists.

Specific Software Features for Special Needs Students

We have avoided prescribing specific software, primarily because software that suits one teacher's methodology and student population may be totally inappropriate for another teacher. Although every teacher has preferences, specific qualities to look for in software from a technical, instructional, and psychological (learning) perspective are discussed to provide some guidelines and criteria. The criteria addressed in this section are comprehensive. Unfortunately, software currently available does not meet them all. If a teacher wants to use the computer in special education, some compromises need to be made. Understanding specific software features will help a teacher select the qualities that are most important to successful use of the computer by her students. This selection process must be based on the teacher's own view of the educational process and whether the experience of using a particular software program is worth making some compromises. These are issues that special educators must consider when they adapt instructional materials to the needs of special education students.

The unique concerns for special education students largely relate to the appropriateness and accessibility of the academic content, what is being taught, and the quality of the instructional process for these students. Technical concerns to be examined are summarized in the following pages.

Flexibility

Flexibility is particularly important in special education because student capabilities vary greatly. For example, variability in academic entry level is important. Software should be flexible enough to be used many times by an individual student and by a large number of students. Software is too expensive to use once or twice for one student and then be put aside because the student has learned a particular skill or, worse, because the student is bored. Although storage space on a floppy disk is limited, one diskette should challenge different students by containing a number of different skills, or a variety of difficulty levels for the same skill in order to challenge the same student over time as his or her skill level increases. For the student who learns slowly and needs many repetitions, a program should have several different presentations of the same materials. The program should also allow a teacher to insert materials. Alternate forms to develop the same skill are also very desirable.

Student or Teacher Control of the Presentation of the Materials

It is extremely helpful to have software that lets the user control the presentation. For example, the rate at which material is presented and/or at which response to a problem must be recorded should be controlled by the user. Student control can be provided by allowing students to enter the answer or press the return key at their own rate. Programs by Hartley have been developed along these lines. Another alternative is to allow the teacher to preset the speed at which words and problems are shown on the screen. Some of the more sophisticated programs, such as DLM's *Arcademics*, let the teacher preset speed; however, even the slowest speed in many programs is often too fast for a special education student with learning problems. The teacher should preview the software and have a student use it to determine if the speed range is acceptable.

Number of Problems or Length of Lesson

To maintain the student's attention, the amount of time devoted to a particular task needs to be regulated by the teacher. If the student's attention span allows him to complete 20 problems and a program only presents 10 problems and then branches into a reward sequence or another task, the software does not meet the student's needs; time on the task is unnecessarily wasted and the student is underchallenged.

Rate and Type of Reinforcement

Some software developers have overdone the amount of reinforcement or included inappropriate reinforcement. Reinforcement is important; however, an intermittent schedule and variable types of reinforcement are most productive for the learner. After using a program a few times with reinforcement after every answer, most students simply ignore the reinforcement and just want to get on with the task. Overuse of reinforcement detracts from the task, wastes time, and becomes boring.

Some reinforcements were developed to entice very young children and some last too long. This makes the software unattractive to special education students who are learning below grade level skills. The graphic displays meant to motivate younger children become a turnoff to older special education students. The time reinforcement takes becomes an issue if time at the computer is limited.

Reinforcement may motivate the student to answer items incorrectly. This occurs when the graphic display on feedback is as interesting or more interesting when the wrong answer is entered. There is a natural tendency to test the limits of any program. If the student discovers that feedback for wrong answers is interesting, the student may be encouraged to give the wrong answer. The most effective way to deal with incorrect answers is to present very bland, unvarying feedback; ask the student to try again; give the correct answer; or blank out the screen. In some cases it is effective to have feedback for incorrect answers aversive or tedious, such as rerouting the student through a tutorial to review information related to the answer. If the rate and type of reinforcement can be controlled, most of these problems can be avoided.

The type of reinforcement presented may be (1) passive, meaning the student is given a written message; (2) active, meaning a graphic display is flashed on the screen, a razzing sound is made for wrong answers, or cheery musical tones are made for correct answers; or (3) interactive, which allows the student to play a game or interact with the computer.

Varying the reinforcement is important, since flashing the same graphic display or seeing "Good job!" over and over again can produce boredom rather than incentive for achievement. Randomization of the type of reinforcing message offered along with control of how much reinforcement is provided can help motivate and stimulate the student.

Another incentive-producing feature is personalized messages. Software can retrieve the name of the student and provide messages such as "Terrific, Joan!", "Great work, Joan!", or "Your score is 100%, Joan. You got every answer right."

Selection of Content

It is helpful if a teacher or student can select and insert content in the program.

Spelling, reading, and language arts programs are more useful if the content can be modified by the teacher. Some programs let the teacher enter vocabulary, spelling words, reading passages, or comprehension questions. This flexibility lets the teacher adapt computer use to student needs and also support curriculum that applies directly to classroom requirements. It also permits interesting materials to be added for particular children or new materials to be added for the slow learner — a truly individualized arrangement.

Other technical features are less complex but equally important. Screen displays should be clear and uncluttered. The program should be user-proof so that if a random key is inadvertently hit the program will not crash or proceed to an unwanted sequence. It should be bug-free so it runs as intended. The program should be easy to use for both teacher and student. Directions should appear on the screen in simple English.

Documentation also needs to be brief and easy to understand. Even a very determined teacher does not want to spend hours deciphering the directions in a disorganized or incoherent user's manual.

The program should also maintain student records, which can be printed, if desired. This helps the teacher determine what skills should be retaught or emphasized, and when a student has mastered a skill and is ready to move on to a more difficult task.

The teaching format (e.g., multiple choice, fill in, and choosing from a menu) should be assessed to determine if it will meet student needs and complement the teacher's curriculum and teaching strategy. Close examination of the teaching format can also determine whether the software will actually teach students or if it is set up as a guessing game. Multiple-choice items should be directly related to a skill that was taught rather than letting the student guess the correct answer. The wording should be clear and unambiguous. Fill-in responses should not penalize the student for spelling problems. The software should allow for a close approximation of the word, give credit for the answer, and also give feedback on the correct spelling.

Making one's choices from a menu on the monitor or on a card can be confining and can imply incorrect rules of English usage unless the teacher clearly indicates that the menu is a limitation of the program, and not an example of correct English usage. *Story Machine* by Spinnaker and *CARIS* by Britannia are examples of software that illustrate menu-selected items. *Story Machine* has a vocabulary the student selects from a card and inputs. In some instances, correct grammatical expressions are not accepted because of software limitations. *CARIS* only allows use of a set vocabulary. Low-level students may generalize that there are limitations within the English language that are not true; similarly, experimenting with language expressions may be limited by these charming and highly motivating programs.

Correction and feedback vary from program to program. There may be no feedback on correct or incorrect responses. Some software lets the student respond incorrectly once, twice, or three times and then presents the correct answer or tells the student to try again. Branching is sometimes used to reteach a segment of a lesson the student missed. For example, if a reading passage is given and the student answers a comprehension question incorrectly, he may then be presented with the segment of the reading passage that contains the answer to the question and asked to respond to the question again.

It is a basic tenet of the authors that the computer be viewed as another tool for instruction, not as *the* teaching tool that will revolutionize the classroom. Teachers must see how the computer can contribute to the child's learning of a particular skill or content, how it can help him express himself more easily in prose through word processing or improved spelling or punctuation. This may be a difficult viewpoint to develop and hold in the face of the revolutionary talk around us, but it is the only way to ensure that the computer will in fact contribute to student learning. Thinking through the goals for the computer *portion* of the student learning plan will help the teacher focus on the unique contribution the computer can make.

In summary, then, the qualities of instructional content need to be examined to make sure that the software provides a valuable experience to the student. The teacher should check to make sure the content is accurate; this includes spelling, grammar, and concepts. It is necessary to be aware of all prerequisite skills needed to use the software; it is not enough to read the documentation to ascertain skill level. Since special education students often have gaps in information and skills, the teacher needs to preview the software carefully and note not only the skill prerequisites but also computer software-related prerequisites, such as how much the keyboard is used or what level of skill is needed to read the directions on the screen.

Suggested Reading

Electronic Learning. The software lineup: What reviewers look for when evaluating software. *Electronic Learning*, 1982, *2*(2), 44-48.

Frankel, P., & Gras, A. *The software sifter: An intelligent guide to buying computer software.* New York: Macmillan Publishing, 1983.

Grimes, L. Computers are for kids: Designing software programs to avoid problems of learning. *Teaching Exceptional Children*, 1981, *14*(2), 49-53.

Hannaford, A., & Sloane, E. Microcomputers: Powerful learning tools with proper programming. *Teaching Exceptional Children*, 1981, *14*(2).

Hannaford, A.E., & Taber, F.M. Microcomputer software for the handicapped: Development and evaluation. *Exceptional Children*, 1982, *49*, 137-142.

Howe, J. Computers: A researcher's view. Special education: Forward trends. *British Journal of Special Education*, 1980, 7(4), 17-21.

Mothner, H., & Shawn, J. Microcomputers are "Macrocontributors" to special education programs. *American Annals of the Deaf*, 1982, *127*, 449-451.

Pennington, J.R. Word processing and teacher evaluation. *Electronic Learning*, 1984, *3*(6), 66-68.

Senf, G. Learning disabilities challenge courseware. *The Computing Teacher*, 1983, *10*(6), 18-19.

Signier, B. How do teacher and student evaluations of CAI software compare? *The Computing Teacher*, 1983, *11*(3), 34-36.

Thorkildsen, R.J., & Williams, J.G. *A brief review of the current status of computers in special education.* Logan, UT: Utah State University, Exceptional Child Center, 1981.

10
Tips for Introducing Teachers and Children to the Computer

This chapter addresses two major issues: the concerns teachers have about computers, and how to deal with them; and suggestions for introducing children to the microcomputer. The chapter closes with teachers relating their experiences in introducing students to computers.

Teachers' Concerns

Teachers' concerns about the technology are many and varied and easy to appreciate, especially at a time when teachers are being blamed for the decline of American schools. In this climate, schools and teachers are being pressed to concurrently restrict themselves to traditional methods of instruction and to adopt a new technology that can dramatically alter the instructional process for many students in the foreseeable future. Thus, while computers are working their way into more classrooms directly and indirectly (through exposure in offices, stores, arcades, and at home), it is increasingly apparent that children are giving rave reviews and teachers are remaining more cautious.

Teachers have a number of concerns about how this new technology may affect their profession. For example, computers are generally viewed as dehumanizing. Visions of a roomful of children, each hooked up to a computer instead of interacting with other children, quickly come to mind. Computer games are pictured as simply drill and practice activities. Often, computers are considered too difficult for an average person to operate. Teachers may ask some of the following questions: What if a computer outsmarts me? What if a computer-hip student outsmarts me? What if a computer replaces thinking? What if a computer replaces *me*?

These concerns are symptoms of what many people are calling *computer anxiety* and are cited as a major factor inhibiting the use of computers in schools. Teachers, like many adults, are generally anxious about their contacts with microcomputers and feel uncomfortable and threatened, either because of the intimidating appearance of the technology (a feeling that children do not share) or their fear, in an era of retrenchment, that microcomputers will make their positions redundant.

This resistance may have other explanations. It may reflect skepticism about the instructional value of computers even while administrators or parents are pushing enthusiastically toward microcomputers. Experienced teachers recognize the microcomputer is not a panacea, as touted, having climbed on other bandwagons in education that promised a lasting "cure." This feeling is bolstered by universal concern about the lack of high-quality instructional software and the unproven value of what is available. Teachers may think they have to become programmers to use a computer, and not be interested.

These teacher concerns are part of the mystique surrounding the computer. The concerns reflect a lack of definition of how teachers can become involved in applications of the new technology in schools. For example, programming skills are not necessary since a major feature of this technology is the ease with which applications can be packaged for the computer novice.

Early work in computer assisted instruction was based on the premise that the quality of instruction could be upgraded by the introduction of teaching machines. Teachers viewed this work as an effort to displace them. The earlier search for "teacher-proof" programs, of which programmed instruction and then CAI were to be the exemplars, demonstrated that teachers are essential to the successful introduction and use of any instructional innovation, including computers. The instructional utility of the computer for the student, especially in special education, depends on teachers.

On a more philosophical level, some educators have argued that the teaching process will become dehumanized with machines (Cunningham, 1977). Magidson (1978) assessed students' attitudes toward the use of *PLATO* computer assisted instruction (CAI) programs. Students enjoyed using *PLATO* and did not find using a machine dehumanizing. This finding was also reported by special education teachers, students, and parents who regarded the use of CAI with special education students positively.

While teachers, like most adults, do not display the same unselfconscious, easy enthusiasm of most children for the computer, there is no concrete evidence that teachers' fear is greater or different than other adults. The difference is that teachers may at times feel under duress, being told, "You will use a computer!" Teachers, like most adults, are unfamiliar with computers and their potential uses. The process of familiarizing school personnel with the realities and capabilities of computer technology should stress the computer as a tool, one they can learn to approach as easily as they turn on their stereo systems. The training should actively work to reduce misconceptions and distortions by using an approach that is hands-on, paced to enable the teacher to master and feel in control, and communicable among colleagues. This approach is stressed to demystify the computer and dispel teachers' fears and apprehensions about the technology.

Introducing Teachers

One must start from a basic premise: No matter how many teachers are willing to accept the microcomputer in their classrooms, teachers will not be equally proficient or enthusiastic about it. A reasonable goal is for all teachers to attain some minimal familiarity with it. Given this, we suggest three levels of competence one can reasonably expect of teachers:

1. Most, or all, teachers should have a minimal familiarity that allows them to approach the computer with relative comfort.
2. Some teachers will be interested and use applications software with their students in the classroom.
3. A smaller cadre will become engrossed in the technology, actively learn to master its elements, and develop their own programs and lessons.

The three levels of involvement with the microcomputer demand different strategies for teacher training and support.

Level One

The first level, which should be attained by all teachers and administrators, involves *a basic introduction* to how the machine and the technology work. This goal can be achieved by having the participants select some application they would like to implement on the computer, and working to attain this self-selected goal to some criterion they or the administrator set. For example, if a teacher chooses to learn word processing, a screen of relatively clean copy — 22 lines — of an essay or a letter might be produced. If a game is selected, mastery should be such that it can be played with a colleague. If learning a program to balance a checkbook is chosen, the program might be applied to one month's checking activity, real or imagined. Teachers might choose to become familiar with *LOGO* or educational software.

This personally-oriented approach may help overcome teachers' sense of strangeness and intimidation through demonstrating some success in an application they choose. The intent is to turn an ambivalent or neutral attitude to a positive one by enabling teachers to do something *they* want to do. For the authors, the word processing application is understood to be so powerful an application that it makes the microcomputer incredibly valuable. For others, the games, balancing a checkbook, or developing a budget may demonstrate very concretely *to them* the power of the microcomputer. Involvement, seeing the computer in concrete terms "for me," seems to be a useful way to demystify it and develop a more positive view. This, in turn, may encourage teachers to consider how it can be useful for students.

The above contrasts with the usual introduction of the computer using a lecture-demonstration format. However, it does not preclude offering the formal materials at the same time. A course could present the rudiments of the technology much as they are presented in this book; discuss other information relevant to using the computer and helpful in its application; and conclude with a review of how a computer works, types of software and how they run, and the educational applications available. Such a course should be in conjunction with the hands-on application.

It is the self-selection and completion of a desired application which should give each individual a personal sense of accomplishment, counter-balancing their sense of discomfort and demystifying the technology. An important objective is to have teachers enroll for Level Two of training, which would help them understand how to introduce the microcomputer into their special education setting.

Level Two

The second level is for teachers who are interested in *implementing the technology* using packaged software with students in their classrooms. The objective of this training is to prepare teachers to install and use the microcomputer in their classrooms.

Each session should consist of hands-on time reviewing and using selected software, and a discussion period. The training could be held after school, on Saturday mornings, or during the summer months. The suggested length of each session, allowing time for both activities, is 2-3 hours.

The following two-part sequence is suggested, with no particular time span for each of the two phases — reviewing software and constructing instructional scenarios. There is no particular need to keep the two phases separate, though becoming familiar with various types of software should precede including CAI in instructional scenarios.

Two introductory sessions might include a review of the materials from Sections I and II of this book: the origin of the computer and how it works, and the uses of the computer in special education.

Phase One

Phase one includes hands-on time reviewing and evaluating selected software chosen by the teacher, covering reading- and mathematics-related programs and other areas. Teachers and administrators preview software, use it, and evaluate its strengths and weaknesses for particular special needs, such as learning styles and reading level. The software evaluation form in Appendix 2 can be used as a guide. The evaluation should be written so it can be shared with colleagues and distributed for review by other teachers interested in the software.

In the second half of the session, participants should present their experiences with and impressions of the software they reviewed; discussing its salient characteristics, the needs it can address, and its weaknesses. The presentation should involve a demonstration of the software using a large monitor at the front of the room which is hooked up to a computer. The discussion should also include other instructional situations in which the software can be used, when in the instructional sequence the software might be introduced, and what instructional procedures might solidify the learning and assist in using the skill learned on the computer in computerless settings. At all times, it is important to think about the computer as one instructional tool among many.

If a district is just starting to use computers with special education students, these evaluations, compiled and circulated, could direct teachers to different software by making available information from colleagues about a broad array of software. This is an important practice for all districts.

Phase Two

In phase two the focus shifts to students. Teachers develop instructional scenarios for specific students, specific special needs, and specific learning styles, searching for appropriate software. Again the stress is on using the computer as one instructional tool in a coordinated instructional program for the student. Each session should leave time to discuss the instructional scenarios each teacher develops for skill-building or knowledge-learning, using this case study format.

The logical continuation of these activities is ongoing meetings to discuss and compare notes on the effectiveness of software used with particular students to meet particular needs, and to examine the instructional scenario and the effective role(s) the computer played. An ongoing users' group is critical to integrating the technology effectively into the instructional system.

Viewing the school as a social system, Berman and McLaughlin (1978) indicate the importance of administrator and supervisor support for the introduction and use, over time, of an innovation like microcomputers. We suggest that teachers be trained with their principal or special education supervisor so that the administrators know what is involved and can support teacher efforts. Since sharing one's experiences with colleagues — especially when one is experimenting with new materials — is very useful, more than one teacher or special education person from a building should be included in this training program.

Level Three

The third level involves a small group of teachers who will *be innovative with the technology*. These computer enthusiasts can be the most valuable staff members to the system because, if supported by the administrators, they can provide an innovative impetus and support to their colleagues. They can learn to write lessons to fill the prescriptive needs of children as requested by their colleagues. Their enthusiasm brings an air of excitement and adventure to the introduction and use of the microcomputer. This group of teachers may or may not know a great deal about computers, but they are willing to learn and immerse themselves in the computer technology. They should be offered opportunities to expand their knowledge in this area. They might have some time allotted each week to support colleagues using the computer and, perhaps, take referrals from teachers to write programs appropriate to the needs of a particular child.

Those whose interests make them skilled in the applications of computers need support and opportunities to express these interests in the school setting. They are valuable assets to a special education department since they can be key to making the use of computers possible as well as innovative, given that the technology is evolving. Their excitement can excite other staff members. Their enthusiasm can be used to help their colleagues be more effective. Often this enthusiasm is not supported fully by school administrators, since computer capabilities do not appear in teachers' job descriptions. The potential contributions of these teachers may be ignored by oversight rather than by design. Their enthusiasm should be tapped by school administrators concerned with enriching their department's capabilities and offerings. As the interview data in Chapter 8 indicate, most teachers learned how to use computers through their own interest and incentive. Few had access to training within their district and fewer still were trained in college because the technology has only recently become available to the nonspecialist.

The primary objective of Level Three training for teachers interested in computer technology is to provide instructional programming experience so their interest can be translated into skills for using the computer: Skills to meet the prescriptive needs of their special education students and to support other teachers' efforts to do likewise. The kinds of training and experiences might include:

1. Learning an authoring or programming language so teachers can write lessons requested by colleagues for students who require skills or knowledge not available to them in existing software or in the district.
2. Developing a referral form so that colleagues can specify the type of software needed. The form would specify the characteristics and content of the program requested, the kinds of reinforcements the student responds to, and the format in which he learns.
3. Discussing lesson formats and broadening the spectrum of available formats for teachers who are not familair with computer capabilities.
4. Teaching workshops for Level One and Two training and developing the content and style of these workshops.
5. Meeting regularly as a group to strengthen understanding of the technology and address applications issues that other teachers have raised.

This vital core of teachers, excited and devoted to the technology, may be critical to successful adoption of computers. These persons do not have to be special education teachers but can be teachers in any subject area — mathematics, computer science — or just computer enthusiasts. Some teachers get really turned on to the computer. Others need the support of their colleagues. If the latter's interest is nurtured and supported, these teachers will gain motivation to become involved with the computer.

Such spontaneous developments occurred in Lexington, Massachusetts schools. A few teachers became involved with microcomputers in the middle 1970s. They kindled the interest of some colleagues and then began writing programs and sharing them, providing materials and support when both were at a premium. They were also able to duplicate their home-written programs since they were not commercially purchased and restricted in use or copyrighted. At a time when computers were rarely even noticed, these special educators found ways to integrate them into their instructional programs, relying solely on teacher interest and initiative. Recognizing this asset, the administration arranged a sabbatical year for the teacher most involved; during the sabbatical the teacher wrote additional software, which he shared with his colleagues.

A teacher comments:

> I was one of those typical sort of computer-phobic type people. Not oriented at all. Never thought I could learn to use it or learn to program it. But another person actually who wrote this program — none of these are my programs — I'm not to the point where I can really write a good program, although I have taken programming and plan to do more. The person who did this, C.R., who's a science teacher, he took a sabbatical and piloted computer use and programs for special ed to use. And he ran a little mini-workshop and introduced me to it and then I began to use a lot of his programs. And then I took programming on my own and I used to expand his programs and modify them for my purposes. This year I'm having a lot of problems because there's now computer literacy, that's required for all students in grade 7. As a result, I borrowed this computer this period. Last year, well, the last four years, I've been able to get the computer any time I needed it, and basically I used it every period. My style as an educator is to work in stations. And each student is doing something different and the computer fits right into it.

After Implementation

After the implementation of microcomputers in special education classrooms one should develop and maintain a continuing forum for teachers to share experiences. Users can share their experiences with specific software for instructional or motivational purposes; the instructional scenarios they used, the extent to which the software or scenario achieved its intended goals, and other experiences they did not anticipate. If results were not as expected, teachers can share whatever changes might be necessary. Some meetings may be devoted to specialized uses of the microcomputer, such as using word processing, graphics, or *LOGO*.

The logic of this approach is simple. To stimulate intelligent adoption of an innovation, teachers can benefit from sharing their experiences and gain a sense of how the technology can be used to address the educational needs of different children. The exchange can be very useful in stimulating teachers' thinking about the technology. It is a strategy for staff development that can be used profitably in most areas of instruction, not only with computer-based applications.

In sum, each school district should develop a capability, including a staff capability, to explore the various instructional applications of the computer. All districts probably have teachers who are or could be interested in microcomputer applications in special education. These teachers represent a means to build these capabilities and allow the district to explore its options. They can be instrumental in introducing and sustaining the adoption of the technology. Special efforts should be made to identify these teachers and to help them get the training and experience to develop their interests. These teachers can spearhead the introduction of the technology within the district. This is a low-cost option using local talent to support and develop this new capability.

Introducing Special Education Students to Use of the Microcomputer

Teachers who have introduced special education students to microcomputers say most become easily entranced. In this section some approaches to introducing students to the computer are suggested, along with the planning required by teachers. The chapter closes with examples from teacher reports of students' first use of the computer.

Planning the Introduction

First, the teacher must know how often, where, and when the students will have access to the computer. Is there to be a computer in the special education room? If so, for how much of the week? Do the students go to a computer center for their computer time? What software is available for the students? Whatever arrangement exists, the teacher has to plan to minimize confusion and to have the students use the computer with care from the very first day.

Assuming the computer is placed in the special education classroom, the teacher must carefully think through its location in the room and the rules for its use. The rules include such details as scheduling use; the number of students who can work with it at one time; when, for how long, and for what types of tasks it can be used; and how nonreading students' can use it. Many of these issues were discussed by the Oregon teachers quoted in Chapter 8.

Aids to Using the Computer

To ensure understanding, posters and chalkboard notices can be prepared to highlight aspects of the computer and so keep details about its use in front of the student for easy reference. One notice might have a picture of the computer, including its parts and the major keys to remember (up/down and right/left keys, control key, and so forth). Another notice could indicate the operations to start and use the computer; pointing to the on/off buttons for the computer and disk drive, the place to insert the disk, and how to boot a disk (load the program). Another might portray the proper way to handle a diskette; red arrows indicating where to place one's fingers, cautions not to bend it, put anything on it, or drop it; instructions to keep it in the container; and so forth. Relevant vocabulary and definitions might be on another poster. Most important would be the presence of a poster that repeats the rules for using the computer. The posters might be developed by class members assigned a class project for developing some initial understanding of the computer. The computer corner, with equipment and posters, should have a distinctive look and serve as a work station in the special education room.

Over time — since the posters will become part of the decor and not be used effectively as a source of information — the teacher might prepare laminated instruction sheets that are placed in a notebook kept near the computer. These can used as references for specific operations.

The teacher must decide how to manage the software library and check-out system to minimize damage and potential confusion, with clear rules for borrowing and returning diskettes. The teacher should also establish rules regarding use of the computer to minimize confusion and equipment breakage. The teacher should require a clear sense of order for its use. Some suggested rules are:

1. Know how to turn on or use the equipment. (Offer a *user's certificate* for students who can use it independently.)
2. No food or drink near the computer area.
3. A maximum of three people can work at the computer at one time.
4. If working in groups, students must work cooperatively.
5. Noise must be kept to a minimum.
6. Ask for help from the teacher or tutor if you are stuck.
7. There is an assigned length of time for each computer session.

Scheduling Computer Use

Scheduling depends on access to the computer — that is, how many machines there are and when they are available. Some special education teachers are fortunate enough to have a computer in the classroom on a regular basis.

Others have to share computers with the entire school or must go to a computer center on a scheduled basis. Scheduling also depends on how much computer time is productive for the student.

If computers are in the special education room, teachers find that scheduling practices evolve somewhat naturally. Some teachers have a sign-up sheet, use the computer as follow-up to a lesson, or have use of the computer contingent upon completion of regular classroom work. In cases in which computers are shared with other classes or computers are in a lab, more rigid scheduling is required to maximize use, and assignments for computer time may have to be developed before the students go to the lab. This discussion focuses on the situation in which the teacher has the computer in the classroom, part or full time.

Length of Individual Sessions

The amount of time spent using the computer depends on the time it takes the student to complete an exercise, the attention span of the student, and the objectives of the student in the special education setting. Teachers are well aware that students lose interest rather quickly if any one instructional tool or technique is overused, especially in a boring, repetitive mode. Even the computer can become boring, particularly if used only for drill and practice; as a result a loss of interest in the computer as a learning tool may ensue. To manage and sustain interest, one should carefully structure access and use the computer in instructional sequences or scenarios which will augment learning achieved in other modes. Teachers usually have students spend 10-20 minutes at a time on drill and practice. This, of course, may vary depending on student needs, the software used, and the tasks on which the student is working.

The Computer as Motivator

Most students want to play games on the computer. This can be a reinforcement for learning completed, on the computer or elsewhere, and a powerful motivator for students to do classroom work. It is especially helpful with those students who have great difficulty completing work.

Some teachers use game playing as a reward for work completed. Other teachers refuse to acknowledge the legitimacy of games as a motivator and do not allow students to use the computer for games in the classroom. Both positions need to be considered carefully.

A reasonable approach is to negotiate an agreement with each student separately on the number of minutes they can earn for a specific amount of work completed — whether workbook pages, a required writing assignment, or part of an assignment (for the child who has difficulty completing and may need milestone reinforcements along the way). The teacher should be pragmatic; seeking reasonable arrangements that the child understands and which will help him complete work and learn in an ordered, independent fashion. Some teachers make the inducement easy to achieve initially and then, as the child exhibits more competent learning or behavioral control, steadily increase the amount of work required to earn "X" minutes of game time. Others make the reinforcement quite difficult for the child to earn from the beginning. There are no guidelines except the empirical one: If the child works harder or completes more work of increased quality, then he is responding to the reinforcer.

One should recognize that game playing can provide educational benefits as well. The student can practice gross or fine motor control using the joystick or other control device and, over time, increase his appropriate response rate. The concern, even with game playing, is to match the rate and complexity of the game with the student's capability so he can attain success and, by continuing to play, get better at it. If permitted to choose any game, the student may choose one that is too difficult for him, resulting in another personal failure. The teacher should maintain some control over what game and the conditions under which the child can play, or at least negotiate it with the student.

The Need for Flexibility

After giving some thought to the rules and the schedule for computer use that will be best for her students, the teacher can decide how to introduce the computer and what the prerequisites for using it should be. Supervised use obviously requires fewer prerequisites than independent use. Deciding on the appropriate level of use depends largely on the student's capabilities, needs, and learning style.

Initially, the rules should be few and simple, but as uses expand the rules may have to change. For the student working with drill programs or games, a time limit per sitting could suffice. One must take care that the rule allowing a student to complete a current task is not abused by a student starting a new task just as his time is almost up. This manipulation would obviously reduce the time available to the other students.

When students write programs or prose on the computer, they need time to develop their products and the customary time limit may not be sufficient; still, one student cannot be allowed to monopolize the class time writing a composition or a program. The teacher may need to formulate rules indicating at what stage in the course of composition or program development the computer may be used. The program may have to be written before trying it on the computer. Considerable notes may have to be written before attempting the composition on the computer. In either case, more time on the computer is needed for these applications. Writing a program may be a group effort; writing a composition is an individual one.

Initial Introduction to the Computer

Introducing special education students to the computer can be done on a one-on-one basis or in small groups, by the teacher or with the help of a peer tutor. Whatever the approach, the goals are to allow each student to use the microcomputer as independently as possible, have a positive experience, feel in control, and be successful.

As in the case of introducing teachers to computers, each student should have immediate hands-on experience with the computer to engender initial enthusiasm. The teacher may use aides, peer tutors, or other students for this or may wish to initiate each student to the computer personally. Managing these initial contacts includes turning the computer on, loading the program, showing how to use the diskette or cassette recorder, and demonstrating how to respond to the chosen program.

Concurrently with this hands-on experience, the teacher may present a curriculum that explains the basic functions of the equipment, how it works, how the students must use it, and so forth. A sample curriculum is presented in the next section. Under the supervision of a peer tutor or an aide, a simple self-instruction module can allow some older or higher-level students to earn a *user's certificate*. This may require some reading ability. The tutor can help here. This type of introduction should cover teaching the simplest fundamentals of starting and using the computer and peripherals, and include a brief program (e.g., the student learns how to write his name and — presto! — it shows up on the display screen as the noun in a preformatted simple sentence).

Suggested Programs for First Experiences

In addition to the specific special needs, age, functioning level, and learning styles of the student, the software available to the teacher will determine what is selected for first-time use. What follows are some suggested programs that may be used by students at various levels.

Hodge Podge, produced by Dynacomp, Inc., is software that may be used with preschool or older children. It allows the student to experiment with the keyboard. The brief documentation best describes what *Hodge Podge* does: "As any key is pressed, a song, animation or picture — related to the key in some way — is heard or appears on the screen." The shift, Return, Ctrl-C, Esc, and Reset keys can be demonstrated with this program. *Hodge Podge* is particularly effective when used with a color monitor.

For students able to read at the third- or fourth-grade level, *Apple Presents Apple*, produced by Apple Corp., is a useful introduction. This program teaches the beginner how to use the Apple computer through programmed instruction. One potential problem with *Apple Presents Apple* is the large amount of text to read on each screen display. However, a lot of latitude is provided in gaining skills: The teaching approach is varied, and incorrect responses are dealt with by branching to tutorials and reteaching the skill that was missed. This is a good program to involve the special needs student with a peer tutor from the resource room or from a regular classroom.

Another route involves using one of the many drill and practice programs developed by Hartley, DLM, Milliken, Milton Bradley, and many other companies. Some of these programs, such as DLM's *Math Arcademics* or Milliken's *Edu-Fun*, are in game formats. The teacher must choose the appropriate skill level for the student, the rate of problem pacing, and reinforcements. This may diminish the student's initial thrill at being in immediate control of the computer. Simulations, such as *Lemonade, Oregon Trail,* or *O'Dell Lake* from MECC and *Survival Math* from Sunburst may also be used as introductions.

If a drill and practice or simulation program is used, the teacher needs to preview it carefully. The directions written on the screen are sometimes above grade level, and sometimes nonexistent, so the teacher may have to explain what to do.

A Suggested Lesson Plan

The following lesson plan teaches students about the computer. We strongly suggest that each lesson include a hands-on component, in which the student actually uses a selected piece of software. The teacher will need to explain rules about access to and use of software, as well as how to solve problems that may arise when using the computer. Using posters and work sheets as guides can make it easier to present the materials to a group of students. It is also valuable for students to have copies of the guides for their notebooks.

These lessons were written for an Apple II or IIe and may be easily modified for use with other microcomputers.

Day One

Objective: The student will learn to identify parts of the computer with 100% accuracy.

Parts of the computer include:

monitor or CRT	cables
keyboard	on/off switch (computer and monitor)
computer	door on disk drive
disk drive	disk drive slot
printer	red light on disk drive
disk or diskette	

Materials: a microcomputer, printer, and floppy disk; ditto sheets or pictures illustrating this equipment.

The teacher points to parts of the computer and names them. The student repeats the name after the teacher. The teacher then points to different parts and has the student name them. This lesson, and those following, should be repeated until the student can reliably identify the parts by talking or pointing.

Day Two

Objective: The student will learn the keyboard functions with 100% accuracy.
Keyboard functions include:

Return	Ctrl
arrows	Esc
space bar	Reset
Rept	caps lock, Tab, Delete
shift	open apple, closed apple
upper-case symbols	difference between the letter "O"
numbers	and the number "0"

Materials: microcomputer, diskettes.

The teacher loads a program and models how the keys are used. The teacher demonstrates how the shift key, Ctrl, Esc, and Reset are used and the effects they may have on the program. The student repeats what the teacher has demonstrated until mastered with 100% accuracy.

Days Three and Four

Objective: The student will learn vocabulary associated with using the computer with 100% accuracy.
Parts of the computer:

monitor or CRT	cables
keyboard	on/off switch (computer and monitor)
computer	door on disk drive
disk drive	disk drive slot
printer	red light on disk drive
disk or diskette	

Keyboard functions:

Return	Ctrl
arrows	Esc
space bar	Reset
Rept	caps lock, Tab, Delete
shift	open apple, closed apple
upper-case symbols	difference between the letter "O"
numbers	and the number "0"

loading	software
drive in operation	program
floppy disk	screen
label	envelope
insert	power supply
peripheral	cursor
error	input
hardware	output

Materials: microcomputer, software

The teacher defines each term and points to the equipment or demonstrates the term. The student points to the equipment and, if he can, defines each part of the computer. The teacher may want to give a written test to determine if the student has integrated the vocabulary. A poster with the terms and the definitions should be posted on the wall; they should also be on ditto sheets in the student's notebook for him to refer to when studying.

Day Five

Objective: The student will learn how to handle a diskette and how to load a program with 100% accuracy.

Materials: microcomputer, diskettes, documentation.

The teacher demonstrates the following steps in handling diskettes and loading the software:
1. How to handle a floppy disk
   a. Remove the disk from the envelope.
   b. Always remember to put the disk back in the envelope and file in the proper place after use.
   c. Never put the disk near heat, bend it, sit on it, drop it, or put anything on the disk, press it, or write on it. Never touch the shiny part.
   d. Always hold the disk where the label is.

2. Loading the disk
   a. Hold the disk label side up, with the label closest to you.
   b. Make sure the disk drive door is open.
   c. Insert disk in drive slot. Slip it in; do not force it.
   d. Close drive door.
   e. The red light on the disk drive goes on and a whirring sound is heard. Never take the disk out while the red light is on.

After the teacher describes and demonstrates handling of diskettes and loading a program, the students should be guided to handle the equipment in a careful manner. Once the students can do this reliably, they will be ready to use the computer with relative independence.

The Process

In small groups the teacher may first model the information to be learned, then lead or prompt the students to give the correct answer, and finally test the students individually to make sure they know the material. Additional equipment may be needed, including ditto sheets of the keyboard and enough diskettes for each student to learn how to hold them properly. The group should be small enough so that each student has an individual turn to identify parts of the computer actually using the equipment. A *user's certificate* (badge or card) may be given to each student who successfully completes this brief introductory course.

Introducing the Computer into a Classroom: One Teacher's Experiences

I found that students had virtually no anxiety about computers. In fact, I have yet to find a student who has refused to try the computer. The excitement was obvious and continued through the four sessions of the clubs over a period of several months. However, I noticed that some students tired of the games near the end of the two-hour club sessions.

***

The computer was introduced in a whole-group lesson. Mechanical instructions were demonstrated, while important commands were written on the board. Also on the board was a schedule for computer usage. Students were responsible for maintaining that schedule. Remembering to go at the allotted time, quitting when the time was up, and rescheduling during conflicts became their responsibility. As far as the overall management, the students were very conscientious about handling the schedule without my having to worry about it. On the few occasions when students did forget, there was always some other anxious person who would remind her.

***

Two problems did arise. The first concerned a rule I had established that a person previously assigned to the computer was allowed to finish the game she was on if her time had run out during the change in schedule. Some quickly realized that if they started up a new game just before their time ran out they could buy themselves a few extra minutes of the next person's time. The rule was then changed to *Your game ends when your time ends.* (This solution would probably not work well if the students were working with a word processor at the time. A lot of writing might be stifled if someone were told they had to quit.)

The other problem centered around the sharing of computer time. In most instances, I gave the children the option of choosing a partner to work with. After a few days, new "friendships" seemed to blossom, particularly if you were a student who was assigned to the computer sometime that day. All the children would volunteer to help you with school work or play with you during recess. There were a few times when conflicts would arise because of these new-found friends. Still, it was interesting to watch the children creatively alter their social patterns.

***

In order to see which combinations of people were the most productive, I organized the first three days so that the children were grouped in a variety of ways. Some groups consisted of a computer club member (who had participated earlier with microcomputers) with a noncomputer club student, a strong reader with a weak reader, a student alone, and a student alone with the option of choosing a friend.

By and large, the grouping that produced the most interaction and the most cooperation in problem solving was when a student could choose a partner. In the other groupings, computer club members tended to monopolize the game time, although they were passing on vital information due to their expertise. A non-reader and a strong reader turned out to be an uncomfortable association. If the two were not particularly good friends, the good reader would not necessarily help out the weaker reader. And a student assigned alone tended to look bored.

However, in a "your choice" pairing, the interaction was quite different. Students always chose partners in spite of the fact they would often choose games not requiring any interaction. The students seemed to create their own reasons for interaction, such as competition (who could get a better score when one person plays a game and the other plays the same game immediately afterwards), encouragement (cheering them on during a particularly thrilling game), and assistance (particularly for figuring out strategies and lower-level skills such as remembering to press return after typing in commands).

***

By the end of the week, it became overwhelmingly apparent that the students were thoroughly enjoying themselves. But was anything good coming out of it beside that? A closer look revealed the students were dealing with many valuable tasks. While the sharper students were given an opportunity to be challenged, the low achievers were given an opportunity to show their expertise in ways they didn't before. These students were extremely motivated to find strategies for playing better.

For example, Dick was a particularly quiet student who had difficulty demonstrating school activities that he could master well. Either his shyness prevented him from revealing strengths, or he had very few school-type strengths to show. Yet he turned out to be the classroom's highest "money-maker" in a game called *Lemonade* in which players earn money operating a lemonade stand but must work with factors which affect operating costs. It turned out that Dick's parents ran a small business and he had picked up some strategies from them.

On the whole, the computer caused very little disturbance to the overall functioning of the classroom. I explained to them that I had to go about my teaching and was thus not always free to deal with their problems. They were to do their best trying to solve the problem and should only come to me if it was absolutely necessary. Generally, the students managed to solve the problems on their own except when a problem occurred involving some programming knowledge.

Introducing computers to nonreaders

Would the mechanics be too difficult? Would playing the games be too difficult? Would not being able to read the text pose a large problem or discourage them? Would working the keyboard be too difficult? Or would playing with the computer motivate them enough to learn their letters, numbers, or words in order to acquire computer literacy?

I was interested in observing what kinds of problems nonreading students would have dealing with the three levels of operating a computer. The first level involves the mechanical aspects of setting up the computer. This included loading the disk, turning the machine on, adjusting the monitor, knowing when the disk was being loaded, and reversing the operation when their time was up. The second level involved game selections. A player needed to choose a game, get the game started and ended. The third level was the ability to actually play the game.

I had aides who were fifth graders helping out. The aides would give a synopsis of the lengthy instructions that appeared on the screen, rather than reading them word for word. One disadvantage was that in their zeal to operate the computer the aides would often do too much for the students. One student complained that he could never type anything for himself.

But, overall, the aides were extremely competent. When a problem occurred, I was amazed to see how quickly they were able to size up the situation. The knowledge they needed in order to assist was really quite minimal. A parent volunteer could probably learn enough to serve as an aide in a matter of minutes.

Getting started with the computer:

How was the computer to be set up? The computer was placed on a large table close to the teacher's desk. Originally, the computer was visible from all parts of the room, but that tended to be too distracting. A cardboard partition was placed on the table, so that the rest of the class could go about its business.

***

On the first day, I gave a short lesson to the whole class about the computer and how to operate it. The children were quickly fascinated by it. An explanation was given about the different features of the computer and basic operating instructions: how to put the disk in, turn the machine on, turn the monitor on, and choose from the menu (a list of the games from which the students merely had to press the letter that corresponded to the game).

I demonstrated two games which they could play on the first day. One game was called *Brickout*, which resembles many of the television-video pong games commonly on the market. The other was *Airplanes*, a game in which the player fires a gun to shoot down airplanes flying across the screen. Both games were designed for one player at a time and both require more use of an attached paddle which serves as controls for both games.

While many of the children were familiar with the pong-type games, none had ever played the *Airplanes* game, which was quickly seen as the more exciting of the two. The children were particularly excited about the graphics of airplanes being shot down, which resembled fireworks exploding.

***

The rules used were:
1. Try to play on the computer as best you can without having to disturb me unless you absolutely have to.
2. Your computer time is when a teacher assigns you to a time.
3. Your computer time is finished when a teacher tells you the time is up, whether you've finished with a game or not.

4. Students are not to hang around the computer to watch when they are not assigned. Any loitering will automatically disqualify them from a turn on the computer that day.

5. Students are not to ask the teacher when their computer time is.

During the first week, children were assigned so that everyone would have a chance to play on the computer. Again they were given the option to choose a partner, and again no one turned down that option even though they often chose programs which were not designed for two players.

By the third week, the children seemed to be extremely efficient at playing with the computer. More games were being introduced and students were having very few problems playing the games. If another adult or tutor was available, I would assign students who could use the extra assistance.

Typing on the keyboard held a particular fascination for them....Students seemed to be very efficient with respect to the mechanics of the computer.

Difficulties stemmed from not being able to get through the preliminary [screens] because they couldn't read text on the screen and were unable to memorize the different operating instructions for each program. For example, [in the review of the operating instructions] I explained how they could start a new program by calling up the menu. One student raised his hand and asked, "But what if we can't spell 'run menu'?" I was surprised to find that they were more concerned with language barriers than with the mechanics.

***

Some students were having a difficult time knowing at what level the computer was working. They couldn't tell the difference between the computer loading up when it was searching for a game, when the game was actually on, or when they were in the middle of instructions. These problems are normally solved by reading the text. Some students have solved that problem by "memorizing" operating instructions for certain games. The difficulty for them is in keeping instructions for the various games separate. While making an honest effort at memorizing instructions, some students would use commands for one game on another.

Some of these problems were alleviated in various ways. One way was by having a friend play with you. Often that friend would help remember instructions or would alleviate some of the burden of remembering how to run a game. For example, if a student were typing "run menu" on the keyboard, the other would be checking the screen for typing mistakes. Or if a student was trying to figure out a specific command, the other might remind her to press return after giving the instructions.

At one point I had noticed some instructions were easier to memorize than others. These instructions seemed to be similar in the way in which the text was constructed. For example, wordy text was extremely difficult to memorize. But less wordy text was much easier, and easier still if the text was "shaped," such as in a short list, or with numbers, or in "block" form. If there was a recognizable figure or character, the students tended to remember that and seemed to associate it with a specific set of instructions. On the whole, the students were plagued with the problem of not knowing how to read and therefore not knowing the directions to follow.

***

In some cases a few students totally misunderstood the intentions of the game. For example, in *Brickout* the object of the game is to control a bar which serves much like a ping-pong paddle, so that an oncoming ball ricochets off the paddle and knocks out the bricks of a well which is displayed at the opposite end of the screen. Two children who were playing the game thought for some reason that letting the ball hit the paddle was an undesirable aspect of the game and proceeded to play "dodge ball" instead. In another case, a student was having an extreme amount of difficulty guessing where the ball might hit and maneuvering her paddle so that the two would meet.

These types of problems were sometimes dealt with through assistance from a partner. Often a player would be fortunate enough to have a partner who knew the intention of that particular game and would clarify the issue, or who had come up with some strategy for playing the game better. For some students, partners gave assistance as to how to move a paddle effectively in order to aim a gun, or track a ball. Early on, I noticed that students were having difficulty coordinating the use of the paddle. I taught a pair how to hold the paddle in their right hand, using their thumb to press the button on the side (often used for shooting), while the left hand maneuvered the dial (often used for aiming or controlling speed).

***

Most of the time a lot of interaction was going on, some of it involving how the time was going to be used and how that time was going to be divided. It was not established at the outset how the children were to share the computer time, which left them to negotiate among themselves. This division usually depended on the games chosen. The students might divide up turns. ("You shoot one and then I'll shoot one.") Or they might divide time according to a complete game. ("You play one game and I'll play the next and we'll see who gets the highest score.") Some partners pro-rated the time. ("You played one long game, so I get to play two short ones.") In general, I was surprised to find that most of the share time worked out quite equitably.

There were, of course, the divisions which worked out more according to personality than to fairness. These included those partnerships where one person was much more persuasive in decision-making. In spite of that, there seemed to be little complaining to the teacher about turn-taking. It's not clear whether this was due to the fear that complaints might result in the loss of that computer time. My own observations lead me to believe that the students simply share a particular goal and that compromises get made while problems get sorted out. In this case, the goal they share is to figure out how to play on the computer. The students seem to be finding out that helping each other out is a good way to get the job done as well as to keep problems to a minimum.

***

In general, it seems that with the right modifications it is quite possible for nonliterate children to begin instruction in computer literacy. Adjustments need to be made with respect to appropriateness of games, revising text, making instructions simpler. The notion of children working on computers alone and not interacting with people should be abandoned since they do seem to like working together. People writing software might note this advantage in interaction by making it possible for more than one person to play a game. Programs could be written where the students need to share the responsibility of solving the problem.

The comments in this section are drawn from a paper by M.G. Quinseatt (1981) entitled "Implementing Computer Technology in a Classroom Setting: An Anecdotal Report of Long Term Use."

Suggested Reading

Cory, S. A four-stage model of development for full implementation of computers for instruction in a school system. *The Computing Teacher*, 1983, *11*(4), 11-16.

Davis, N. Yes, they can! Computer literacy for special education students. *The Computing Teacher*, 1983, *10*(6), 64-67.

Electronic Learning. Inservice workshop: An eight part staff development series. *Electronic Learning*, 1983-84, (1-8).

Hall, K.A., & Knight, J. *Continuing education (in-service) for teachers via computer assisted instruction: Final report.* (Bureau of Education for the Handicapped). University Park, PA: Pennsylvania State University, Computer Assisted Instruction Lab, 1975. (ERIC Document Reproduction Service No. ED 111 327.)

Helmick, M.A. Attitudes of special educators toward classroom applications of computer technology, individual educational programs, and Skiltrac. (Doctoral dissertation, University of Cincinnati, 1979). *Dissertation Abstracts International*, 1979, *40*, 1357A-1358A. (University Microfilms No. 79-19, 332.)

Lawson, H. The holistic approach to introducing computer systems. *The Computing Teacher*, 1982, *10*(2), 43-49.

Lewin, A.W. "Messing about"; Six easy steps for getting started with computers. *The Computing Teacher*, 1982, *10*(2), 14-17.

Taber, F.M. *Microcomputers in special education: Selection and decision making process*. Arlington, Virginia: Council of Exceptional Children, 1982.

Vochell, E., & Rivers, R. Computer literacy for educators: An applied programming approach. *The Computing Teacher*, 1983, *10*(8), 61-63.

11

The Computer as Helper: For Teachers and Administrators

Computer Use in Diagnosis of Learning Needs: Expediting and Improving the Diagnostic and Program Planning Processes

Computers can facilitate the diagnostic process by helping to schedule timely assessments, identify appropriate assessment materials, and store the assessment information gathered. They may even be used to test the student at some time in the future.

A computer helps to ensure that students referred for testing are evaluated without delay using the appropriate materials. Scheduling, in accordance with the timelines required by state and Federal regulations, can be easily tracked and monitored. Using the computer to identify the appropriate assessment tools, double-checked by the individualized education program (IEP) team leader or a specialist, can help to ensure fair, nondiscriminatory, and comprehensive assessments keyed to the student's suspected disabilities. Staff members can increase their knowledge of assessment tools. Staff specializing in specific assessment areas, such as intelligence, academic, and modality testing, can learn about other test materials in their own areas and become familiar with assessment procedures in other special needs areas. Communication among professionals can also improve.

165

In addition, criteria for eligibility for a special education service can be specified, resulting in more informed diagnostic judgments and program planning decisions. The location of assessment tools available within the district or outside the district can also be indicated. A computer can be used to indicate specialized resources for referral, ensuring use of the community's resources. Quite simply stated, the practice of using computers to identify assessment tools broadens the base of knowledge among district assessment personnel.

A computer can chart a student's response to particular programs and identify successful and unsuccessful program elements. Staff can then understand the student's preferred learning styles—what works for the student. A well-constructed, computer-based data file, carefully thought through, can significantly enhance programming decision making since student responses to program elements will be routinely entered in a student's computerized file.

Data gathered regarding the overall performance of students within a program format can be used to evaluate current programs for children with particular needs and objectives, and to structure future programs. Schools can gather information about the effectiveness of particular programs for children with similar objectives. Students can then be assigned programs based on the actual responses of children with similar needs or objectives, not the "best guess" approach generally used by clinical practitioners. Detailed information about outcomes demonstrates to parents and appeals hearings the appropriateness of a proposed program for the student.

In sum, a computerized information base can enrich the assessment and program planning process, broaden the capabilities of the assessment staff, and make assessment and program planning more appropriate and timely to the child.

Current Applications of this Approach

Professionals are experimenting with the use of computers to facilitate the diagnosis of handicapped students. The Educational Services: Diagnostic Educational Management (ESDEM) assists parents and professionals in the diagnostic and decision-making processes regarding special education students. Instructional data are collected by ESDEM that aid in evaluating and monitoring student progress. According to Parelius (1978), ESDEM is advantageous because it provides more informed communication with parents and students in nontechnical formats, easy access to stored information by teachers, individualized IEP objectives, and printouts of IEPs.

A San Diego, California clinic has developed a computerized data-collection system that stores and retrieves information on learning disabled students who were diagnosed at the clinic (Adams, Richards, & Brao-Ternger, 1980). This system is used to prescribe treatment and follow student progress. It provides easy access to data and may be utilized in conducting both longitudinal and short-range group studies.

Limitations of Computer Use in the Diagnostic Process

It is unlikely that computers will ever constitute the major or sole basis for the diagnostic process, since inflexibilities and limitations in the type of data that can be accepted and processed preclude this development. However, their use to monitor information, aggregate data, and alert staff to inconsistencies in current procedures can be invaluable.

Computerized IEP Development and Support Systems

Public Law 94-142 requires that every child between the ages of 3 and 21 who has been identified by the public school system as in need of special education services must have a written IEP intelligible to parents and staff. This requirement also involves consent forms, organizing assessment procedures and data, scheduling and planning meetings, and developing clear statements of findings, goals, and objectives.

The regulations for P.L. 94-142 require that the individualized education program for each child include:

- A statement of the child's present level of educational performance;
- A statement of annual goals, including short-term instructional objectives;
- A statement of the specific special education and related services to be provided to the child and of the extent to which the child will be able to participate in regular educational programs;
- The projected dates for initiation of services and the anticipated duration of those services;
- Appropriate objective criteria, evaluation procedures, and schedules for determining, on at least an annual basis, whether the short-term instructional objectives are being achieved (Code of Federal Regulations, 300.346).

Price and Goodman (1980) examined the costs associated with developing an IEP and found that "the writing of the document and gathering of supportive diagnostic data, in that order, account for the major time expenditures in the overall document development process." (p. 449) Teachers were concerned because the "IEP development process did indeed make demands on both personal and instructional time." (p. 453) Developing an IEP is time consuming since it must contain much information gathered from a variety of sources.

The tasks that take the greatest time are conceptualizing and writing the goals and objectives. To assess the student's progress systematically, the objectives should be written so the behaviors can be measured; hence, the behaviors must be observable. Many teachers do not have the training or expertise in task analysis to write short-term objectives that effectively reflect the long-term goals that have been targeted (Walker, 1978). Translating curriculum into observable and measurable behaviors that reflect skills to be taught is often difficult, even for a well-prepared teacher. A teacher may be able to analyze the tasks in an area of special need and write short-term objectives in some areas, but not every teacher has expertise in all academic and behavioral realms.

Teachers phrase objectives and analyze tasks differently. When the objective is not stated precisely by one teacher, another teacher may not understand what the student can do or needs to learn. For instance, an objective relating to addition may be written in innumerable ways but essentially mean the same thing. Similarly, an objective can be open to misinterpretation. The following is an example of this phenomenon:

1. When Ralph is given ten problems containing two one-digit numbers, he will add those numbers with 90% accuracy.
2. Given ten one-digit numbers, Ralph will be able to add those problems accurately 90% of the time.
3. When given ten addition problems, Ralph will add them with 90% accuracy.

There is a vast difference between the first two objectives and the third. Although all three objectives are written correctly, the third objective does not give enough information to preclude misinterpretation. There is a slight but important difference between the first and second objectives: The second objective may indicate that the student can add ten one-digit numbers with 90% accuracy as opposed to two one-digit numbers.

Producing consistently high quality IEPs, especially in a timely fashion, is often a problem for teachers and assessment staff. In many instances the goals or objectives are poorly specified, or the required information is not present on the IEP form. A computerized data bank of goals and objectives can provide some uniformity and precision in objective writing. It can also provide significant savings in labor and costs if goals and objectives are stored by subject area, level, and special need area. The quality of goals and objectives can be improved. Precise but jargon-free goals and objectives can be carefully written, using the staff's expertise in their areas of strength. Accessing the goals and objectives by computer improves the timeliness of response in developing IEPs and reduces writing and typing costs by secretarial and professional staff.

With computerized assessment information, staff and parents can clearly see how the student is doing and agree on the long-term goals and short-term objectives from a computer listing. Since many goals dictate specific objectives, objectives could be generated from a data bank stored in the computer to save laborious writing and typing. Developing a computer file for the child creates a data base from which to monitor the child's progress in the program.

A concern among some practitioners is that standardization of goals and objectives may make an individualized process appear like an assembly-line product. However, what the computer does is allow more time for analyzing the child's special needs and producing a readable product that reflects those needs rather than spending the time and physical labor on manually writing or typing the goals and objectives onto an IEP form. The computerized objectives bank allows expensive, skilled staff to use their expertise where it matters: in the assessment and determination of an educational plan. The computer does the secretarial work. In addition, the software should allow goals and objectives to be written specifically for a given child, should the computerized bank prove insufficient.

Many districts have generated noncomputerized lists of goals and objectives to write IEPs. Three major problems are linked with this approach. First, some districts number the objectives, and the IEP may list the numbers instead of the objectives on the form. While this saves work, it does not communicate information readily to parents, teachers, and students. A second problem is that teachers may use this preprinted list to check off particular goals and their associated objectives. This often results in an IEP that is too lengthy, difficult to read, and which contains much irrelevant material. A third problem is that teachers might use the list to identify the student's objectives and then copy or type them onto the IEP form, wasting many hours in a clerical task.

A computerized system can solve these three problems. A staff member enters the numbers into the computer, which then prints out the goal or objective related to the number. This provides easily read information specific to the student and saves teachers many tedious hours formulating or transcribing objectives. Another major benefit of standardizing objectives on a computer is that objectives can be more easily shared among concerned staff. Regular classroom teachers are often unable to contribute to the IEP writing process because of a lack of training in writing goals and objectives. Providing them with a listing of goals and objectives allows them to participate by referencing the master list or adding to it.

Individual educational plans are typically retained in the central office or are locked in the special educator's file cabinet. Many staff members cannot and do not examine the contents of the IEP to ensure that the child's program is relevant to the stated goals and objectives, or to understand the child's current strengths and weaknesses. While the special educator may consult the IEP, he often does not do so until the annual review and update. Having the IEPs available on a computer allows special and regular education staff to access them easily and update them when a student meets an objective. It enables the staff to ensure that the planned program is being presented in a coordinated fashion. Clearly, access must occur with safeguards for confidentiality of identifiable personal information.

Some Examples of Current Usages

Public schools are using or developing the use of computerized IEP support systems. Implementation of these systems requires adequate funds and careful planning of software selection (Bracken, 1981). The Newton Public Schools in Massachusetts implemented such a system to reduce the paperwork related to IEPs and progress reports and reduce the time between a team evaluation and the implementation of a completed plan. Most special education teachers in Newton no longer transcribe student IEPs. Instead, teachers use a booklet containing goals and objectives compiled by the district curriculum coordinator and experts in each curriculum area. Coding sheets are used by teachers to indicate goals and objectives for students. When the coding sheets are completed, they are sent to data processing: One week later a printed IEP is received. If the child has a unique educational need, additional objectives are handwritten onto the IEP. Special education teachers appear to be pleased with this system because paperwork is decreased and more time is allowed to provide services to students (Huff, 1981; Massimo, 1981; Silluzio, 1981).

Another example of an IEP- and report-generating system is available from Learning Tools, based in Cambridge, Massachusetts. The software is flexible, allowing districts to set up a computerized system to meet their specific needs. A listing of goals and objectives, stored as a data bank on the computer, was developed by 20 special education teachers in New Hampshire, using Learning Tools' *Curriculum Management System.* The Southeastern Regional Educational Service Center in Derry, New Hampshire is helping to install this software in over one third of the districts in the state. Districts are using the software to generate IEPs and reports and to access data banks of goals and objectives, using this data bank as is or revising it to meet their own specific needs.

In South Dartmouth, Massachusetts the special education director is using this same software; however, he has set up the system so that teachers use their own individual data banks of goals and objectives. Each teacher has created a data bank and has a printed copy of it. The teacher specifies the goals and objectives for the student to work on and sends this information to the central office, where the secretary is then able to generate IEPs.

In summary, public school systems are using the computer to produce educational plans and store and retrieve information.

Advantages of a Computerized IEP and Support System

1. Districts find it easier to ensure timely compliance with the requirements of P.L. 94-142.
2. Assessment and curriculum staff can pool their knowledge from their areas of expertise in writing precise goals and objectives.
3. Assessment staff do not regenerate, de novo, goals and objectives for each IEP. Instead they can concentrate on collecting data and making intelligent judgments regarding the child's special needs and how to plan the child's program.
4. The quality of the IEP can be improved as can the staff's understanding of its elements.
5. Regular classroom teachers are able to participate more fully in the process of planning and implementing programs for handicapped students.
6. Curriculum objectives are held constant across program elements of classrooms. This minimizes differences in interpretations among program staff, maximizing understanding and communication so all staff are pulling together with the same knowledge and awareness of the goals and objectives for a child.
7. A computerized printout can be individualized.
8. Administrators can access the information for reporting to Federal, state, and local agencies.
9. Administrators can access information for planning and evaluation.

Computer Managed Instruction in Special Education

Computer managed instruction (CMI) is another potentially valuable application for facilitating the education of special education students. Five computerized components provide a comprehensive CMI program useful in special education.

The first component is the data bank of goals and objectives from which IEPs are written. The second and third components consist of IEPs and progress reports for each student. The fourth component is test items written by special educators in the district for each objective. These are used to test a student's progress. Tests are taken on-line by the student, or teachers can request a printout of a test covering a specific objective. The student's responses are fed back into the computer file, thus making available current achievement levels related to objectives. The fifth component involves matching instructional materials with methods available in the district for implementing the goals and objectives. Teachers can add to this methods and materials bank as new methods and materials are found or developed.

Illustrations of CMI's Potential Uses

Use of IEP and Diagnostic Information

One of the problems in the implementation of P.L. 94-142 is that once the diagnosis has been completed and the IEP written, the information from these two sources is put aside and not often used by the teachers to guide instruction. The teacher may (and usually does) proceed with "instruction as usual," never referring to the diagnostic information or IEP until it is time for writing a new IEP. This phenomenon was clearly observed by Yurchak and Mathews (1980), who stated:

> A striking aspect of our cases is how seldom the child's IEP goals are used as a reference point for assessing progress; in no case did teachers, specialists, or parents explicitly and systematically question whether the goals of the IEP had been met. (p. 64)

A computer-managed system makes student information more accessible and can yield instructional programs related to the prescribed goals and objectives. In addition, information can be shared to provide more consistent and interrelated instruction. Improved accessibility of information aids teachers in following recommendations formulated from the diagnosis and the IEP.

Sharing Curriculum

A CMI system can enhance the special education teacher's instructional repertoire. The system might contain information about materials and methods available for teaching some set of objectives. Thus, the teacher does not have to rely on familiar materials and methods but can be informed and updated as to the latest equipment and techniques available. When a teacher finds materials or methods that prove effective with students, the information can be shared district-wide via the data bank.

For example, if a student needs remediation in reading, the objective might read:

> The student will read orally a 100 word passage (2.5 grade level) with 98% accuracy and 80% comprehension.

The CMI program could indicate a number of reading programs that might be used to instruct the student. The entire printout might read:

> The student will read orally a 100 word passage (2.5 grade level) with 98% accuracy and 80% comprehension.

Grade Level: 2.5

1. "A King on a Swing": Level D (orange); SRA Basic Reading Series by Rasmussen and Goldberg***linguistic method***supplementary materials: workbooks; Miss Keenan's supplementary dittoes (Willard Elementary); supplementary reading; teacher's guide

2. DISTAR II by Engelmann and Becker***direct instruction— synthetic phonics approach***teacher scripts; small group presentation; supplementary material: work sheets

3. "Sounds of Laughter" by Martin Jr. and Brogan. Holt Rinehart and Winston***sight word approach—high interest*** supplementary materials: teacher's edition, annotated

4. ACTION Books Library 2, Scholastic Book Service***high interest—low vocabulary***junior high interest level; supplementary materials: spirit masters

Information sharing need not be limited to academic areas. Objectives to be worked on could be related to behavior management problems. The printout might read:

> The student will attend all classes and arrive at those classes on time for one week (month, quarter, semester) 95% of the time.
>
> 1. See Mr. Hickey (counselor) to set up a behavioral program.
>
> 2. Set up a home/school program; student will be given a mutually agreed upon reward by parents for reaching goals.
>
> 3. Set up a token reward system for the student.

    4. Write a contract with the student; set mutually agreed upon reward.

    5. Send the student to guidance counselor for counseling.

Data Keeping

A CMI system permits teachers to focus on providing appropriate instruction, as opposed to performing time-consuming clerical tasks. An aide or clerical staff member can enter student data for the teacher and help special education teachers keep systematic data regarding student progress. This should facilitate the process of planning instruction that reflects the student's current achievements and goals. Teachers can avoid reteaching skills and concepts already learned. Since the methods and materials used to instruct an individual student are entered, those that are productive or unproductive can be indicated. The ongoing record shapes the instructional program for the child over the years.

It is extremely trying for a special education student to shift from one instructional method to another to accommodate teacher preference. For example, if a special education student is taught one year with a linguistic approach and the following year with a sight-word approach, it is likely the student will have difficulty succeeding. Unfortunately, instructional-method shift does occur because communication among teachers is often limited and teachers rely on their own methods and materials. Equally debilitating is teaching a student with a method that has already failed. This can happen when there is no record of what instructional methods were used in the past.

Facilitating Group Instruction

Unless a resource room is well organized, teachers and aides often spend excessive time instructing students on a one-on-one basis. This is not always necessary since a number of students visiting a resource room at different times of the day are probably working on the same or similar skills. Instructing students individually can also be counterproductive for a special education student, since the student may become overly dependent on this teaching format and may feel unable to learn unless he has the teacher's undivided attention.

A computer-managed system helps a teacher group students appropriately. For example, a computer can identify all special education students at a particular school who need to learn the same or similar skills. The students can then be grouped by criterion-referenced tests to determine skill level. Students working on the same skills at a similar level can visit the resource room at the same time and be given instruction in small groups. The teacher's instructional time is maximized and the students learn to work in groups, as in regular classes. The teacher does not have to do the clerical work that grouping requires. Those teachers who currently organize small-group instruction without the aid of a computer do not have to waste 2-4 weeks of valuable instructional time every September setting up the groups.

The Student Progress File

The IEP and progress statements stored in the student's computer file can be readily shared with parents, teachers, and the student. The parent feels more confident about the education the child is receiving. The teacher examines the student's skills and learning styles more objectively based on the accumulated evidence of his response. As Yurchak and Mathews (1980) point out, attractive, compliant students are often wrongly assumed to have more skills than they actually possess, and unattractive or noncompliant children may not be given credit for their accomplishments. Subjectiveness of this sort is avoided with an easily available student data file. The student can also be motivated by the concrete proof of progress over time.

Evaluating New and Existing Programs

A computer-managed system can help to evaluate newly adopted instructional programs. Research projects can be conducted within the school district with relative ease if data on each student are accessible. Progress of groups of children can be examined and program allocations shifted or modified on the basis of concrete data as opposed to intuition or brief observations.

Current Uses of CMI

Engelmann and Carnine (1982) at the University of Oregon are developing computer assisted instruction (CAI) software that has CMI components embedded within the instructional programs. CAI lessons are sequentially planned, and student data disks automatically provide a review of previously missed items, as well as a periodic review of items mastered in prior lessons.

A six-volume data bank of goals, objectives, and resources has been developed by the Kendall School in Washington, D.C. The *Curriculum Management System* from Learning Tools was used to computerize this extensive curriculum, allowing staff at the Kendall School and others throughout the country to locate resources to meet objectives within the curriculum. These resources include workbooks, texts, films, filmstrips, learning activities, and field-trip ideas.

Lehrer and Daiker (1978) field tested the computer-based information management system *HELPS* (Handicapped Education Learners Planning System) in Ohio. They state that this system provides "educational objectives, instructional activities, curriculum materials, and supportive information for teaching handicapped learners." Formative results of field testing indicate that *HELPS* is useful for the IEP decision-making process; creating an awareness of available materials, methods, and instructional sequences; measuring student progress; and facilitating communication. Problems with *HELPS* involve teachers' resistance to acting as a classroom manager and their difficulties with understanding and implementing the methods and materials listed on the system.

A team of special educators at Indiana University is working on a computer project that provides "a data-based cascade of services that will facilitate academic, social, and vocational achievement of mildly handicapped high school students in the least restrictive environment" (Haus, Olskin, Olson, Polsgrove, & Rietz, 1981). One component of the Indiana University project involves data collection that allows teachers to monitor student progress toward specified objectives.

Limitations of CMI Use

Given the requirements for its use, CMI must be approached with caution. Software should meet specific student, teacher, and district needs (Smith, 1981). Programs may need to be written by data processing staff, or existing programs may have to be modified. In either case, the assistance of a qualified programmer may be needed. The program must support instruction, be convenient to use, and be easily accessed by teachers who may be resistant to the technology. The program should not be so complicated that it impedes instruction. Furthermore, teachers should be committed to the use of CMI and thoroughly trained.

Special educators should be alert to a potential overdependence on CMI. Using a data base may improve instruction (Rosenberg & Sindelar, 1981), but effective teaching techniques must be available to support its use. The system must become a tool to facilitate the teaching of children.

Summary of Advantages of Using CMI

1. CMI coordinates diagnostic information and IEP documents to help teachers use them to guide instruction.

2. CMI serves as a resource to inform teachers about materials available in the district to teach specific concepts and skills.
3. CMI relieves the teacher of the tedious clerical task of keeping data on student progress.
4. Teachers can share methods and materials that have been successful in teaching students specific concepts and skills.
5. CMI aids student transition from grade to grade or teacher to teacher by providing uniformly-stated information regarding achievement.
6. CMI improves communication between special educators and regular classroom teachers regarding student progress.
7. CMI helps teachers and administrators group students for instructional purposes.
8. Communication with parents can be improved with a data base system that informs parents of their child's progress.
9. Information reported to parents on student progress is objective rather than subjective.
10. CMI can motivate students.
11. Administrators can use CMI to evaluate newly adopted programs and overall effectiveness of programs.

Administrative Use of Computers

Directors of special education programs find computers extremely useful for planning, evaluating, and reporting to local, state, and Federal agencies. Student data that is kept up to date and stored in a computer can provide easy access to information, help coordinate service delivery, and decrease paperwork. A well-designed software system allows the director to focus on managing a program and keeping closer contact with personnel by organizing and allowing access to the information that is necessary to gather, maintain, and report on their program.

When considering administrative use of computers in special education, as with all computer-related decisions, the admistrator must make the basic decisions about *software* before considering the *hardware*, unless there is hardware already available. However, the process of *implementation* — putting the system in place — is very important but frequently ignored, jeopardizing the entire enterprise. Also, considerable funds may have to be budgeted, depending on the complexity of the system design.

Software

Anyone deciding to have a computer address a range of problems should realize that the software that will do the job must be selected first, followed by the hardware the software will run on. The software, then, is critical, and its capacities and flexibility should be carefully examined to be certain it meets administrative needs. Two important technical characteristics are its user-friendliness and user-definability.

User-friendly means the software is easy for a nontechnical person to use. A menu with commands in English, rather than computer jargon, should allow the user to choose from a number of options. The term *menu* is used because it may be compared to a restaurant menu. The user selects one option after another to complete a task. The menu shapes and guides the behavior of the user, allowing him to select desired components of the program and exit from the program easily. The menu or commands allow the user to choose from such options as "edit," "quit," "see," "insert," and "delete."

For ease of use, menus and commands should be selected with a single key rather than with whole words. Single-key action is timesaving and avoids typographical errors which force repeated typing. Computers are typically programmed to accept precise information: They do not tolerate a misspelling or an incorrect expression; thus, single-key action avoids a great deal of frustration.

If an incorrect key is hit, the software should provide an error message that is easily understood. A beep or a message written in English should indicate that required information was not supplied or the action requested is not possible. The user should not be presented with computer jargon or have to refer to a manual to find out what is wrong. Errors should be handled at the keyboard or on the monitor.

Another user-friendly feature is an action-reaction sequence. Whenever a key is struck, the software should respond immediately. If the software is looking for information and the user is waiting for something to happen, the software should provide a signal that it is indeed looking. This response might be a row of asterisks or dots moving across the screen, or it might be a written message stating what the software is doing (e.g., loading, memorizing, recalling).

A critical feature, often overlooked, is the software manual, usually referred to as documentation. It should be jargon-free and easy for the nontechnical person to understand. Sample screens should be included to assist a user in learning how a program works. The documentation should contain an index as well as a table of contents. A well-written index gives the user quick access to specific information without reading through many pages of text.

Finally, demonstration systems that show capabilities and illustrate how to set up a data base are helpful. A demonstration gives the user a starting point and may approximate what the data base might look like.

The second technical feature, *user-definability*, refers to the flexibility of the software: The user should be able to adapt and expand the system to meet current and future needs. Every school district maintains and manages information that is district-specific, as well as information oriented to state and Federal requirements. The user's needs will change over time, especially as he becomes more sophisticated in his understanding of the program's capabilities and its ability to meet a broader range of his needs. The software should allow the user to adapt the data base and analysis possibilities to unique needs. A system that is truly flexible lets the user print reports with specific information in a specific sequence. For example, a special education director may want a listing of students by handicapping condition while the secretary may need a listing of special education students by school. These options and many others should be available.

Support for Administrative Needs

While technical features are important, they are ineffective unless the software supports administrative needs. The director should make a "wish list" of the tasks the computer should perform. Obvious tasks include producing information for local, state, and Federal reports, as well as such aspects of the local special education program as:

- what specific procedures were used to evaluate students
- whether evaluation practices across schools are consistent for a given suspected disability
- whether IEPs were developed or reviewed on time
- if students have been reevaluated as required
- which students should be reevaluated
- who is responsible for reevaluation
- the precise number of students served by a given teacher
- how many students are scoring below grade level
- the progress made by program or skill area.

With this wish list in mind, the director can seek out software to address these needs. If one inquires openly, without preconceptions, many unanticipated needs that can also be handled by software will be identified. The basic instructions are: Ask as many questions as possible! Explore possibilities freely! Shop for software looking for unexpected applications! While the goal is to have software that ultimately will help improve instruction and services, an adequate software system will at least help fulfill state and Federal regulations and provide access to information for planning, evaluation, and monitoring, thus releasing managerial and supervisory time.

We have indicated the computer's potential to aid in production of individualized educational plans and to manage the instructional process. While no one software package is likely to allow for this range of possibilities, a good maxim may be that the more dedicated the system is to particular functions — that is, the more it has specific, preset formats for particular forms or categories of information or reports — the less likely it is to be amenable to new or different types of problems. A minimum requirement should be that software obtained for management and reporting of information be compatible with software for developing IEPs or managing an instructional system.

A special education director may choose to obtain software from three sources:

- a company that sells microcomputer software specifically designed for special education
- an organization that sells or leases prepackaged software for a mainframe computer
- a programmer who develops software specifically for the director's needs.

Use of each of these sources has its pros and cons.

The director who hires a programmer to develop the software for microcomputers or a mainframe can have software tailored to meet the district's specific needs. While this may seem to be the most desirable situation, it may not be. A programmer is expensive, will take considerable time to develop and debug a workable system, and demands a considerable expenditure of energy by the director or data manager to ensure that the desired capabilities are built into the software. These capabilities should include flexibility to expand and adapt the software over time, and clear documentation to allow users to access it. It is unlikely that a program of this type will be compatible with commercial packages unless this compatibility is specifically requested when the contract is negotiated. Compatibility is difficult to add later. When the program is in place, the programmer or a surrogate must be available to maintain the software and make changes as needed. Other programmers may not be able to do this unless the original program design is clearly and explicitly documented at the time of development. The authors are aware of many excellent programs developed on projects that were unusable when the project staff dispersed. The contracting agency had not made any commitment to maintain the program in advance; hence it had not required transportable documentation. While all data processing approaches involve some considerable expense and thus an extended time commitment of support to justify their costs or even see tangible benefits, hiring a programmer is probably unnecessary unless the data base is very large or the hardware is already available within the district.

Prepackaged mainframe management systems are available from state agencies, service districts, and private companies. These systems offer preformatted reports to meet state and Federal requirements. Some may be relatively inexpensive if the district has terminals in place. They may also be easy to obtain if the district has an established relationship with the county service district or state agency. Mainframe systems may have limitations. The number of *fields*—items of information per student—is usually limited simply because they are predefined. Access to the computer is usually limited by excess demand. The turnaround time to produce reports may be lengthy unless a terminal and printer are available within the district or in the administrative offices. If a terminal is available locally, the operator has to know how to access the data, format them, and print out the reports. This usually requires a sophisticated understanding.

An increasingly viable option is to purchase prepackaged microcomputer software—those dedicated to special education functions, more general packages that can be adapted to these functions, or general packages to supplement the specialized packages. There are several dedicated packages for special education administrative needs. The benefits include increased flexibility in the system, control of the data bank, and independence from a central data processing system. However, someone in the special education department has to assume responsibility for organizing, maintaining, managing, and accessing the system. The specialized packages run on a variety of popular microcomputers such as the Apple II, the IBM Personal Computer, and DEC professional computers; and the packages vary in degree of flexibility and capacity. Restrictions may include a limited number of fields or an inability to store information on a large number of students. A *hard disk* may be added on to the microcomputer system to circumvent the limited memory.

An example of a dedicated package is *APS* (Administrative Planning System) provided by Learning Tools. *APS* lets a director of special education maintain, manage, and report information on a large or small number of students; the amount of information that can be stored is extensive since *APS* is used with a hard disk. The system permits the user to specify an appropriate format to print information to meet local, state, or Federal requirements for reporting or to meet planning and program evaluation needs.

An interesting option to explore with the help of a knowledgeable programmer is a combination of a relatively simple (and inexpensive) dedicated package for special education report generation combined with one of the data base packages in more general use (such as *dBase II* and *Lotus 1-2-3*) to provide a virtually unlimited range of options for organizing the data base system and even generating the reports. An interested member of the special education office must become involved in the design and maintenance of this open-ended system. An advantage of purchasing commercial packages is that the software developer supports its software. The buyer can call the software developer with questions. For popular software, there are user groups in the area, accessible by telephone or by electronic bulletin boards. The potential uses of these general purpose packages are very broad, though they may have to be installed by a programmer familiar with the system to meet the specifications of the director or staff. However, the system can be extended by the programmer as the director and staff become familiar with its parameters and determine new functions for the computer.

It should be mentioned that programmers can be extremely useful as consultants to design and implement the system, select the software packages and hardware, train staff, and adapt software packages to maximize flexibility. Since considerable funds are involved, with implications for the future, this may be a cost-effective procedure.

Hardware

The choice of software packages should dictate the hardware to be purchased, except when a programmer is hired to develop software or a school system is locked into using certain hardware, such as a district mainframe. For the director starting without access to equipment or choosing to develop an independent capability in the department, the absolute rule of thumb is that software should be selected before hardware. The discussion of the nature and capacities of hardware in Chapter 3 provides some guidelines for the aspects of hardware that one should consider. Many will be dictated by the software, but it is possible to buy a basic system that will allow the software to run without fancy add-ons. As the staff becomes proficient with the software, the system may be expanded to meet new options, reducing the one-time costs somewhat and allowing the interest in expanded uses to define further investments.

Implementation

As mentioned earlier, the director and staff should develop a wish list of tasks for the computer to perform. To make the system operational, the needs must be defined, and responsibility for the system's operation assigned. Staff who evidence a strong interest in making this system work should be selected.

The time needed for start up must be recognized and budgeted. The purchased software must be adapted to the wish list, and this may be done best by a programmer or other person familiar with the software. Entry forms for data may have to be designed unless the software already has forms or allows for direct entry of data. Manuals have to be written or adapted so that users in the district enter materials correctly. A data-entry system must be developed and assigned to the secretarial staff. The programmer may also train the staff to use the system. Simultaneously, the staff must be helped and supported to provide current and new data in a timely fashion; and a method for entering these and past data must be developed. It must be decided how far back in time the data base will be developed and how. Staff time is then required to enter the student data.

Tactically, it is wise to start small and carefully so that the staff or director are not overwhelmed by the computer or the software. The implementation timeline should not burden the staff. A series of "dry runs" should be made to detect any bugs before an aspect of the system is widely implemented. Rather than being swept up by the initial enthusiasm and excitement about the computer, one is better off moving slowly and cautiously. First, make sure the system is operational and demonstrate in small ways how it will add to the capabilities of the department. For example, generate a local school district report or a preprogrammed state report to illustrate that managerial, supervisory, or secretarial time to generate these reports can be reduced. Concurrently, involve interested staff in an IEP development system on a small scale (if this is a direction selected). If another pilot application can be launched, start it, but make certain each experience results in a successful application.

Success will feed upon success, and failures will defeat ultimate acceptance of the computer. It is best to consider what can reasonably and successfully be carried out in small steps, developing islands of receptivity or acceptance rather than imposing the total burden on an unwilling, unconvinced staff.

Recognize that the miracles ascribed to the computer require investment of time and energy as well as money. The computer, regardless of the hype, is not a panacea. Although computers help the director, they cannot make decisions, make a disorganized program organized, or solve all the administrative hassles many directors experience. The computer is a tool to be used with discretion by the special education director and staff.

Suggested Reading

Brown, N.P. CAMEO: Computer-assisted management of educational objectives. *Exceptional Children*, 1982, *49*, 151-153.

Crawford, J.L. Computer support and the clinical process: An automated behavioral rehabilitation system for mentally retarded persons. *Mental Retardation*, 1980, *18*, 119-124.

Electronic Learning. Microcomputers for the special education administrator. *Electronic Learning*, 1984, *3*(5), 39-43.

Killen, J.R., & Myklebust, H.R. Evaluation in special education: A computer based approach. *Journal of Learning Disabilities*, 1980, *13*, 440-444.

Lehrer, B.E., & Daiker, J. F. Computer based information management for professionals serving handicapped learners. *Exceptional Children*, 1978, *44*, 578-585.

Martin, E. Microcomputer applications to special education administration. *Forum*, 1980, *6*(4).

Ragghianti, S., & Miller, R. The microcomputer and special education management. *Exceptional Children*, 1982, *49*, 131-135.

Whitney, R.A., & Hofmeister, A.M. *MONITOR: A computer based management information system for special education*. Logan, UT: Utah State University, Exceptional Child Center, n.d.

Wilson, K. Computer systems for special education. In J. Dominguez & A.W. Weston (Eds.), *Educational Applications of Electronic Technology*. Monmouth, OR: WESTAR, 1982.

Wilson, K. *Computers for special education management: Progress potential and pitfalls*. The ERIC Clearinghouse, 1981.

Wilson, K. Managing the administrative morass of special needs. *Classroom Computer News*, 1981, *1*(4), 8-9.

12
Microcomputers: Making the Technology Work in Schools

What should the special education department do to manage the introduction of microcomputers into the school district? What do we advise?

There are three areas in which decisions must be made:

1. Training staff as leaders in this area, and acquainting the entire staff with the technology;
2. becoming familiar with software; and
3. addressing the hardware options.

Training Staff

The uses of microcomputers in school *and* special education settings are now being defined. In order to develop the computer capabilities of the special education staff and explore instructional applications in this rapidly changing environment, it is necessary to have persons who can introduce and support the new hardware, software applications, and peripherals in the district. To make the technology work in schools, it is critical that staff support the introduction of computers and use them constructively with students. For this to happen, school districts must develop ways to help staff become familiar with how microcomputers work and how they can be used for instruction.

Each school district, then, should focus on two areas:

1. Identifying staff who are interested in learning about and using computers in their classrooms and directing them to courses outside the system to develop an understanding of microcomputer uses in classrooms.
2. Developing in-service courses to acquaint all teachers, administrators, and specialized staff with the nature and functions of microcomputers.

Introductions

In discussing how to introduce the microcomputer to teachers in Chapter 10, we identified three levels of competence and involvement which can reasonably be expected of teachers: a minimal familiarity that allows every staff member to understand the essentials of the computer; a second level for teachers interested in using applications software with students in their classrooms; and a third level of teachers and staff who become very involved and adept with the technology.

All teachers, administrators, and staff should complete the introductory workshop series which focuses on some personally selected application *they* would like to implement on the computer. This personal selection of an application enables participants to see the potency of the microcomputer. The task chosen is less important than the fact that they value it and commit themselves to attaining some competence. This approach can be contrasted with more formal training which focuses on how the computer works, etc., but is also flexible enough to include that information.

The second level is for teachers interested in using packaged software with students in their classrooms. After an orientation, these teachers would become familiar with the software available in the different areas of student needs, learn how to evaluate and critique software, and learn how to incorporate the computer into a plan for teaching specific skills or information. We call this plan an *instructional scenario*. The logic of instructional scenarios and some sample scenarios are presented in Chapter 7. Second level teachers are not interested in learning to program; they simply want to be able to use microcomputers for instruction.

The third level of competence is that of the enthusiasts or "zealots" (Hanley, 1983): teachers, specialized staff, administrators who will be the leaders in the technology in the district. These staff members will develop a more sophisticated understanding of microcomputer technology and can provide support for their colleagues; ultimately they may provide the in-service training. They can learn to write lessons to prescription using programming or authoring languages. Their enthusiasm brings an air of excitement and adventure to the use of the microcomputer.

Teachers at all three levels need encouragement and support from administrators. All should be encouraged to meet and exchange experiences in a users' group. Users' groups extend each participant's understanding of the technology, increasing teachers' sophistication with software and broadening their range of applications. Users' groups should be a tradition encouraged within each school district.

User groups might be organized within a district or across districts. Organization across districts allows for more variety of interests and a larger pool of teachers. Groups might have different foci:

1. Special education teachers interested in remedial and special education instructional applications
2. Regular and special education teachers interested in particular applications, e.g., *LOGO* or word processing to improve writing and language arts
3. Regular and special education staff interested in learning a new application or about new peripherals (This group might meet for a series of sessions and then reconvene to compare notes on their classroom experiences.)
4. Parents and students interested in participating

Different kinds of support are required for each level of participation. Introductory level participants require encouragement, particularly to attend users' groups. Continued exposure and conversations with colleagues may prompt them to use microcomputers in their classrooms.

Teachers using computers in their classrooms need hardware and software budgets in order to utilize the new applications they discover. They will want to grow with the applications and perhaps have access to persons who can write, or help them write, particular lessons for a student. The administrator must anticipate this and provide budgetary support for software, training opportunities, additional peripherals, etc.

The enthusiasts both need support and give support. These individuals are important resources for their colleagues and the school district. Studies of the early implementation of microcomputers in schools indicate that enthusiasts predominate, are self-interested and self-taught. They teach others, lead in-service teacher training, and enrich users' groups. Often an enthusiast learns to program, converts other teachers, and keeps them supplied with programs. They represent a rich resource that supportive administrators can use with little additional investment. Administrators must support this resource by making equipment, training, and time available.

When There are No Resources for Training in the District

In many districts, this zealot group will not emerge or will not be sufficiently knowledgeable to provide in-service training or leadership. The special education director, or an interested group of teachers and staff, will have to seek other resources. Likely resources are local colleges and universities, especially those with special education training programs. Also important are the intermediate education agency and the regional office of the state department of education. A neighboring district may have already introduced microcomputers or be interested in becoming a partner in the search for resources.

If there are no resources for orientation and training in any of these agencies, it is necessary to search for resources somewhat farther afield. The state university in your state or a neighboring state may have staff involved. These staff may be able to suggest persons in your area who can serve as consultants to help plan and provide training. The special education director, however, should define the district's goals and plans for action with the consultant and some participating teachers.

We have emphasized that special education applications are a rapidly evolving area of practice. Computer consultants will not necessarily be able to help special educators use the technology with students unless paired with a knowledgeable special educator. They will be most useful in helping teachers and staff understand the technology, how to use computers, and, perhaps, where to locate interesting software for instructional and administrative applications. Consultants can be very useful as technicians, while a subset of teachers explores how to translate various applications into instructional uses for special needs students.

Computer magazines can supply considerable information to help locate software or interesting applications. The Office of Special Education of the U.S. Department of Education has funded several projects to examine applications of computer technology to special education. The Technology and Marketing Branch can help identify these resources as can the Council for Exceptional Children, the Association for Special Education Technology, and Federally-funded regional resource centers in special education (see Appendix 3).

This need to explore instructional applications is a major reason to move thoughtfully and carefully into the area of microcomputers.

1. Create a planning team of teachers and staff, and/or the administrator of special education to meet and develop a three-year plan for introducing and implementing microcomputer technology in classrooms.
2. Become familiar with the technology before moving district-wide. Our suggested approach is to identify interested staff and provide them with the encouragement, time, support, and budget to take courses outside the district as well as the software and hardware to use in their classroom when they demonstrate competence with the technology. These staff should meet in a users' group, and can also serve as the planning group in a small district.
3. Create opportunities to understand the potential of microcomputers. For example, develop a relationship with a local facility, or develop a facility within the district, to experiment with the software and hardware available for different computer systems. Regional centers, colleges and universities, and intermediate educational units may have these facilities and make them available to cooperating school districts. Other resources to cultivate are local industries or businesses that are knowledgeable about computers. Their staff are often interested in educational applications, and might be interested in helping teachers learn about computers while they learn about educational applications.

This is a period of capacity building, in which the focus should be on developing capabilities among the special education staff. The zealots will continue to develop their own understanding and share it with their colleagues. The zealots' enthusiasm will interest other staff. These capabilities will need continued cultivation and support. If supported, they will enhance staff's understanding of the uses of the technology.

Becoming Familiar with Software

We have purposefully placed becoming familiar with software ahead of hardware because it is critical to remember that software makes computer applications possible. Software dictates what can be done and so dictates the hardware to be purchased. There is instructional software for particular machines that is not available for other systems. But this situation is changing rapidly as popular software is rewritten for the popular machines. Thus, though Apple has the most instructional software, popular software is becoming available for the Commodore 64, TRS-80, and so forth. There do remain proprietary sources of software unique to one machine. For example, since the Acorn's development was subsidized by the British government for instructional applications, and Acorn is currently committed to entering the U.S. market, it is worthwhile for schools to become familiar with software packages compatible with the Acorn.

Our argument is that, ideally, the body of instructional software found to be useful should determine the hardware to be purchased. The earliest experiences of teachers and administrators should be with software — working with a particular software package and understanding its strengths and limitations. By working with different programs, experienced teachers develop a sense of whether particular software is useful, as well as a better sense of how to view, use, and gauge the utility of a package, or elements within a package, for particular student needs.

Descriptions of software abound but are generally too subjective to allow a special education teacher to know how the software can be used with special education students. Having special education teachers prepare a written evaluation helps expose specific strengths and weaknesses of a software package. Having the evaluations on file allows other teachers in the district to identify software they may find useful with a particular student. These in-district evaluations will also reflect district instructional philosophy and be more applicable than those available in journals. The process of evaluation is particularly important for special educators because they often have to adapt instructional materials to student needs. Special education teachers must develop a more sophisticated sense of the ways to view and use software in order to meet needs for which it may not be intended by the software developer.

The software evaluation instrument presented in Appendix 2 can be modified or duplicated for use in a district. It suggests many important evaluation features. Other elements may be added to this form as evaluators become more sophisticated and specific needs are clarified.

Locating Software for Trial

A major dilemma is how to find software to review without purchasing it in order to review it. There are several sources of software, some of them available free of charge. For example:

1. Microcomputer journals print programs for the reader which can simply be keyboarded.
2. Members of user groups often exchange programs they have written. Members bring diskettes to meetings. Groups advertise programs in

their newsletters or on electronic bulletin boards. Many electronic bulletin boards allow programs to be copied (downloaded). The National Association of State Directors of Special Education (NASDSE) in Washington, D.C. sponsors an electronic bulletin board through a facility called Special Net to which school districts and individuals can subscribe (see Appendix 3).

3. Some software is available simply for the asking. A listing of such public domain sources is available in Appendix 3.
4. Software developers, distributors, local stores, teachers from other districts, and university resource centers will often demonstrate software for teachers and staff.
5. Computer shows display software. Tell the salesperson what your needs are, ask what software is available, and describe your experiences with the products on display. This is important feedback for software developers to hear.
6. Neighboring school districts may have software that staff can observe being used with students.

There are also other less exotic means of obtaining access to software. Many software companies will allow potential buyers, especially school systems, to preview programs. When ordering a package, request that it be sent "on approval" for preview, subject to approval of the buyer.

Increasingly, universities, colleges, intermediate educational districts, and larger school districts are collecting software for examination at their curriculum libraries, media centers, or teacher centers. These centers may allow teachers taking courses preview privileges and offer workshops in which courseware is examined. As their collections improve, such centers will become an increasingly valuable source of software for examination.

Addressing the Hardware Options

Hardware purchases should be dictated by the software available. Major issues are the administrator's timeline and whether the district has already purchased microcomputer systems. If there is no time pressure to introduce the computer for instructional purposes, then strategies for introduction can be developed. In any event, a plan for implementation should be developed.

Hardware capabilities are changing rapidly. The MacIntosh from Apple Computer features many non-keyboard options for its software. These may be particularly useful for low functioning and physically handicapped students.

The next generation of personal computers will be based on larger core memory. The earliest machines had 8K or 16K of memory: Today's tend to have 48K or 64K. The next generation of home and small personal computers suitable in price for schools will likely have 128K. Larger core memory means that software with more sophisticated capabilities can be developed for microcomputers. Simultaneously, the range of peripherals suitable for students with disabilities will continue to grow. Many of these may be compatible with popular systems.

Adaptations will be available to upgrade or add to the capabilities of current machines, much as add-on memory boards are available now. School districts committed to one system should investigate upgrading their equipment rather than replacing it: The industry for add-on hardware is extensive for popular computers.

In this period of rapid change, staff should review software for instructional applications for each of the major computers. The variety of applications, even the characteristics of the same software (e.g., the various versions of *LOGO*) can be compared and contrasted. The staff should be aware of differences in versions of the same software. Also, specialized classrooms for the visually or aurally impaired and the physically or multiply handicapped have different instructional needs, and should use the computer differently. To conduct this hardware and software review, districts may purchase, lease, rent, or arrange for a loan of hardware.

What Do We Know about Managing Microcomputer Instruction?

There are several sources of information beginning to be available. Many comments in this section were drawn from Thormann's (1982) study, summarily presented in Chapter 8; interviews conducted by Budoff (1983); and a study currently underway (Hanley, 1983).

The Adoption of Microcomputers

Two stages describe the adoption of microcomputers for instruction in schools. In the first, individual teachers teach themselves the technology. Often they purchase a system for home use and bring it to school, or the school buys one for them to use. They, in turn, interest other teachers, and support them in their classroom efforts. In the earliest days, these enthusiasts also wrote their own software and offered it to their colleagues. These individuals characterize the "zealot" stage (Hanley, 1983) — what we refer to as Level 3 participants, the enthusiasts (see Chapter 10). These individuals are important in popularizing the technology in their districts.

The second stage is the district-wide introduction of microcomputers. Unlike the earlier stage, training is formally offered by the district to teachers and the placement of equipment in classrooms is often more formal. Whereas the zealots may have brought their own equipment into classrooms and then received equipment from the district; in the second stage, administrators often feel the teacher must qualify to receive the equipment. New users must be trained and demonstrate their understanding before they are provided with microcomputers. In one district, teachers were not given microcomputers until after they completed an 8-week in-service training course that included hands-on experience and written reviews by the teachers of at least three educational software programs. In another district, the teachers were trained and then required to develop a formal plan demonstrating how they would use microcomputers in their classrooms.

Patterns of Organization

Two patterns of organization have developed. A typical *centralized* pattern is likely when a district-level administrator plays an early and major role in adopting microcomputers. A *decentralized* organization emerges when interest and expertise are concentrated at the school building level. In these instances, the instructional applications are often initiated by classroom teachers. Administrative personnel become involved in response to teachers' growing interest, requests for more equipment, and needs for technical assistance and training. District-level program directors can ensure that microcomputers will be available to teachers within their programs by authorizing equipment purchases from program funds (e.g., special education funds), and ensuring priority use of microcomputers by teachers and students.

Factors other than the centralized or decentralized pattern seem important to the growth and utilization of microcomputers. Persons with key skills and authority are essential. Skills should include recent or current teaching experience as this encourages appropriate integration of microcomputer use within the classroom. These persons require access to or control over administrative resources to assure that supporting resources continue to be made available. Persons with these skills can work as a formal or informal group, and the group may or may not work at the district level.

Most Districts Establish Formal "Coordinator" Positions

In most cases, coordinators are school-based teachers or consulting teachers who have been involved with microcomputers. Some of these teachers are formally appointed, but many more represent the voluntary assumption of these responsibilities by teachers. Decentralized or school-based coordinators are expected to fulfill their other educational responsibilities; coordination is considered to be a part-time responsibility. Microcomputer coordination is viewed as simply another function of already established roles — special education consulting teacher, career counselor/coordinator.

Does a Coordinator Make a Difference?

Even when the administration is not particularly supportive or interested in microcomputer applications, teachers seem to identify their own resource persons among the staff and rely on them for technical assistance and guidance. Coordinators play a key role in expanding teacher knowledge by being key developers and presenters of in-service training on microcomputers for other district staff. Coordinators who are perceived as most effective by teachers are those who have already had microcomputer experience in the classroom.

Case studies indicate that some of the most successful uses — in terms of the number of special education teachers and students involved, and the diversity and extent of applications made — occur in districts where microcomputers are available to both special and regular education users. In many of these cases the differences in applications between the two groups are essentially transparent — training for personnel is the same, and the software and approaches to the microcomputers are identical.

The Coordination of Administrative/Instructional Use

In districts that plan "mixed" uses — administrative and instructional — specific microcomputers should be allocated to either instructional or administrative applications, and resources (such as software) should be allocated to support both types of uses. When administrative applications are added to an instructional system, additional computers should be purchased. This expansion of the resource base of the system, with training for new users, increases local expertise and knowledge, and local support. Administrators who have used microcomputers are usually more supportive of instructional uses.

Hanley (1983) reported an interesting feature of microcomputer use. The introduction or expansion of administrative applications did not bump instructional applications, which had been the negative experience of many teachers with a prior history of instructional applications on mainframe and minicomputer systems. Dedication of different microcomputer systems to different functions is seen positively as a way to ensure system availability for each function.

Students can also be directly involved in administrative applications. Entering data, updating files, and operating business software can be meaningful, vocational experiences.

Adminstrative Leadership

Hanley (1983) reported that special education administrators often have not been directly involved in the development and management of microcomputer systems. He ascribes a number of reasons.

- Special education administrative staff were relatively few in number and their time was heavily allocated to other tasks: assessment, placement, keeping records, generating reports, etc.
- The impetus for instructional applications came from the teachers; it was a "bottom-up" phenomenon and the knowledge base for instructional applications was decentralized — in the school buildings and classrooms.
- In an atmosphere of reduced local budgets and increasing demands for services, special education administrators were often reluctant to provide funds to purchase microcomputer equipment. Special education teachers, therefore, relied on equipment provided from other sources, e.g., regular education. In using this equipment, the teachers interacted more often with other administrators (principals, microcomputer coordinators) than with the special education administration.

In addition, Hanley (1983) reported special and regular education applications were often very similar. He suggests that applications particularly beneficial to handicapped students tend not to occur in school districts which do not have special education administrative leadership in microcomputers. He concludes:

> Ultimately, special education administrators may have to take a more active role in the planning and management of microcomputer systems to encourage more specialized use of this technology in programs for handicapped students.

In Closing

The microcomputer can be used for a variety of applications in special education that can make it enormously valuable to administrators, teachers, and students alike. It can serve as tutor and tutee, showing the student how to learn more effectively; keep records and produce reports for the administrator; and be used as a word processor by staff to write reports, or by students to improve their writing and language arts. It can remove much of the onerous work of producing an individual educational plan as well as be used to monitor the student's instructional progress, access the instructional library, and help the teacher identify other exercises appropriate to the student. Potentially, it can vastly enrich the educational experiences of the students, and provide intellectual stimulation and practical aid to the teacher.

The applications of microcomputers to special education need careful thought and planning for the potentials of the technology to be tapped for the students. The technology is complex, can be intimidating, but can be very exciting as well.

Special education administrators must, minimally, allocate funds for ongoing costs to effectively support microcomputers in special education. Provision for the following must be included:

1. Funds to involve groups of educators in planning and microcomputer applications. Such groups should include district-level staff (e.g., assistant superintendent or special education administrator), the zealots, and the newer enthusiasts — all represent a critical knowledge base for applications.
2. Costs for training teachers initially, and for helping them maintain and increase their understanding and uses of the technology.
3. Funds for maintenance and repair of the equipment, and insurance.
4. Funds for continuing additions to the software library.
5. Funds for peripherals such as printers, interfacing cables, voice devices, graphic pads, etc.
6. Funds for occasional consultations with persons working with special education applications or the technology.

In addition, there are other requirements. The coordinator of microcomputer systems should work to create an assisting network in its multifaceted features. The coordinator should develop access to electronic bulletin boards such as SpecialNet, identify local societies of computer users, locate users' groups in the community, identify sources of software in the area, and so forth. Mundane needs must be addressed. A reliable person to service the computer and peripherals should be identified. A staff member should be assigned the task of clipping interesting articles for circulation and identifying new and interesting devices or applications software. Resource persons in the area should also be identified and enlisted to support the effort.

Buying locally offers distinct advantages. Local vendors often service equipment and offer technical advice and backup. They can also be made aware of the district's needs and, if their knowledge and interest in instructional applications is cultivated, they can become specialized resources for new applications and developments.

The promise of this technology is vast but we cannot emphasize enough the need for administrative leadership and support. The special education administrator must lead the staff or encourage and support leadership by interested teachers. The microcomputer can bring a dramatic expansion of the tools available to special educators to work with special needs students, and also provide aids for the disabled student to minimize the effects of disability. Hence, we feel it is important for all school districts to become involved with the technology.

While computers are increasingly available in regular education, special educators are only beginning to become involved. Their continuing unfamiliarity with this exciting technology causes their special needs students to be denied the instructional opportunities an informed staff could provide. Special educators must be introduced to microcomputers and their instructional applications. The special education leadership must be particularly supportive and encouraging so that special educators acquire a level of knowledge sufficient to tailor the instructional use of microcomputers to the needs of special education students. Microcomputers can be an invaluable teaching tool for the special educator.

The past decade has seen enormous strides in reducing the gap in opportunities between regular and special education students. The microcomputer technology may be critically beneficial to special education students who have been unmotivated and failing. The excitement of the computer can stimulate their classroom learning. Yet special education students appear to be lagging behind in their access to microcomputers in schools, especially in the specialized applications from which they could benefit. It is important to recognize that applications for special education students will vary from those for regular education students. Special education administrators and staff must make microcomputers as accessible to special needs students as they are becoming to regular students, and structure this access to best meet the needs of special education students. To fail in this task is to deny a major benefit to students in critical need!

References

Adams, J., Richards, J., & Brao-Ternger, B. Data storage and retrieval system for use in a learning disabilities diagnostic clinic. *Journal of Learning Disabilities*, 1980, *13*, 539-541.

Beck, J.J., Jr. The microcomputer bandwagon: Is it playing your tune? *Directive Teacher*, 1982 *4*, 27.

Becker, W., & Carnine, D. Direct instruction — An effective approach to education intervention with disadvantaged and low-performers. In E. Lakey & A. Kazkin (Eds.), *Advances in child clinical psychology* (Vol. 3). New York: Plenum, 1980.

Berman, P., & McLaughlin, M.W. *Federal programs supporting educational change, Vol. VIII: Implementing and sustaining innovations*. R-1589/8-HEW, May 1978. (Available from the Rand Corporation, Santa Monica, CA.)

Bracken, P. *IEPs and technology*. Unpublished manuscript, 1981. (Available from OTIS, 1200 Hwy. 99 North, P.O. Box 2680, Eugene, Oregon.)

Budoff, M. *Integration of a microprocessor based computer in special education resource room: Some case studies*. Final Report, Grant No. G008100280, U.S. Department of Education, Office of Special Education Programs, Field-Initiated Studies, 1983.

Carnine, D., & Silbert, J. *Direct instruction reading*. Columbus: Charles Merill, 1979.

Cunningham, W.G. The need for dialogue between educators and technologists. *Phi Delta Kappa*, 1977, *58*, 450-62.

Engelmann, S., & Carnine, D. *Theory of instruction: Principles and applications*. New York: Irvington Publishers, 1982.

Gagne, R.M., & Briggs, I.J. *Principles of instructional design (2nd edition)*. New York: Holt and Winston, 1979.

Goldenberg, E.P. *Special technology for special children: Computers to serve communication and autonomy in the education of handicapped children*. Baltimore: University Park Press, 1979.

Hanley, T.V. *Microcomputers in special education: Organizational issues*. Arlington, Virginia: SRA Technologies, Inc.; and Washington, D.C.: COSMOS Corporation, 1983.

Haus, G., Olskin, B., Olson, J., Polsgrove, L., & Rieth, H. *An application of a computerized IEP and student progress monitoring system*. Paper presented at the 59th annual international convention of the Council for Exceptional Children, New York, New York, April 1981.

Huff, P. Personal communication, September 5, 1981.

Lehrer, B., & Daiker, J.F. Computer based information management for professionals serving handicapped learners. *Exceptional Children*, 1978, *44*, 578-585.

Magidson, E. Student assessment of PLATO: What students like to dislike about CAI. *Educational Technology*, 1978, *18*, 15-19.

Massimo, J. Personal communication, September 13, 1981.

Papert, S. *Mindstorms: Children, computers, and powerful ideas*. New York: Basic Books, 1980.

Parelius, A. *Monitoring-evaluation system*. Paper presented at the World Congress on Future in Special Education, Sterling, Scotland, June 25-July 1, 1978. (ERIC Document Reproduction Service No. ED 157 332.)

Price, M., & Goodman, L. Individualized education programs: A cost study. *Exceptional Children*, 1980, *46*, 446-453.

Quinseatt, M.G. *Implementing computer technology in a classroom setting: An anecdotal report of long term use*. Paper presented at a conference of the National Institute of Education, 1981.

Rosenberg, M., & Sindelar, D. Computer-assisted data management of instructional programming. *Education Unlimited*, 1981, *3*, 37-40.

Shannon, C.E. A symbolic analysis of relay and switching circuits. *Transaction of the American Institute of Electrical Engineers*, 1938, *57*, 713+.

Silluzio, V. Personal communication, September 13, 1981.

Smith, R.W. Improving instructional management with microcomputers. *Occasional Paper*, 1981, *1*.

Thormann, M.J. *Public school use of computers in special education*. Ed.D. dissertation, University of Oregon, 1982.

Trachtman, P. Putting computers into the hands of children without language. *Smithsonian*, 1984, *14*, 42-51.

Wade, T.E. Evaluating computer instructional programs and other teacher units. *Educational Technology*, Nov. 1980.

Wager, W. Issues in the evaluation of instructional computing programs. *Educational Computer*, Sept.-Oct. 1981, 20-22.

Walker, H. The individualized educational program (IEP) as a vehicle for delivery of special education and related services to handicapped children. In *IEP: Developing criteria for the evaluation of individualized education program provisions*. Washington, D.C.: U.S. Office of Education, 1978.

Walter, R. *The eleventh edition of the secret guide to computers*. Boston: Russ Walters, 1984.

Weir, S., Russell, S.J., & Valente, J.A. LOGO: An approach to educating disabled children. *Byte*, 1982, 7, 342-360.

Yurchak, M.J., & Mathews, R. *The final report of findings (The Huron study of the quality of educational services provided to handicapped children from the perspective of the child, the family, and school personnel)*. Cambridge, Mass.: The Huron Institute, 1980.

Appendices

APPENDIX 1

Hardware Features and Technical Considerations

This Appendix briefly deals with details of hardware components in current use. Some software considerations are discussed, such as the use of storage media for data files. It is important to remember that the tide of technology is rushing in at a rapid rate. Some of this information may be out of date by the time you read it. On the other hand, many of the exciting developments described here and in the computer periodicals are still emerging. It usually takes some time for the latest breakthroughs to trickle down to affordable, reliable applications and mass-produced components.

For the reader's convenience, the material in this Appendix is divided into categories. CPUs are not included because they are discussed in detail in Chapter 3, especially in the sections entitled *Processing in the CPU, CPUs are Not All the Same, CPUs and Memory,* and *CPUs and Operating Systems.* Categories are presented here in the following sequence:

- Communications
- Input Devices
- Memory
- Operating Systems
- Output Devices
- Storage Devices and Media
- Storage and Files

Sub-categories, as well as *their* subcategories, are arranged in alphabetical order.

Communications

Here *communications* refers to the various means by which information can be transmitted between one computer and another or between a computer and peripherals. *Peripherals* are input and output devices, disk and tape drives, terminals, and even other computers acting like "dumb" terminals.

Baud rate: The speed at which bits of data are transmitted. Commonly used rates are 300 and 1200 baud but rates less than 100 and more than 9600 are possible. Most devices allow the user to select from three or more rates as needed. Transmitter and receiver must be set to the same speed: If a computer sends information at 1200 baud and a printer accepts it at only 300 baud, something is likely to be lost along the way.

Bus: A hardware unit for carrying data. All computers have buses within the CPU. Some provide external buses as well for adding on multiple peripherals or system enhancements.

Interface: A hardware unit, a software unit, or a combination of both that allows communication between two units not specifically designed for each other.

Modem: The name is derived from a contraction of *modulator-demodulator*. A modem allows two computers or a computer and a terminal to communicate through standard telephone lines. At the input end, it converts digital signals from the computer into audio signals for transmission. At the output end, it converts sound into digital signals. A modem is needed at both the input and output end. Some computers, especially portable models, have built-in modems. Some units can be set up to dial a given telephone number or to answer incoming calls. Direct-connect modems plug directly into modern telephone jacks, bypassing the telephone itself. More primitive models use an *acoustic coupler* that provides a special cradle for the telephone handset. These are not as reliable for transmitting data as the direct-connect.

Network: A wiring and interface arrangement by which many computers, terminals, and peripherals can share resources, such as storage, facilities, data, and printers. This technology is making rapid progress, even to the point of allowing communication between otherwise incompatible hardware units. Networks may require special Operating System capabilities.

Port: An electrical connection through which a computer communicates. The CPU has one or more ports of its own, and the computer provides one or more ports for the user to connect peripheral devices. A device and the port it is connected to must be of the same type, unless a special interface can be found.

> **Parallel port**: Allows data to be sent more than one bit at a time; for example, 8 bits can be sent simultaneously over 8 parallel wires.

> **Serial port**: Allows data to be transmitted one bit at a time over a single wire. (Other wires are required for grounding and for sending messages such as "Are you ready for more?" and "Yes, go ahead.").

Robot: Listed here because it often combines both input and output, involving two-way communication with the outside world. Robots can see, hear, measure, sort, count, lift objects, walk, talk. They can be programmed to perform specific tasks such as putting wheels on automobiles. Some things they do as well as humans. Robots can also be very entertaining to build and program and a number of make-it-yourself kits are on the market at surprisingly low prices.

Terminal: Another input-output device. Many terminals look just like desktop computers — they have keyboards and video screens even though they have no CPUs. Most computers can pretend to be dumb terminals. Mainframe computers and microcomputers with multiuser Operating Systems serve several terminals at one time. A printer can be called a terminal, especially if it has a keyboard for sending data and instructions to the computer.

Input Devices

The list of input devices below is generally limited to those that are readily available and intended for direct input — by humans — of data and instructions.

Digitizer tablet: Requires software that knows how to interpret the input signals. Using a digitizer tablet is rather like drawing or writing or tracing on a sheet of fine graph paper. Each square is given a pair of coordinates, x and y. A square 5 inches in from the left margin and 4 inches up from the bottom might have an x coordinate of 500 and a y coordinate of 400. If your writing instrument entered that square, the values 500, 400 would be sent to the computer (in binary).

An obvious use of the digitizer tablet is for entering graphics — anything drawn on the tablet can be stored in code form. It can then be reproduced on the screen or sent to a graphics printer. The tablet can also be used to enter responses to multiple-choice tests and questionnaires. The program associates certain blocks of squares with certain questions. With the right software, digitizer tablets can even be used for handwritten entry of letters and numbers. Their standards of legibility are somewhat higher than ours — some day they may be used to teach penmanship.

Joy stick: Widely used in video games. To use a joy stick, you tilt the stick on its base in any direction. The cursor, spaceship, or other indicator moves around the video display screen in response. A skillful user can guide the cursor through an intricate maze. Another use of joy sticks is for moving the cursor to a desired location in a context provided by the software, as in selecting from a menu. The user can press a button on the joy stick to indicate "This is my selection."

An educational game for beginning readers might display the word "CAT" on one side of the screen and pictures of a cat, bat, hat, and mat on the opposite side. A player could use a joy stick to "point" to the picture that he thinks matches the word. (See also *Paddle* and *Mouse*.)

Keyboard: The most commonly used input device. Most people feel comfortable with a keyboard — perhaps because of its similarity to a typewriter keyboard or because the keys are labeled with familiar symbols. Children with low-level motor skills who have trouble with handwriting find it relatively easy to use a keyboard.

Keyboards are rarely purchased as stand-alone units: They usually come built into or ready to plug into the same cabinet as the computer or CRT. Plug-in models are equipped with cords so you can position them comfortably. A recent innovation uses infrared signals instead of a physical connection: The keyboard can be moved freely up to several yards from the receiver, as long as there is no wall or similar object in between to interfere with the signals.

The buyer of a computer system may not have a choice of keyboards. If a choice is available, the buyer should look for comfort and ease of use. Remember, the keyboard is one of two hardware elements with which the user will spend the most time.

The differences between one keyboard model and another are so subtle that you might not notice them in a brief trial period. In the long run, they can make a big difference. Variations include the size of the key top, spacing of keys, amount of pressure required to activate a key, sculpturing to keep the fingers from sliding off the keys, and location of seldom-used keys. On some models the "home keys" (F and J) are identified by special sculpturing as an aid to correct hand positioning for touch typing.

Braille keys: Standard key tops are replaced with keys that are not only marked in the usual way but also embossed in braille. These are helpful to the blind, and sighted persons using them may become familiar with braille in the process.

Caps lock key: Essential if the keyboard and computer support upper and lower case. This key is different from the shift lock on a typewriter: It makes all alphabetic characters come out upper case, but has no effect on numbers and special characters. Thus, to get a "%" instead of a "5", the normal shift key is used.

Cursor control keys: Four keys usually labeled with arrows (up, down, left, right). Cursor control keys let the user position the cursor at any point on the screen for input. They are convenient for such applications as editing text. They do require appropriate software: The program must keep track of the cursor's location, but it must not treat the use of these keys as input of data or instructions.

Dvorjak keyboard: Instead of standard QWERTYUIOP layout, the Dvorjak arranges keys according to frequency of use and ease of typing. For example, all vowels and the most frequently used consonants are on the middle row of alphabetic character keys. The Dvorjak keyboard on a word processor is claimed to increase productivity by 50% or more once the user has learned it. (The QWERTYUIOP layout, by the way, was actually designed to slow the typing pace so that mechanical typewriters could keep up.)

Function keys: Special keys used to enter commands with one keystroke. The keys are labeled with their functions. A word processing system might provide Append, Edit, Save, Print, and so on. Once again, the function must be recognized by the software program or the Operating System.

> **Programmable function keys:** Usually labelled F1, F2, F3, etc. A great convenience for people who bother to learn how to use them. The user can define and redefine key functions at will. The function may be a command or a string of text. Some systems have a 128 character limit. When the function has been defined for a key, it can be called up with one keystroke.

Key sound control: Many keyboards are silent, and you might think that desirable. However, some of us who have used a typewriter are so used to audio feedback that silence is disconcerting — if we don't hear the key, we are not sure we touched it. Many computers add an artificial click; some let you control the loudness of the click; some let you add a small beep.

Membrane keyboard: Found in some of the more inexpensive computers. Membrane keyboards use a flat surface with printed keys instead of raised, separate keys. One problem is the lack of tactile feedback. To compensate, a bell or other mechanical sound may be provided.

Numeric key pad: A separate bank of keys like that on an adding machine. It is handy for entering numeric data.

One-hand keyboard: Advertised as a revolutionary device that permits rapid text and data entry with only one hand. (It's not clear whether there are models for left-handed users.) The device is small, not much larger than a pack of cards, and provides a small number of keys, all of which can be reached without moving the hand. The keys can be used singly and in combinations to provide at least as many characters as a normal keyboard.

Light pen: By-passes both keyboard and cursor. The user holds a pen-like object connected to the computer by a cord and touches the screen directly. Special hardware is required to detect and identify the point of contact and special software is needed to interpret the input. Software permitting, light pens can be used to draw and edit graphic images on the screen with great precision. (See also *Touch screen*.)

Mouse: A device held in one hand and rolled about the tabletop. Its motion is echoed on the video display. One or more buttons are provided to enter predefined commands. The most common use of a mouse is for selecting from an array of options, but some claim the mouse is good for drawing graphics. For that purpose, however, a digitizer tablet might allow greater precision.

Mechanical mouse: Uses rotating balls in contact with the table top or other surface to detect the motion. It functions better on slightly rough surfaces than on formica or glass.

Optical mouse: Must be used on a board marked with horizontal lines in one color and vertical lines in another color. The mouse uses a light beam and reflectors to sense and count the lines being crossed. It is said to be more durable than the mechanical mouse. However, the user must pay close attention to alignment.

Paddle: Works rather like a joy stick or mouse but has less freedom of motion. The user turns a knob on its base, and an associated bar, like a long cursor, moves up and down or back and forth along a straight line. Paddles are used for a great many action games; in these the true cursor often represents something like a hockey puck or soccer ball. Under the control of the program, the cursor whizzes about the screen and bounces off paddle bars, obstacles, and screen edges. The angles of reflection follow at least some of the laws of physics. Parents of youthful addicts say that joy stick and paddle games develop excellent hand-eye coordination. (See also *Joy stick* and *Mouse*.)

Reader: Not intended for interactive applications. A reader converts whatever it reads into binary codes and is particularly valuable for fast entry of prepared material. Coded data input from readers is often sent directly by the CPU to disk or tape for magnetic storage.

> **Bar code reader**: So far, used mostly in supermarkets and automated warehouses. The bar codes are those rectangles of wide and narrow black lines on cereal boxes and other prepackaged items. A bar code reader scans the lines very quickly. The binary code it sends to the CPU identifies the item and can be used to retrieve description and price or to update an inventory file. At least one general-purpose printer on the market can print bar codes. Both printers and readers are becoming less expensive.
>
> **Mark sense reader**: While punched-card readers sense punched holes mechanically, mark sense readers are optical devices that detect black marks. They are useful for entering data from multiple-choice tests and survey questionnaires in which boxes are checked or bullets filled in. They can also read punched cards if the cards are backed by a black surface. Like other input devices, mark sense readers must be supported by programs.
>
> **Optical scanner**: Modern units can read printed or typewritten copy easily and rapidly, recognizing any given character in a number of typefaces and sizes. They are often used in newspaper offices to feed copy from ordinary typewriters into computer storage. One scanner can keep up with several typists. Optical scanners are not yet very skilled in reading handwriting.
>
> **Paper tape reader**: Reads continuous paper tape coded with holes, like that used on teletypewriters. Data are written onto the tape with a *paper tape punch*. Paper tape readers have been in use for many

decades, and are still being manufactured, but are not likely to be used with modern computers. Their functions have been taken over by modem communications and by magnetic storage.

Punched card reader: Reads stacks of cards with holes whose locations represent data or program codes. The holes may be punched with a manually operated *keypunch* or automatically by computer with an output device called a *card punch*. Punched cards, like paper tape, have been used for decades but are seldom seen in new computer installations.

Touch screen: Requires special hardware, which can sometimes be added to a standard CRT. As the name implies, the user merely touches the screen, usually with a finger. One means of detecting the touch and its location is by optical sensors ranged around the screen's edges. Because of the size of human fingers, control is less precise than with a light pen. The primary use of touch screens is for selecting from an array of choices (such as a menu) presented by the software.

Voice digitizer: Breaks down the wave forms of human speech into "slices." Each slice is converted to a group of binary codes. Code groups are compared to standards, each of which represents a word in a vocabulary file. Voice digitizers are used by workers whose hands are occupied with manual tasks, as well as by persons who have lost the use of their hands.

Most voice digitizers have very limited vocabularies and also must learn to recognize the individual speaker's voice. They become confused if the regular speaker has a cold. High-pitched voices also cause confusion. However, this technology is advancing rapidly.

Memory

As noted elsewhere, the computer can be said to use three kinds of memory. One of these is generally referred to as storage (see *Storage*). The other two are Random Access Memory (RAM) and Read Only Memory (ROM). The CPU can access these very quickly by memory address because it is wired to both memories directly. By contrast, reading or writing information on disk or tape storage requires mechanical drive action and assistance from the Operating System to find the right location.

Addressable memory: The total memory that can be addressed by the CPU. Addressable memory includes both RAM and ROM. An 8-bit CPU cannot make use of more than 64K of memory without special assistance. A 16-bit system can address many megabytes.

In evaluating various systems, one is apt to forget that ROM must be included in addressable memory. If an 8-bit system has 48K of RAM and includes or requires a 16K ROM chip for any reason, the limit of 64K has already been reached.

> **Bank-switching**: Refers to a technique for increasing the amount of addressable memory. For example, an 8-bit CPU can work with 128K of RAM in two 64K banks. A *memory management unit* takes responsibility for switching access from one bank to the other. As far as the CPU is concerned, it only sees 64K.

> **Virtual memory**: Another way of circumventing normal limitations. This approach uses disk as an extension of RAM. It swaps bytes between RAM and disk as needed. Its use has generally been confined to large systems running large programs.

RAM: Random Access Memory works with microscopic switches that can be turned on or off, by means of electric current, to represent bits of data or instructions. RAM is actually not accessed randomly but under the very precise control of the Operating System and other software. Any byte in RAM can be read or written to at any time.

RAM is used for temporary storage of programs and data copied into it from disk. It also stores input from the keyboard or other devices and whatever data is generated by the CPU. Depending on the system, it may also have to accommodate the Operating System and an interpreter. Obviously, the more memory the better. Fortunately, more memory is becoming less and less costly.

> **Battery-backed RAM**: Ensures the survival of the RAM contents in the event of a power failure.

> **NOVRAM**: Non-Volatile RAM, also called EEPROM (Electronically Erasable Programmable Read Only Memory). The bit switches in these chips can be reset, as in RAM, but will then remain fixed, even without electricity, as in ROM. So far, this form of memory has the disadvantages of slower access and greater power consumption.

> **User memory**: Usually refers to the amount of RAM that is not reserved for the Operating System and other software required by the

CPU. If the operating system is in ROM, user memory and RAM may be the same.

ROM: Read Only Memory is memory in which software has been made permanent — programs in this form are called *firmware*. ROM chips cannot be changed as the program is in the form of fixed switches. The contents of ROM chips are secure even without electricity. The CPU can read faster from ROM than from RAM.

Some systems use hard-wired ROM chips to store always-needed programs such as Operating Systems and interpreters. Some of these, however, do offer other options: The normal CPU/Operating System team can be bypassed by inserting a board with a different CPU accompanied by its own Operating System in a ROM chip. In a sense the user then has two computers, even though they may not read each other's disks.

Some systems provide for the insertion, removal, and replacement of various ROM cartridges. Game cartridges for home computers are one example. Another is the removable ROM cartridge that controls the variable typefaces of certain printers.

Operating Systems

Chapter 3 discusses the various functions of Operating Systems in some detail, as well as their relationship to CPUs, disks, languages, and programs.

Command language: Each Operating System has its own set of commands that users can call on without the support of any other software. For example, DIR to display a disk directory, ERA followed by file name to erase a file, PIP to copy files from disk to disk, and STAT to see how much free space is left on a disk. Some command languages are easier to use than others. Unfortunately, there is no standard terminology.

Concurrency: Also called *multi-tasking*. Allows the user to carry on more than one task with one CPU. One program can run in the "background" and another in the "foreground." Also, the user can interrupt one program, call up another, and return to the first where it was interrupted.

Multiuser system: Usually, a system in which several users at several terminals share the same CPU and disk storage. Multiple users can even access the same data files. The CPU is assigned to one user for a fraction of a microsecond, to another for the next fraction, and so on. (The fractions of time are sometimes called "time slices.") The Operating System has responsibility for time slice scheduling and data integrity, in addition to its normal duties.

Multiuser capability is provided by most if not all mainframe and minicomputer systems. Among microcomputers, the majority are still single-user systems. However, as microprocessors and disk storage approach the power and economy of mainframes, more multiuser operating systems will become available. At least one multiuser system on the market provides a separate microprocessor and RAM for each user, while all users share the same hard disk.

Network system: Establishes and maintains communication paths between computers in a network configuration. (This is not the same as multiuser systems which are usually built around one processor.) Networks may connect computers that are in the same building, miles apart, or both.

Output Devices

The output of a computer, one might say, is the point of the whole thing. Before buying a software package, sitting down to write a program, or even acquiring a computer, the logical thing is to decide what output is wanted, in what form, and for whom. Many computers can make use of all the devices mentioned below, although some may require special interfaces. Some of these devices may require special software that is not available for every computer.

Printer: Used primarily for text, but some models have graphics capabilities. Printers have come a long way in the last decade. More and more features are available at ever lower prices. It is important to remember that printing is controlled primarily by software. Special features usually require special software support.

> **Impact printer**: Works somewhat like a typewriter, using a ribbon between the paper and the print head. All impact printers are noisier than non-impact printers.
>
> > **Band printer**: Big workhorse used mostly in busy data processing departments. Now being offered in smaller sizes at lower prices.

Dot matrix printer: Works with a moving print head that contains a matrix (rectangle) of tiny movable pins. According to the character code received, the necessary pins are projected against the ribbon and each pin prints a small dot. The more dots, the clearer the character.

New models are extremely flexible. They can print draft copy at very high speed, correspondence-quality copy at lower speeds, and graphics as well. The user may specify compressed print, expanded print, or double-size print. Some use multicolored ribbon and variable dot density to produce shaded color graphics.

At least one manufacturer controls the typeface by codes stored in ROM cartridges. By changing the cartridge you can change the typeface. Three or four cartridges can be inserted at once, allowing you to mix typefaces in the text. With some units, you can also create special characters and small graphics, store them on disk, and insert them in the text as you would any normal character.

Formed character printer: Produces *letter quality* print like that produced with a good electric typewriter. This category includes *daisywheel* and *thimble* printers, the names referring to the shape of the changeable printing element. The print head moves along the line, and each character code received makes the element spin to place the right character in front of the hammer that will make it print. Changing the typeface requires changing the print element—a rather clumsy procedure to carry out in the middle of printing text.

Line printer: Prints an entire line at once. Like the band printer, its speed, reliability, and cost make it most suitable for large data processing centers where massive reports are being printed 24 hours a day.

Non-impact printers: Have their advantages, of which the greatest is that they are quiet. They cannot make carbon copies. Most require special paper, special ink, special chemicals, or other supplies that add to the operating cost.

Electrostatic and electrographic printers: Quieter and faster than any impact printer. May require special paper. Can produce graphics, but not in color. Similar in many ways to the *thermal printer*.

Ink-jet printer: Relatively expensive but becoming less so. Can print anything in black and white or color.

Laser printer: Relative newcomer. Can print anything in black and white, is incredibly fast, and is correspondingly expensive.

Plotter: Does not print at all, but actually draws with pens. Can draw almost anything and is excellent for color graphics. Plotters require special software, but some are very reasonably priced.

Thermal printer: Similar to the *electrostatic/graphic printer* but uses a different chemical process to produce the image.

Printing features: The importance of each of the following features depends on the primary use, frequency of use, and location of the unit. Thus, you may not care if a printer is noisy, as long as it is in somebody else's office. You may not care if it is simple and slow, as long as you enjoy exclusive use.

Buffer memory: Text and data are often sent to a printer faster than the printer can print. The buffer takes up the slack. When the buffer fills up at the input end, the computer is told to wait until there's room. The bigger the buffer, the better. Some vendors offer interfaces with capacious buffers included.

Clarity of print: In general, the formed character printers are better than dot matrix printers at producing clean crisp characters. With dot matrix printers the clarity is a function of the dot density.

Color: Produced with colored ribbon on formed character printers, multicolored ribbon on dot matrix printers, colored ink on plotters and ink jet printers. Generally, the last two provide the brightest colors and sharpest images.

Connector cable: Unless you purchase a complete, ready-to-go system that includes a printer, you usually need to have a special connector cable made up. The cable consists of wires to connect "pins" at the printer connection with pins at the computer port. It seems as though every make of computer and every make of printer has its own pin assignment—the computer may send a message on pin 6 that the printer looks for on pin 17. Anybody handy with a soldering iron can buy the parts and make up the cable if the pin assignments are known, but user manuals do not always tell what those assignments are.

Descenders: A descender is the part of certain lower case letters, such as *g* and *y*, that is printed below the base line. Some dot matrix printers with small matrices do not print below the base line, and letters that should have true descenders appear deformed. Printed text looks better, and is easier to read, with true descenders than without.

Graphics: An increasingly popular feature, available with some quite inexpensive dot matrix printers. Plotters are designed primarily for graphics. Laser printers handle graphics as easily as text. Very limited graphics can even be produced with a formed character printer. In all cases, special software is required.

Interface to computer: A printer may offer a serial interface, a parallel interface, or both. The type used must match the computer's port. There are differences among interfaces. Even the common RS-232C connector is not completely standardized. If computer and printer do not match, a special interface is required.

Justification: Many users like to see pages of text neatly lined up, or *justified*, on the right as well as the left. One means to this end is to insert extra spaces between words where necessary. A more sophisticated method is *microjustification*. With this method, any extra space is evenly distributed between characters and spaces throughout the text line. Either method can be used with proportional spacing.

Keyboard: A printer with a keyboard can be used as a typewriter by itself or as a computer terminal. Input and output appear on the paper instead of the screen. This option is offered with some expensive formed character printers and with others intended for use as remote terminals.

Noise level: Noisy printers seem to become more noisy with use, though this is purely imaginary. Acoustic cabinets can be purchased for most printers. Thermal, electrosensitive, ink-jet, and laser printers are virtually silent.

Paper feed: If you plan to purchase only one printer, it is preferable to have one that can handle all types of paper stock: Single sheets and envelopes, paper rolls, and pin-feed.

>   **Pressure or friction feed**: The paper is gripped by rubber rollers as on a typewriter. Roll paper (from a large roll) and fan-fold paper feed continuously; single sheets must be inserted one at a time. Alignment is up to the user.

Sheet feeder: An attachment that stores a few hundred single sheets of paper and feeds them to the printer. Expensive but much easier than feeding them by hand.

Tractor feed: Also called *pin-feed*. Eliminates hand feeding at very little cost. The paper is continous, fan-folded, with perforations along the folds and holes along the sides. The tractors have pins that fit the holes and pull the paper along. This permits perfect alignment and registration. The paper can be preprinted with user-specified forms or letterheads. If you do not like the holes, you can buy paper, even fine quality bond, with perforated hole strips that tear off to leave a neat edge.

Paper width: Common maximum widths that printers can accommodate range from 8 to 14 or more inches. The number of columns for printing text depends on the pitch (characters per inch) at which the text is printed.

Spacing or pitch: Most printers can be set to either of the two standard pitches available with electric typewriters: 10 characters to the inch or 12. A few offer 16 pitch. Some can be controlled by software to print at almost any pitch.

Proportional spacing: Results in very handsome copy, similar to that in a book. Not a common feature. With true proportional spacing, the *m* is wider than the *n* and the *n* wider than the *i*.

Speed: Formed character printers are limited in speed because the printing element has to spin to the correct position for each character. Their speeds range from 12 to 55 cps (characters per second). Dot matrix printers are usually faster; quite inexpensive models print at 130 cps or better. Line and band printers print at speeds of 2,000 lpm (lines per minute), while electrostatic printers manage 18,000 lpm and electrographic 30,000 lpm. Some ink jet printers offer speeds of up to 45,000 lpm, others use lower speeds to achieve higher print quality. Laser printers combine very high speed with versatility and clarity of print.

Spooling: This convenience is provided by software, but it is related to printing and nothing else. Spooling means that one or more print files can be written on disk and then sent to the printer at any time with one command. The printing is then automatic, leaving the user — and the computer — free to do other things.

Variable type: Formed character printers allow changes of typeface but this must be done manually by changing the print element. Some dot matrix printers provide many typefaces and varying sizes through programmed codes or ROM cartridges. Ink-jet and laser printers can print anything the software can define.

Video display: The most commonly used output device for interactive computer systems. As of this writing, nearly all video displays are cathode ray tubes (CRTs) just like those used for television. Many home computers are even designed to use television sets for their displays. *Plasma displays*, the latest wrinkle in display technology, have one big advantage over CRTs — they are thin and flat. Because of the high cost per square inch, plasma displays have so far been limited in size to 10 or fewer lines of text. The price is falling, and their use and usefulness will expand.

Most desktop computers and terminals come with built-in video displays. Other computers may not include any display: The user is expected to hook up a separate *monitor*, which must of course be compatible with the computer.

Video displays vary greatly, not always according to price. The following features should be considered in their evaluation.

Character size: Controlled by software, but the lower limit is determined by the *resolution* (see below) of the screen. As in a printed book, large type makes reading easier for small children and visually handicapped persons. On the other hand, more text can be displayed on the screen at one time if the characters are small. Some systems allow the user to select from a range of character sizes or height-width ratios. This feature is most likely to be found in systems offering graphics.

Color: Multicolor, actually, as we mean the combinations of 8, 16, or more colors, both foreground and background. Color has great appeal, especially for children, and can clarify distinctions and associations among separate elements of a display. A color CRT and special software are required.

Even among monochrome CRTs there is some choice: Green on black, white on black, grey on amber. Studies in Europe determined that amber was the easiest on the eyes for long-term use, but other studies disagree: There is no clear consensus. For continuous reading of text, the clarity of the characters may be the most important factor in reducing eyestrain.

Descenders for lower case: Each character displayed on the screen has a rectangle of space reserved for it. Within that rectangle is a smaller one from which dots are selected to form the character. (This block of dots has to be smaller so that the characters do not all run together.) On some displays this smaller *print block* rests on the base line rather than extending below it. In this case, the tails of the lower case *g, j, p, q,* and *y* cannot be shown below the base line. These characters end up looking rather odd, with their tails tucked up under them. The difference is small but sometimes annoying and might add to the difficulties of dyslectics and others with reading problems.

Graphics: Recently introduced in business systems but included in small home computers as a matter of course for years. Graphics have proven to be a valuable communications tool. Image quality depends primarily on screen resolution (see below). The determining factor is the size of the smallest area that can be controlled.

On some systems, the smallest block of dots that can be controlled is the *character block*. In text mode a given block may display one of the standard text characters; in graphics mode it may display a graphics character (such as a bar, diamond, or triangle); in either mode it may be an empty block set to dark or light or color. In true graphics systems, the software can control *pixels*, which are much smaller. A typical character block is 10 x 10 pixels; thus the pixel is 100 times smaller than the character block.

With low-resolution screens or *character graphics*, the effect is grainy or blocky. Curves and diagonals look stepped. High-resolution screens with *pixel addressing* can produce smooth curves and realistic images, but at a very high price. Fortunately, there are many alternatives between the two extremes.

Resolution: Indicates the number of pixels on the screen. A pixel is the smallest area that can be individually lighted or colored. Dedicated graphics equipment may provide resolutions of 1,280 x 1,024 pixels, while inexpensive monitors and television sets typically offer around 256 rows by 192 columns on the same size screen.

Screen size, in inches: Measured on the diagonal. The 13-inch screen is the most common size in current use, presumably because it is comfortable for the user. Large screens are difficult to view in their entirety, and small screens may feel confining. However, portable computers with screens as small as 5 inches on the diagonal have been popular, and some displays used for word processing have screens measuring more than 20 inches. The optimum screen size for any purpose depends on the desired character size and the number of lines and columns.

Screen size, in lines and columns: A great deal of packaged software has been written for the common screen layout of 24 or 25 lines top to bottom and 80 columns (characters) across. At present, many of the home computers used in schools allow for a maximum of 40 columns.

Voice synthesizer: The potential applications of this technology are so many and varied that a great deal is being invested in its development. The voice synthesizer calls on groups of binary codes representing discrete sounds, syllables, or words and produces recognizable speech through a speaker. The quality of the sound varies in rather the same way as the quality of graphic images — by the size and number of individual particles that can be defined.

However, to store all the codes representing all the nuances in 5 seconds of true human speech would fill an entire floppy disk. One solution is to store code groups representing phonemes. If there are enough phonemes on file, they can be assembled in various combinations to form a large number of words and even sentences. A dictionary of words and their associated phonemes is still required — one researcher predicts that written language will evolve (or devolve) into phonetic spelling so as to be easily recognized by computers.

Those working in this area are finding ways to reduce or even eliminate the mechanical, robotic sound of synthetic speech. While researchers are perfecting voice synthesis, future users are planning for its most effective applications.

Storage Devices and Media

Storage is the computer's third memory — long term but capable of being revised. Storage disks and tapes can be placed on-line by mounting them on the computer system drives for instant access. When not in use, they can be stored anywhere, and often are. It is surprising how fast disks and tapes can accumulate and how easily novice users can become confused as to what is on which. Prospective computer users are advised to plan a catalog system and stick to it from the start.

In 1980, storage capacity was a major factor in computer costs. In 1984, the price of storage is a relatively minor consideration, and storage capacity can usually be expanded after initial purchase. Many microcomputers permit *daisy chaining* disk drives. Many vendors offer built-in hard disks with multimegabyte capacity as an option. Many other vendors offer hard disks with special interfaces to allow access by various computers. Meanwhile, whether for on-line or backup storage, tape is very inexpensive and becoming more so. (See also *Tape storage.*)

Disk storage: Almost all microcomputers today offer disk storage. Most provide two disk drives in their standard configurations. Those that provide only one drive or only tape as a standard feature usually offer disk drives as optional add-ons. An important feature of disk storage is that the computer can access any part of an on-line disk almost instantaneously.

> **Disk drives:** The mechanisms for making the disks go around, and for rapidly positioning the *head* at any location to read or write the magnetically coded bits on the disk surface. A disk drive can only handle one size of disk and only one type. However, for a given size and type the drives of several manufacturers may be interchangeable.
>
> **Floppy disks:** While indeed flexible, they do not flop. As of 1984, there are three standard sizes: the 3-inch microfloppy, the 5¼-inch mini-floppy, and the 8-inch floppy. However, the actual capacity of any floppy disk is not standard: It is related less to its diameter than to the drive design (e.g., whether it can access both sides of the disk or just one) and the *format* (see below).
> Compared with *hard disks*, floppies are inexpensive and convenient. They can be easily removed from the disk drives and replaced. This convenience does mean they are more subject to damage from careless handling.
>
> **Format:** The organization and density of storage on a disk. The available surface of a disk is divided into *tracks*; each track is divided into *sectors*; each sector can store a specific number of bytes. Formats differ in number of tracks, sectors per track, and bytes per sector. Many computer manufacturers develop proprietary formats. In this case, the Operating System includes a format routine which ensures that the Operating System will be able to read its own disk, and other computers will not.
> A *hard-sectored* disk has been given a format by the disk manufacturer, a format that cannot be changed. *Soft-sectored* disks allow formatting by the user, to accommodate the various proprietary formats. Storage capacity depends on the format: For example the same 5¼-inch minifloppy may store 80,000 bytes with one format and 400,000 with another.

Hard disks: Allow considerably more storage than floppies, as well as faster reading and writing. Like floppies, hard disks come in many sizes, not necessarily related to their storage capacity. With the new Winchester technology, a hard disk the size of a minifloppy can store many megabytes. Most hard disks are fixed in place, and programs and data must be transferred to other devices for back-up. Some are paired with removable disks, providing the ideal combination of capacity and flexibility.

Laser disks: A disk that stores information by optics rather than magnetism. The laser writes a bit of data by changing the surface at a given point from amorphous to crystalline, or vice versa. The crystalline surface is highly reflective, the amorphous is not, and so the bits can be read optically. One firm predicts the storage of 5,000 pages of text on a 2-inch disk.

A more important feature of laser disks is that they are already in use for audio and video recordings. When the problems of nonstandardization and incompatibility are solved, a single disk will be able to store music, pictures, and movies side by side with computer text, data, and software.

Tape storage: The tape media used for storage in computer systems range from standard audiotape cassettes and special data tape cartridges to giant reels. For general purposes, the main advantage of tape storage over disk is its low cost. It is very useful for backing up disk files: Data and programs from an entire hard disk can be copied onto tape for safekeeping; then if the disk files are destroyed, they can be restored from the tape.

Tape storage also has some definite advantages for classroom use. (1) If a system can use both disk *and* tape, programs stored on tape free up disk space for data files. (2) Tape cassette cartridges are less vulnerable to careless handling than disks. (3) At least one popular and inexpensive home computer uses two-track tape; one track can be used to record and play back voice or music or sound effects, the other to store programs. Both tracks are read simultaneously.

Tape cassettes have two major drawbacks. (1) Loading programs from cassettes may take two or three minutes, as opposed to a few seconds from disk. (2) Tape *must* be read sequentially. It cannot provide, as disk storage can, instant access to given data. The first of these drawbacks is merely a nuisance, a matter of time and convenience. The second is more important in that it severely limits the usefulness of tape for data files.

Storage and Files

Computer files are just like office files in that everything has its place. Computer files offer the advantage that information can be retrieved without disturbing the files themselves. This is done by *copying* whatever we want into memory instead of actually moving it.

Disk files: The Operating System, working with the disk controller, allocates space for files as they are created. It writes into a *disk directory* the name, type, and starting track and sector of each file. Most users never know exactly where a file resides on its disk, but most users never need to know — the Operating System keeps a perpetual up-to-date inventory of all files.

ASCII file: American Standard Code for Information Interchange (pronounced "asky"). ASCII is a widely accepted code in which numbers are assigned to all the standard letters, digits, and punctuation marks as well as special noncharacters such as line feed and backspace. ASCII files store everything in this code, using one byte per character.

ASCII files can be read very easily by the computer without any special software and can be copied directly from disk to the screen or the printer, or transmitted by modem, without losing any characters.

Programs and numeric data, by contrast, are often stored in *binary coded decimal* or some other space-saving code. Only computer experts and the software that created the file can make sense out of these codes. If you copy such a file directly to a screen or printer it will be illegible.

Data file: A file containing data, usually in a well-defined format of records and fields within records. As with office files, one should be able to access any record at any time — the progress record of one student, the schedule of one teacher, the students enrolled in one class. For handling data, *random access* and *ISAM* files are the most convenient.

ISAM data file: Indexed Sequential Access Method. The ISAM method creates and maintains a sorted index for each data file. The index stores a *key* for each record in the data file. The key might be a name on some systems; on others the key must be numeric. Stored with each key is the location of the associated record in the data file. This allows instant random access to any given record. Because the index is always sorted, it can be used to access the data file sequentially but in sorted order, as would be required for printing reports.

Program file: A file containing a unit of software. Unlike data files, these are usually read from beginning to end, so no random access or index is needed. If the program in the file has already been translated, by a compiler or an assembler, the CPU can read the file but most users cannot. If the program is still in source code form, it can be read by the same interpreter used in writing it. If it is in ASCII code, it can also be read by users.

Random access file: Permits instant access to any given record by its record number. Usually the records are stored in the same order they are entered. They must be sorted every time a printout in sorted order is required.

Sequential file: A method of file organization that does not permit random access. Sequential files are not really suited for data: To find Wagner one has to look at Anderson, Bach, Beethoven, Chopin, Debussey.... This kind of file is used mostly for programs and text.

Text file: A file containing text, which may include numbers as well as letters. Text files are usually created with the aid of a word processor. Text editors, which existed long before word processors, can also be used but are much less powerful. Word-processed files often include a great many special characters, and even unprintable characters, for controlling the printed format. If copied directly from disk to screen, text files may be only partly legible.

Tape files: On tape, all files are treated sequentially, regardless of the type of file. When a disk is backed up on tape this does not matter: If the disk must be restored, all files will automatically be read back in sequence. (Disk back-up and restore operations generally use large tapes.)

The sequential nature of tape becomes a problem when working with disk files and newly created programs. In reading from and writing to tape cassettes, the Operating System cannot keep track of what is where. Instead, the user must note the location counter on the tape drive/reader. It is very easy to save one program or data file on top of another, whether by choice or accident.

APPENDIX 2

Software Evaluation Form

This software evaluation instrument is currently in use in school districts. It suggests many important features for evaluation.

This form may be modified or duplicated for your use. It is assumed that you will add other elements to this form as your evaluations become more sophisticated and specific needs are clarified.

Evaluation and Planning for Use of Instructional Software
with Special Education

Title _____ Version _____

Producer _____ Address _____

Subject _____ Grade Level _____ Cost _____

Type of Program: __Drill & Practice __Tutorial __Simulation __ Game
     __ Word Processing __Programming

Type of use: __Drill & Practice __Drill & Practice after lesson
     __Integral part of lesson __Focus of lesson __Motivation/reward

Hardware requirements:

Documentation: For teacher ____ For student ____

Adequacy of documentation (e.g., clear, concise, step by step)

Time to load program _____

Amount of time to complete one segment of program_____
              to complete entire program_____

Accuracy of content (e.g. grammar, spelling, subject matter)

Prerequisite skills needed

Prerequisite skills to teach

Flexibility

    1. Choice of entry level

    2. Control Speed/Rate

    3. Change vocabulary or other variables

    4. Choose number of problems presented

    5. Choice of rate and type of reinforcement

    6. Allowed to leave program

Reinforcement

    1. Passive (e.g., good, not right)

    2. Active (graphics)

    3. Interactive (e.g., play short game, move to different level)

    4. After each correct answer

    5. Varied

    6. Personalized

    7. Related to response

Corrections

    1. None

    2. Only enter correct response

    3. __1,__2,__3 incorrect, then problem presented again

    4. Branch to an easier or harder problem

    5. Branch to a tutorial

    6. Response to user errors (e.g., beep, written message)

Technical Aspects

    1. User-proof

    2. Screen display (e.g., uncluttered, no distracting info)

    3. Ease of use (e.g., student can work independently, with a peer)

    4. Randomization

Educational Planning Considerations - record keeping

Maintain student interest?   Why?   How?

Teaching approach -- Does it differ from your philosophy?
If so, how?

Teaching format (e.g., multiple choice, free response,
                        reading passage with questions)

Prerequisite on-line directions to teach students.

Stated goals and objectives of program

Additional or other goals and objectives for your students

Generalization and/or follow-up (e.g., instruction, work sheets,
exercises). Be specific.

APPENDIX 3

Resources

Regional Resource Centers

Great Lakes Area Regional
  Resource Center
Ohio State University
101 Student Service Building
154 West 12th Avenue
Columbus, OH 43210-1390

Mid South Regional Resource
  Center
University of Kentucky
128 Porter Building
Lexington, KY 40506-0205

Mountain Plains Regional
  Resource Center
Utah State University
Exceptional Child Center — UMC 68
Logan, UT 84322

Northeast Regional Resource
  Center
Trinity College
Colchester Avenue
Burlington, VT 05401

South Atlantic Regional Resource
  Center
Florida Atlantic University
1236 North University Drive
Plantation, FL 33322

Western Regional Resource
  Center
College of Education
University of Oregon
Eugene, OR 97403

Resources for
Locating Software or Interesting Applications

Association for Computing
  Machinery (ACM)
1133 Avenue of the Americas
New York, NY 10036

Association for Development of
  Computer-Based Instructional
  Systems (ACDIS)
ACDIS Headquarters
Computer Center
Western Washington University
Bellingham, WA 98225

Association for Educational Data
  Systems
1201 16th Street, N.W.
Washington, DC 20036

Council for Exceptional Children
1920 Association Drive
Reston, VA 22091

International Council for
  Computers in Education
Department of Computer and
  Information Science
University of Oregon
Eugene, OR 97403

Microcomputer Education
  Applications Network
256 N. Washington Street
Falls Church, VA 22046

National Association of State
  Directors of Special Education
  (NASDSE)
1201 16th Street, N.W., Suite 610
Washington, DC 20036

National Council of Teachers of
  Mathematics
1906 Association Drive
Reston, VA 20091

National Science Teachers
  Association
1742 Connecticut Avenue, N.W.
Washington, DC 20009

Technology and Marketing
  Branch
United States Department of
  Education
Office of Special Education
Washington, DC 20202

Bulletin Boards

Handicapped Educational
  Exchange (HEX)
11523 Charlton Drive
Silver Spring, MD 20902
(301)593-7033

Special Net
National Association of State
  Directors of Special Education
  (NASDSE)
1201 16th Street, N.W., Suite 610
Washington, DC 20036
(202)822-7933

Sources of Public Domain Software

Boston Computer Society
One Center Plaza
Boston, MA 02108

Softswap
Micromputer Center
San Mateo County Office of
  Education
333 Main Street
Redwood City, CA 94063

Sources for Software Reviews

Courseware Report Card
150 West Carob Street
Compton, CA 90220

Pipeline
Conduit
P.O. Box 388
Iowa City, IA 52244

MicroSIFT News
MicroSIFT
Northwest Regional Educational
  Laboratory
300 S.W. Sixth Avenue
Portland, OR 97204

Robert Purser's Magazine
P.O. Box 466
Eldorado, CA

School Microwave Reviews
Dresden Associates
P.O. Box 246
Dresden, ME 04342

Educational Software Directories

Educational Software Directory
Sterling Swift Publishing
  Company
P.O. Box 188
Manchaca, TX 78652

Educator's Handbook and
  Software Directory
Vital Information, Inc.
350 Union Station
Kansas City, MO 64108

K-12 Micromedia
P.O. Box 17
Valley Cottage, NY 10989

Opportunities for Learning, Inc.
8950 Lurline Avenue
Chatsworth, CA 91311

Queue
5 Chapel Hill Drive
Fairfield, CT 06432

Reference Manual for
  Instructional Users of
  Microcomputers
JEM Research, Discovery Park
University of Victoria
P.O. Box 1700
Victoria, BC V8W 2Y2
Canada

Scholastic Mocrocomputer
  Instructional Materials
904 Sylvan Avenue
Englewood Cliffs, NJ 07632

School Microware Directory
Dresden Associates
P.O. Box 246
Dresden, ME 04342

Sources for Courses
TALMIS
115 North Oak Park Avenue
Oak Park, IL 60301

Commercial Software Sources

This is a partial list of commercial sources for educational software. Many more companies exist. Inclusion in this list does not indicate a recommendation of either company or product.

AB Computers
252 Bethlehem Pike
Colmar, PA 18915

Addison-Wesley Publishing Co.
2725 Sand Hill Road
Menlo Park, CA 94025

Apple Computer Company
10260 Bandley Drive
Cupertino, CA 94017

Atari, Inc.
1272 Borregas Avenue
Sunnyvale, CA 94086

Avant-Garde Creations, Inc.*
P.O. Box 30160
Eugene, OR 97403

BLS, Inc.
2503 Fairlee Road
Wilmington, DE 19810

Broderbund Software
1938 Fourth Street
San Rafael, CA 94901

Cactus Software
1442 N. McAllister
Tempe, AZ 85281

Commodore Business Machines
3330 Scott Blvd.
Santa Clara, CA 95051

Computer-Advanced Ideas, Inc.
1442A Walnut Street
Berkeley,CA 94709

Computer Software/Books R Us
16 Birdsong
Irvine, CA 92714

Conduit
P.O. Box 388
Iowa City, IA 52244

Control Data Corporation
8100 34th Avenue South
Minneapolis, MN 55440

Creative Computing
39 E. Hanover Avenue
Plains, NJ 07950

Curriculum Applications
P.O. Box 264
Arlington, MA 02174

Developmental Learning
  Materials
One DLM Park, P.O. Box 4000
Allen, TX 75002

---

*These publishers have preview policies. Contact them for the specifics of their policies.

Dilithium Software
11000 S.W. 11th Street,
Beaverton, OR 97005

Earthware Computer Services
P.O. Box 30039
Eugene, OR 97403

Educational Activities, Inc.*
1937 Grand Avenue
Baldwin, NY 11510

Educational Audio Visual, Inc.
Pleasantville, N.Y. 10570

Edu-Soft
Steketee Educational Software
4639 Spruce Street
Philadelphia, PA 19139

EduTech
303 Lamartine Street
Jamaica Plain, MA 02130

Edu-Ware Services
22035 Burbank Blvd.
Woodland Hills, CA 91367

Follett Library Book Co.
4506 Northwest Highway
Crystal Lake, IL 60014

Hartley Courseware, Inc.
P.O. Box 431
Dimondale, MI 48821

Holt, Rinehart & Winston
    Publishers
School Marketing Dept.
383 Madison Avenue
New York, NY 10017

Houghton Mifflin Co.
One Beacon Street
Boston, MA 02107

Instructional Communications
    Technology*
10 Stephar Place
Huntington Station, NY 11746

Interactive Education
2306 Winters Drive
Kalamzaoo, MI 49002

J.L. Hammett Co., Inc.
Hammett Place, P.O. Box 545
Braintree, MA 02184

John Wiley & Sons, Inc.
605 Third Avenue
New York, NY 10158

K-12 Micromedia*
172 Broadway
Woodcliff Lake, NJ 07675

Krell Software
1320 Stony Brook Road
Stony Brook, NY 11790

Kvitle Kourseware
15510 Heimar Road
San Antonio, TX 78232

The Learning Company
4370 Alpine Road
Portola Valley, CA 94025

Learning Tools, Inc.
686 Massachusetts Avenue
Cambridge, MA 02139

LINC Resources, Inc.
1875 Morse Road
Columbus, OH 43229

Logo Computer Systems
368 Congress Street
Boston, MA 02210

Math Software
1233 Blackthorn Place
Deerfield, IL 60015

Mathware/Math City
4040 Palos Verdes Drive, N.
Rolling Hills Estates, CA 90274

MCE, Inc.
157 S. Kalamazoo Mall
Kalamazoo, MI 49007

McGraw-Hill Software
1221 Avenue of the Americas
New York, NY 10020

Microcomputers in Education*
4148 Winnetka Avenue, N.
Minneapolis, MN 55427

Micro-Ed, Inc.*
P.O. Box 444005
Eden Prairie, MN 55344

MicroPro International
99 Fourth Street
San Rafael, CA 94901

Milliken Publishing
1100 Research Blvd.
St. Louis, MO 63132

Milton Bradley Co.
443 Shaker Road
E. Longmeadow, MA 01028

Minnesota Educational
   Computing Consortium
2520 Broadway Drive
St. Paul, MN 55113

MUSE Software
330 N. Charles Street
Baltimore, MD 21201

Opportunities for Learning*
8950 Lurline Avenue
Chatsworth, CA 91311

Quality Education Design*
P.O. Box 12486
Portland, OR 97212

Radio Shack
Educational Division
400 Tandy Atrium
Fort Worth, TX 76102

Random House School Division
400 Hahn Road
Westminster, MD 21157

Reston Publishing Co., Inc.
11480 Sunset Hills Road
Reston, VA 22090

Scholastic, Inc.
904 Sylvan Avenue
Englewood Cliffs, NJ 07632

School and Home CourseWare,
   Inc.
1341 Bulldog Lane
Fresno, CA 93710

School Courseware Journal
4919 N. Milbrook
Fresno, CA 93725

Science Research Associates
155 N. Wacker Drive
Chicago, IL 60606

Scott, Foresman & Co.
1900 East Lake Avenue
Glenview, IL 60025

Spinnaker Software Corporation
215 First Street
Cambridge, MA 02142

Sunburst Communications*
39 Washington Avenue
Pleasantville, NY 10570

Teaching Tools
Microcomputer Services
P.O. Box 50065
Palo Alto, CA 94303

Terrapin, Inc.
222 Third Street
Cambridge, MA 02142

Texas Instruments
P.O. Box 53
Lubbock, TX 79408

Universal Systems for Education
2120 Academy Circle
Colorado Springs, CO 80909

Xerox Education Publications
245 Long Hill Road
Middleton, CT 06457

About the Authors

Dr. Milton Budolf received his Ph.D. in Human Development from the University of Chicago. He is Director of the Research Institute for Educational Problems in Cambridge, MA.

Dr. Budolf is co-author with Alan Orenstein of *Due Process in Special Education: On Going to a Hearing* and has published articles on the instructional use of microcomputers, learning potential assessment, mainstreaming, labelling, and children's conceptions of handicapping conditions. He is co-author with Susan Conant and Barbara Hecht of *Teaching Language-Disabled Children: A Communication Games Intervention*. Dr. Budolf is currently conducting a study on the use of authoring languages by special teachers.

Dr. Joan Thormann earned her doctorate in Education at the University of Oregon, specializing in the area of computer use in special education. She taught special education students in public and private schools (levels k through post-secondary) for eleven years and has held faculty positions at a number of colleges and universities. Dr. Thormann is currently employed as an educational consultant and conducts a number of workshops regarding use of computers in special education. She also works for a software development firm in Cambridge, MA.

Dr. Thormann is co-author with Metzger and Ouellette of the booklet *Learning Disabled Students and Computers: A Teacher's Guide Book*, and has written articles about special education and the use of computers in special education.

Ann Gras is an enthusiastic self-taught programmer. She designed and wrote custom mainframe applications for newspapers before starting a microcomputer consulting firm in 1979.

Ann Gras is co-author with Philip Frankel of *The Software Sifter* (Macmillan, 1983).